THE DEVIL'S CHILDREN

A History of Childhood and Murder

Loretta Loach

ICON BOOKS

Published in the UK in 2009 by
Icon Books Ltd, Omnibus Business Centre,
39–41 North Road, London N7 9DP
email: info@iconbooks.co.uk
www.iconbooks.co.uk

Sold in the UK, Europe, South Africa and Asia
by Faber & Faber Ltd, 3 Queen Square,
London WC1N 3AU or their agents

Distributed in the UK, Europe, South Africa and Asia
by TBS Ltd, TBS Distribution Centre, Colchester Road
Frating Green, Colchester CO7 7DW

This edition published in Australia in 2009
by Allen & Unwin Pty Ltd, PO Box 8500,
83 Alexander Street, Crows Nest, NSW 2065

Distributed in Canada by
Penguin Books Canada,
90 Eglinton Avenue East, Suite 700,
Toronto, Ontario M4P 2YE

ISBN: 978-184831-019-3 (hardback)
ISBN: 978-184831-066-7 (paperback)

Typeset in 11.5 on 16pt Minion by Marie Doherty

Printed and bound in the UK by
J.H. Haynes & Co. Ltd.

To Jlo, to whom I owe everything and more.

About the Author

Loretta Loach has an extensive background in television documentaries, as well as a PhD in History. The most recent historical drama documentary she has worked on was *Queen Victoria's Empire* for Channel 4. She has appeared on Radio 4's *All in the Mind* and has written for the *Guardian*, the *Observer* and the *New Statesman*.

ACKNOWLEDGEMENTS

A number of people have guided me through, though they might not have known it. Friends who were first puzzled and perhaps troubled by the subject matter have nonetheless encouraged me to continue. Among them are: Nel Druce, Nick Hewlett, Julia Henderson, Mandy Merck, Lynne Segal and Jude Watson. The rest know who they are and I am grateful to them all.

I am also thankful for the support of the history team in the School of Social Sciences at Kingston University and especially Dr Andrea Tanner. Alison Whyte was a constant source of critical encouragement and Corrine Westacott and Paul Bryers offered useful advice. Wendy Moore's helpful hints were much appreciated when canvassing the interests of publishers and I am glad the idea found its way to Simon Flynn at Icon who understood its place and purpose from the beginning.

A number of willing helpers assisted with research including Sharon Goulds, Dermot Bryers, Yinka Williams and the enthusiastic Nigel Hargraves in Australia who guided me through the archives. David James Smith helped me with material for chapter 10 and Heather Shore, Nicholas Orme and Pamela Dale found time in their busy academic lives to kindly respond to email inquiries. Joshua Lowe saved me from a technical nightmare and consultant Adrian Timothy saved my life!

Finally, I can't thank enough all the young children I have spent time with over the years, especially my nieces Liffey and Annie and my nephew Jose. Also Michael, Lucy, Hilary, Chloe, Woody and dear Cosmo, not forgetting Bill and Tom. Being with them, and seeing them grow, has been a constant reminder of how curious, occasionally bad-tempered, and utterly fun-loving children can be – assuming, of course, that they are lucky enough to be born into safety and comfort.

CONTENTS

LIST OF ILLUSTRATIONS

Prologue

*There is no original sin in the human heart, the how and why of
the entrance of every vice can be traced.*
JEAN-JACQUES ROUSSEAU

When Blake Morrison was writing his book *As If*, his attempt
to understand the murder of James Bulger in 1993, he returned
home to south London for a weekend while the trial was in recess.
He described being at a dinner party with friends where the talk,
inevitably, turned to the trial and then his own involvement with
it. They asked how he could bear to sit there every day, and did
he not find it upsetting? When he replied that he found it interesting, he received looks in return as if to say 'ghoul, sicko', and
the subject was changed 'to something less awkward, our own
children'. It's a reaction I recognise.

There is nothing more separate in our minds than children
and murder. We know that parents sometimes kill their children
– 33 in the past year according to figures from the Home Office
– and occasionally strangers kill children. But a child who murders another child, though rare, is different because of what it
appears to represent about childhood. When Mary Bell killed
two little boys in 1968 and James Bulger was killed by older
boys in 1993, the effect was shattering. It challenged the old idea
of childhood innocence as if, somehow, the pool of purity had
become contaminated.

It is surprising that, given how powerless children must feel,
and how frustrated and angry they can become, that there are not

more cases in which a child is killed by another child. For those of us who enjoyed the pleasures of an unsupervised 1960s childhood, dangerous encounters with violence were not unfamiliar. One story told to me by a friend made a particular impact.

When he was about eight years old, Martin was playing with a group of boys far away from the watchful eyes of adults. Among them was a willowy blonde boy who was slow, shy and diffident about adventure. Bored with whatever game they had been playing, one of the group suggested that this boy, Keith, be locked in the underground den they had all built. They gathered around the bewildered boy in a threatening circle and shoved him into the makeshift tomb. A piece of corrugated iron was laid over the entrance and bricks were placed on top. There was laughter at his pathetic pleas to be let out, and it was only when his hopeful cries turned to those of terror that he was safely released. Similar personal stories of cruelty have been told by the writers Andrew O'Hagan and Blake Morrison, and they have their deadly fictional counterparts in *Lord of the Flies*, *The Midwich Cuckoos*, more recently in Toby Litts's *Deadkidsongs*, William Sutcliffe's *Bad Influence*, and most devastatingly of all in Lionel Shriver's cleverly complex novel *We Need to Talk About Kevin*.

But what was important about Martin's story and the other remembered accounts was that the terror they had elicited from their captive was the cue for them to stop, whereas for some of the children in this book it became a cue to carry on. Yet the question of whether deliberate intention to kill, in the same sense as we might think of it applying to adults, plays any part in these kinds of crimes, has preoccupied many individuals in the legal and psychiatric professions. In fact, as I found through this research, the issue has confounded lawyers and scientists for over two centuries. Forming an intention to kill, becoming conscious of that desire and then acting upon it, is difficult to fathom in an adult, let alone a child. In the nineteenth century, when the psychological sciences were in their infancy, murder and its motivation was a subject that doctors puzzled over. Excited by this whole new scientific area, they became gripped by the problems of how mental states affect extreme behaviour and criminal actions in particular. For a child standing trial for murder, their deliberations were significant; to illustrate just how significant, in chapter 7 I have diverged from the child-on-child focus of the rest of the book to include a criminal case tried at the highest court in the land in which a boy was accused of poisoning his grandfather. Doctors appearing at this trial offered testimony that stretched common-sense belief about culpability and challenged widely-held assumptions about what it means to be an agent of your own actions.

We think of these killings as a modern phenomenon perhaps because often, after well-publicised incidents, commentators rush to suggest that they are spawned by the excesses of a contemporary culture of violence. Yet the evidence of some of the earliest cases on record shows that these crimes have much older precedents. Long before guns, drugs and computer games, there were children who killed other children, sometimes in double murders. How did people perceive these young perpetrators in centuries past? How were they punished, and what does their treatment tell us about how the communities of times gone by identified the boundaries between childhood and adulthood?

Journalistic books on the subject of a child killing a child, though by no means vast in number, focus on the factual details of recent, twentieth-century cases. Only one book, by Patrick Wilson, has any historical content, though unfortunately it says little about the context of the killings or of the wider opinions they gave rise to. As they appeared in the moment, these murders suggested callousness and evil. Sudden, cruel and fatal, they were seen as monstrous acts committed by children who were deemed only halfway human, inspired, perhaps, by the devil. Yet behind the stories of such crimes lie personal tales of hardship, abandonment and deceit. This account uncovers the disturbing worlds of these children's childhood; sometimes treated no better than slaves, a number of them found themselves lost and floundering in the harsh responsibilities of adult life, while others roamed like vagrants amid the dank alleyways of England's growing towns and cities. These cases are rare, but they reveal the enduring link between children's emotional disturbance and its eruption into devastating acts of rage.

However, not all of the killings can be identified in this way. Among the medieval cases in particular are some accidental killings, which were significant in helping to establish the rules governing a child's criminal responsibility. Religious opinions about children's moral capacity and their ability to distinguish between good and evil had a bearing upon legal considerations of their culpability. In one ill-fated case, a harmless game turned violent, and death occurred because of one boy's terror of being found out. But if attitudes towards these children could ever be thought of as a test of society's humanity then, at least up until the mid-nineteenth century, it failed. The spectacles of suffering displayed in these early stories involve children as young as four being confined to the darkness of St Albans prison, a child being publicly hanged in front of weeping onlookers outside Maidstone prison, and another being transported overseas to a life of hard labour. Sympathy and benevolence towards child criminals was slow to flourish, and it was not until the mid-nineteenth century that sensibilities finally changed enough to make severe punishments incompatible with new ideas of what childhood should be. Even youths who were seen as having taken a wicked path in life were seen as deserving of rescue, protection and education. Although the child who killed posed a challenge to these optimistic ideas of reform and redemption, the treatment of such children also became a measure of how far Victorian society believed itself to have advanced.

This attentiveness to children, while not always positive in outcome, was nonetheless a defining moment in our modernity; it is here that our interest in childhood began. The eighteenth-century philosopher Jean-Jacques Rousseau had played an important part in this change: he had introduced the idea of childhood innocence.[1] Portrait painters of the 1780s followed with their own depictions of childhood as an Arcadian vision of purity, and later the poet William Blake identified the threat to childhood innocence in the form of adult exploitation, which he conveyed in his affecting poem about the plight of the chimney sweep. Fairytales of the 1860s were full of children protecting their own virtue from the supernatural forces of evil, and in the works of the novelist Charles Kingsley, corrupt adulthood was redeemed by the 'smiles of innocent children'. Men, he said, 'see the heaven they have lost – the messages of baby-cherubs, made in God's own image'.[2] These portrayals, together with Rousseau's romanticism, are widely seen as the basis of modern beliefs about childhood, and the moral ideas that emerge from this period continue to influence what we adults think about children's education and behaviour.[3] Furthermore, they have a direct bearing upon the opinions we hold about child killers.

In his book on education, *Emile*, Rousseau attempted to demonstrate that man, in his origins and infancy, is naturally good: 'Vice and error, alien to his constitution, are introduced into it from outside and imperceptibly distort it.'[4] His argument was in part directed at his predecessor, the philosopher John Locke, who held that the human child was neither good nor evil but a *tabula rasa* (or blank slate), waiting to receive the inscriptions of

experience.[5] Both were enormously influential in shaping changing attitudes towards childhood in the eighteenth century, in
that both emphasised the importance of a deliberate focus upon
a child's individual moral identity. But their opinions about a
child's nature and capacity could not have been more different.
As Peter Coveney argues in his book *The Image of Childhood*,
Locke's theory of education concerned itself with 'the swift creation, through controlled environment, of the rational adult man.
It seldom considered the nature of the child as a child. Treated
as a small adult, the child was to be trained out of his childish
ways into the moral and rational perfection of educated man-
hood.'[6] The idea that a child was capable of reason was inimical to
Rousseau who believed the stage was marked by reason's absence.
For him, a youth might appear to learn, indeed can appear to
learn quite quickly, 'but nothing sinks in'. In his view, a child's
'shining polished brain reflects, as in a mirror, the things you
show them ... the child remembers the words and the ideas are
reflected back: his hearers understand them, but to him they are
meaningless.'[7]

In modern history the child who kills is continually interpreted through the ideas of both Rousseau and Locke. In *Emile*,
Rousseau describes a boy killing a bird without knowing what
he does. He conveys the idea of a boy killing in innocence, and
argues that he should not therefore suffer eternal punishment. A
number of twentieth-century writers have evoked the philosopher's ideas in their commentary on the notorious Bulger case,
as did Gitta Sereny in her perspective of childhood as a state of
innocence.[8] Yet, at the same time, modern lawyers argued that
a child above the age of ten has the ability to reason between
right and wrong, and should no longer receive special protection through the legal presumption that he cannot.[9] Reason and
romanticism are the concepts that have governed the thinking on

children's capacities, particularly when they have committed the crime of murder. They acquire different formulations institutionally, through the law and criminal justice system; scientifically, through developments in the field of psychology; and popularly, through the medium of newspapers and pamphlets. These ideas of rationality and innocence are implicit in the interpretations made about child murderers not only in the nineteenth century, but also in our thinking today.

There are no universal truths to be distilled from this book. The chronology that it follows is not intended to suggest any statistical significance about the rate at which these crimes occur or to highlight any growing trend. If it appears that there are more contemporary cases, this is partly to do with gaps in the record. From the late fifteenth century assize records are patchy because the clerks responsible often destroyed bundles. Also, given the fact that murder is not a common crime, and children committing it even less so, it is unsurprising that statistical accounts do not appear. Even if it were possible to tally the numbers, they would carry no real significance because they are so small.

The judgement and opinions that were made about these cases differed in their details and varied according to time and place. The views held about the children and their crimes were often contradictory and were guided by emotional, moral and political concerns often external to the facts of the case. Symbolic meanings do, at intervals, attach to these crimes, not least because the child who murders becomes representative of its opposite, the child who does not, and it is partly through these contrasts that a moral identity for childhood is shaped on a wider public stage. Other more specific meanings depend upon the context in which the offence occurred. As the historian Heather Shore has argued in her book on juvenile crime in early-nineteenth-century London, when the spectre of criminal children was worrying the city's inhabitants, 'the murderous juvenile was used as a device, as a conduit through which were expressed societal doubts about the role and future of youth'.[10] While paying close attention to the ways in which these crimes were represented – which are fascinating for the multiple meanings they yield – I also wanted to trace the very real ways in which the children committing them were treated and punished at the hands of the criminal justice system.

Youth crime is an abiding concern, and with 27 killings of youngsters in London alone before 2008 had ended, this is understandable. The death toll includes ever-younger children, with perpetrators of the same age, but these gang crimes have to be understood very differently from those recounted in the pages that follow. Tragic and disturbing though these stabbings and shootings are, their causes are not the same. They are more to do with aberrant peer group behaviour and the particular model of masculinity that these adolescent boys have chosen to live by. Principally, these killings are often (though not always) drug-related, with youngsters from low-income families and with dismal prospects being lured by the generous financial inducements offered by older gang members. Moreover, the way these lawless, swaggering teenagers arrive at their crimes – what psychologists might refer to as their 'developmental pathway' – is in contrast to the trajectories of the killers in this book. There may be areas of overlap, but in the main, the actions of the 'devil's children' are a one-off, and their origins tend to lie in the traumas of physical or sexual abuse, learning disability and the mental ill-health of their parents.

In fact, what is striking about a number of these children's stories from the past is how similar the probable causes of their offences are to the ones that might be highlighted today. Many of them suffered loss and abandonment; they were beaten or relentlessly chastised; and at least one, and possibly more, was sexually preyed upon by adults. Where they did live in families, these were more often than not places of danger. However, hundreds of other children, at least up until the end of the twentieth century, endured similar pains and misfortune but were never involved in murder. Their experience comprises part of the historiography of childhood in which children's vulnerability to exploitation, poverty and death is described and analysed. Children who kill, however, have a particular psychological vulnerability that the early science of psychiatry attempted to understand. By including this as a major theme of the book I hope to give these children a place in the history of childhood, because their repellent crimes have so often put them outside it.

Psychiatry was only one area through which these crimes acquired meaning; the other areas being religion, law and politics. All of which makes this a book as much about grown-ups as it is about children. Adult confusion over how to make sense of these crimes is part of this story, as are adult anxieties about childhood and moral responsibility, which were, and still are, challenged by the horror of such killings.

Fortunately, cases in which a child kills another child are exceptional, many years elapse between episodes and not all incidents make dramatic headline news – for example, there have been at least fifteen other such cases over the last century that do not feature in this book. But were another killing to capture media attention in the way that recent prominent cases have done, per- haps this history will be of some use. The judge's comment in the trial of James Bulger's killers that his murder was an 'act of unparalleled evil and barbarity' gave a sense that the tragedy was archaic or primitive, and therefore beyond intelligibility. But such events have precedent, and previous cases serve as a reminder that, behind the immediate media furore, there will be a story with meaning that might make all the difference to our response.

Chapter One

FALLEN ANGELS

In his angels he found wickedness.
OLD TESTAMENT, JOB 4:8

In the museum of a small medieval town in central Italy, there is a picture of the Virgin Mary of a kind that is not often seen in churches of the region. Painted in rich golden colours, this Virgin is brandishing a gnarled club that she is using to chase away the devil who is about to take possession of a child. Kneeling at the side of the Madonna is the child's mother, her hands joined, imploring the Virgin to banish the demon. In the fifteenth century, this was a popular icon. Some scholars say it is based on medieval stories where a child is given to the devil by its mother in a moment of exasperation. Others believe it was used as a warning to parents not to delay infant baptism, because if they did their child might die and go to hell. But it is also a picture about the temptation of evil and the idea that wickedness is something that can take over a child's being. An echo of this belief has survived, irrepressibly, throughout the centuries. It can be seen written in the legal indictments of children who have killed, right up until the end of the nineteenth century. They were said not to have the 'fear of God before their eyes', but to be instead 'moved and seduced by the instigation of the devil' to commit their atrocious crimes. It is also marked in the epithets of evil used by the judge who tried the killers of James Bulger in 1993, and in much of the subsequent press coverage.

We might think that a child killing another child is a uniquely modern event, but cases can be found in the official records of the Middle Ages – the King's Rolls. Alongside the high-profile crimes of treason and murder, many involving nobility, there are other criminal cases selected, we can only assume, for their unusual nature and because they were useful for judicial precedent. This was the period in which a child's culpability in law, and in religion, began to be discussed. It was the era in which fixed ages of moral and legal responsibility were enshrined, which would last for more than 700 years.

Contrary to what we might expect, the medieval world was as preoccupied with the issue of where childhood ended and adulthood began as we are today. Cases of murder involved people in troubling matters of judgement, conscience and responsibility. When it came to a killing committed by a child, the earliest recorded cases reveal a picture of medieval lawyers struggling to accommodate the exceptional nature of such a crime. In theory, the ancient principle of absolute liability was applied equally to children as to adults – if one child injured another, the latter's parent or guardian took vengeance upon the former simply because he had done wrong, but in practice, considerable uncertainty existed over how to view child killers.

Up until the end of the thirteenth century, a child who had killed either accidentally or deliberately was kept in jail along with adults and the insane, to await the arrival of the royal justices who travelled the realm to hear cases on behalf of the King. In 1249, four-year-old Katherine Passeavant was kept in St Albans jail; its thick dank walls enclosed her in darkness.[1] She had killed another child by opening a door too swiftly, thereby pushing the infant

1. Madonna del Soccorso *(Our Lady of Succour)*, Tiberio d'Assisi *(1486–1524), in the Museum of San Francesco in Montefalco, Umbria.*

into a vessel of boiling water. It now seems tragically obvious that the girl had meant no harm, but in the medieval world the tools of legal investigation were blunter than they are today and she was sent to prison. Evidently, her anguished father could not withstand the sight of his little daughter languishing in jail until the arrival of the King's justice, which could take many months, so he wrote directly to the King who eventually ordered the local sheriff to release the child. She was fortunate. It was a pitiless system for children and for some a pardon could arrive too late, as it did for two boys who both died in prison while awaiting their trial, one of whom was only six years old.[2] During the same period a seven-year-old boy, Robert Parleben, was imprisoned because he had accidentally killed a girl while they were guarding cows together. One of the cows was straying into the corn and the young boy threw a stick to divert it, but the girl was standing in the way, took the force of the blow and was killed instantly. He waited for three years before receiving a pardon from the King.

Nowadays a police investigation establishes whether a killing was accidental or deliberate, but in medieval times a coroner was charged with this duty. His office, established shortly after the Norman Conquest, required him to report to the visiting justices in Eyre any cases arising under the pleas of the Crown, especially those relating to murder or manslaughter. If a charge was made against a named person by a parent, guardian or neighbour of the victim, a warrant would be issued for his arrest and questioning. The coroner sat with a jury of local men who – as well as viewing the body of the deceased, together with the person who first found it – heard other evidence, including that of the accused. When the questioning was over, the jury detained the child in custody until the trial or released him on bail. It did not matter if the killing had been deliberate or accidental, the coroner did not have the authority to discharge him.[3]

In one case, a ten-year-old boy who had shot and killed another by mischance was sent to appear before a county court and acquitted, but when the King's justices were told of this decision, they imprisoned him and fined the county for allowing the boy to go free.[4] It was the King's prerogative to decide upon a child's guilt or punishment, and the accused generally had to wait upon the arrival of His Majesty's justices.

The fact that children had to submit to the same legal processes as adults, that they were arrested for murder and kept in prison, amounted to a recognition that, just as adults could be involved in serious acts of violence, so too could children, and only the King or his justices were competent enough to decide their guilt or innocence. Some infants involved in a killing may have been so by chance, but such acts of violence could also be malicious. In 1299 Justice Henry Spigurnel, who served under the reign of Edward I and his successor, tried the case of eleven-year-old Thomas of Hordlegh in Maidstone, Kent. The local jury found that the boy had killed a five-year-old girl with a hatchet when she was trying to stop him stealing her family's bread. The justices found the accusation to be true and the boy was sentenced to death. Spigurnel recalled the case fourteen years later:

A lad of eleven years was once found guilty before me of having stolen certain chattels and of having killed a child. Now he carried the dead body of the child into a close, and hid it under some cabbages; and the fact that, after having killed the child, he also hid its body was taken as evidence of his heinous malice and he was condemned. So in this case, this lad had committed this felony entirely of his own conception, without any suggestion from his parents; and he must suffer judgement.[5]

Yet Spigurnel's case notwithstanding, this penalty seems to have been rarely used for children and, as this case suggests, for only the most severe offences. The fact of infancy was usually presented specially, so that a pardon could be obtained. Even in cases where there was some question over deliberate intent, such as that of Alice le Ster aged six who, it was believed, meant to kill a girl on the beach below her when kicking stones off a cliff-top, a pardon was granted. The inclusion of infants in the system of the King's pardon reflected the belief that while very young children were capable of crime, they could not always unambiguously be held responsible for it. The system was a useful way of protecting a child who had killed from the full punishment meted out to its elders, but it also delayed the establishment of a proper definition over the legal status of children.

It was not until the end of the thirteenth century that justices started to take a different view of a child's legal standing regarding murder. Rather than recommending them for a King's pardon but leaving the child imprisoned until it was received, sometimes more than a year later, judges used their own discretion to acquit the very young on their age alone. Though Anglo-Saxon kings had mentioned the age of seven as a mark of infancy, it now had a more lasting significance in English common law.[6] During the trial of two young brothers indicted for manslaughter, Henry Spigurnel said that a child ought not to suffer judgement if he committed his murderous deed before reaching the age of seven years. By the fourteenth century the King's Rolls recorded that 'an infant under the age of seven years, though he be convicted of felony, shall go free of judgement because he knoweth not of good and evil'.[7]

The fact that the medieval period saw children as young as four being taken from their family and locked up in the darkness of an ancient abbey is unimaginable from a modern perspective. The practice changed when it was ruled by precedent that a child under the age of seven was incapable of crime because of his lesser intellect. But the years beyond this brought considerable uncertainty, and engaged lawyers and theologians in abstract matters of religious doctrine and legal principle that would have direct relevance in the exceptional case of child murderers. At what age could a young person be said to pass from ignorance to understanding, and therefore become morally culpable either through sin or crime? If a child was believed to be too young to understand good and evil, then how could she or he knowingly commit such a heinous crime? The striking feature of all this, as we shall see throughout the stories in this book, is that each time a child kills another child these questions are asked, albeit in a different form. In essence, the question we are always asking is the same: what can a child's moral thought and understanding really encompass?

Growing Up With Guilt

The context in which these questions were asked at the start of the 1500s was one of change.[8] The Western Church was undergoing a transformation; a religion that had once been about observation of external rules became more a matter of the individual heart. A greater emphasis was placed on the state of people's souls and on the capacity for personal understanding. Children continued to be regarded as sinners from birth, as the theologian and Church of England clergyman Thomas Becon expressed when, in 1550, he asked: 'What is a child or to be a child?' He gave the reply: 'A child in Scripture is a wicked man, as he that is ignorant and not exercised in godliness.'[9] Children could be saved, however, and 'given victory over death and the devil' by faith, and by opening their souls to the Saviour. The spread of change in this period, linked to the historical upheaval of the Reformation, was aided by the publication of new catechisms, which became an essential pedagogic tool for the education of children.[10] The question-and-answer style of these pamphlets, which were published in their thousands, was aimed at ensuring that a child understood the meaning of the doctrines they were expected to live by. The sacraments of the Church, and in particular the Lord's Supper, or Communion, symbolised among other things the 'bread' of sincerity and truth. An understanding of its meaning for the spirit and soul of those taking part in it was crucial in order for its spiritual benefits to be realised. It was a principle already established in Catholic Christianity by St Paul's letter to the Corinthians:

> Whoever eats the bread or drinks the cup of the Lord in an unworthy manner will be guilty of sinning against the body and blood of the Lord. A man ought to examine himself before he eats of the bread or drinks of the cup. For anyone who eats and drinks without recognising the body of the Lord eats and drinks judgement on himself.[11]

The focus on personal salvation in the reformed Church meant that it was concerned not just with the formal, outward detail of religious expression, but with the inner world of motives too. These were the powerful but hidden agents of moral behaviour. Scripture was the best guide to moral action, but the requirements of confession demanded that some attention be given to the more obscure motives for behaviour that are only recognisable through conscience. The Reformation emphasis on education used the catechism to prepare a child for confirmation, for which he or she also had to make a personal confession to God. This dialogue with one's conscience gave the confessor an awareness of culpability for which he must atone. Luther believed that a deeper understanding of the rites of the Church developed as a child matured and that this maturity was marked by the sacrament of confirmation, which was only administered to those who had attained the years of discretion; that is, twelve or fourteen years old.[12]

In England throughout the sixteenth and seventeenth centuries, hundreds of catechisms were published. Religious instruction was especially significant in the turbulent times of the seventeenth century; its wider purpose was to secure national stability and religious orthodoxy, but its personal function was to achieve spiritual understanding.[13] Studying the catechism was seen as a preparation for adulthood, which for a whole range of religious, civil and legal purposes began as early as twelve. In order to be able to take on the duties and responsibilities of adulthood, the child had to be trained to understand their significance. Standards of moral conduct were measured by knowledge of the catechism, but so was a knowledge and understanding of God. It was, in effect, the beginning of a practice wherein children were taught proper moral behaviour that also had a secular dimension. The young were being culturally monitored and their thoughts, habits and actions were being judged not only by the authority of God, but by parents, teachers and priests.

Sir Matthew Hale, who had been lord chief justice under Cromwell and had survived to be reinstated by Charles II, believed the catechism was essential to a child's moral education, and he insisted that his older children send their progeny early to learn it:

So that they may take in the true principles of religion betimes, which grow up with them, and habituate them both to the knowledge and practice of it; that they may escape the danger of corruption by error or vice, being antecedently seasoned with better principles.[14]

Before a child could receive the sacrament of confirmation, an examination of the candidate's knowledge of the catechism had to take place. The test established not only the truth of a child's understanding, but also his guilt. Having the intention to tell the truth and not deceive was a necessary quality of a child seeking confirmation; the fate of his soul depended upon it. In this process of verifying a child's comprehension we can see the religious influence over the law, in that it was a process directly analogous to the legal test about knowledge of good and evil which a youngster was subjected to in a criminal court at the age of eight.

At the time Hale was writing, ecclesiastics no longer sat on the King's Bench but the laws of England were still Christian in character, which meant that questions about moral discretion in children were bound up with legal questions over knowledge of right and wrong. Each sphere was concerned with issues of moral culpability; in religion it was responsibility for sin, and in law it was liability for crime.

Hale was the most important lawyer in the land of his time, and it was his legal opinion that did the most to clarify a child's criminal responsibility in English law. His *History of the Pleas of the Crown*, published after his death in 1676, provides a link between medieval law and the Restoration period. In deciding on a child's liability for crime, Hale declared: 'If it appear by strong and pregnant evidence and circumstances, that he had discretion to judge between good and evil, judgement of death may be given against him.'[15]

This test of moral discretion had been the subject of some debate among earlier jurists. At issue were not only the technical problems involved with setting fixed age boundaries, which in any event could not be properly verified without an effective system of birth registration which was not introduced until the nineteenth century, but a wider issue of judgement, specifically an adult's judgement about a child's state of mind. If there was wickedness in a child's mind when committing a criminal act he was considered blameworthy, since guilt can only be ascribed to someone whose thoughts or intentions have been bad. It was not acceptable that a jury should simply infer bad intent because an action itself was wrong; intention had to be proved. Attending to the accused's state of mind was a difficult task for any judge or jury, but even more so when it involved children above seven years of age.

Sir Edward Coke, the most renowned jurist of the late Elizabethan era, believed that both the madman and the child under fourteen were without full discretion or understanding:

> In criminal causes, such as felony etc, the act of a madman shall not be imputed to him, for that in these causes *actus non facit reum nisi mens sit rea* (the act is not guilty unless the mind is blameworthy) and he is *amens (id est) sine mente*, without his mind or discretion ... and so it is of an infant until he be the age of 14 yrs.[16]

The above maxim assumes that the insane person, and by analogy the child, is incapable of having a guilty mind. Yet in the majority of cases an insane individual who commits a violent crime obviously has a will to harm his victim, as indeed a child sometimes does. The issue of intention was in need of refinement. In order for a criminal act such as murder to be fully regarded as intentional, the killer must be deemed capable of understanding the crime. A child might mean to kill without any real understanding of what death means. In this sense his or her intention is so limited as to be almost meaningless.

It was clear by the time Hale was writing that under common law a child of seven was incapable of criminal intent, but the matter was less clear for a child of nine or ten. Like previous jurists, Hale had made an analogy between children under fourteen and the insane to say that both were without understanding, but he later refined the example. In the case of madmen he drew a distinction between complete and partial insanity:

There is partial insanity of mind … some persons that have a competent use of reason in respect of some subjects, are yet under a particular dementia in respect of some particular discourses, subjects or applications; or else it is partial in respect of degrees; and this is the condition of very many, especially melancholy persons, who for the most part discover their defect in excessive fears and griefs, and yet are not wholly destitute of the use of reason.[17]

Similarly, a child above seven years, though regarded by law as without full discretion until the age of fourteen, could be deemed partially capable of understanding. Thus Hale wrote:

An infant without Age of Discretion kills a man, no felony; as if he be nine or ten years old. But if by Circumstances it appeareth he could distinguish between good and evil, it is Felony.[18]

In other words, in some circumstances it might be justly inferred that a child demonstrated that he not only intended his crime, but he also understood that it was wrong. This would be expressed by the Latin *doli capax*, derived from the word *dolus* meaning deceit, guile and wilful fraud. A child lying about a crime he had committed or trying to conceal the evidence for it might demonstrate this. In 1629 a boy of nine was hanged for burning two barns, 'it appearing that he had malice, revenge, craft and cunning'.[19] Almost a century later, the distinguished lawyer Sir William Blackstone wrote to the same effect, arguing that 'the capacity of doing ill, or contracting guilt, is not so much measured by years and days, as by the strength of the delinquent's understanding and judgement'.[20] Blackstone drew upon the authoritative opinion of his predecessor:

Matthew Hale gives us two instances one, of a girl of thirteen who was burnt for killing her mistress; another of a boy still younger that had killed his companion, and hidden himself, who was hanged; for it appeared by his hiding, that he knew he had done wrong and could discern between good and evil; and in such cases the maxim of law is *malitia supplet aetatem* (malice supersedes age).[21]

Throughout the century following Hale's death in 1676, jurists and justices of the High Court discussed the liability of children under fourteen to conviction and execution for capital offences. In deciding upon a child's understanding of a crime he had committed, the test of moral discretion was consistently applied. The jury had to decide if the young criminal had guilty knowledge and understood that what he did was wrong. Hale had given the example of concealment as proof of mischievous discretion and just grounds for judging a child's guilt. But the common law is similar to stones in a building; it is built up case by case, year by year. A child who killed another child was so rare that any judge confronted by such a case had to consider it afresh, relying on the works of Hale and others for guidance. One case in the eighteenth century became a turning point in the consolidation of the law on such crimes: it involved a young workhouse boy aged ten, who killed a girl half his age.

'The Devil Put Me Upon It'

William York was ten years of age when on 5 August 1748 he was tried at Bury St Edmunds for the murder of five-year-old Susanna Mayhew.[22] His destitute parents had abandoned him and his two younger sisters to the parish of the small Suffolk town of Eye. William was apprenticed to a local villager, John Cutting, who also took in the two girls.[23] It was not uncommon for tenant farmers to buy children from the poorhouse to help them with work on the farm; the victim, Susanna, was also a pauper child living with the Cuttings.

On the day of the murder, Cutting and his wife had left early in the morning to go to work. The boy was put in charge of the children, and they were all in bed when the Cuttings left the house. On their return that evening, Susanna was missing and, when asked where she was, William answered that he had got her up that morning and dressed her, but did not know where she had gone. A search was made in the ditches and pools of water near the house, in case she had fallen into them. During the search, Cutting noticed that a dung-heap near the house had been newly turned up, and when he went to look, he found the body of the child about a foot deep under the surface; she had been 'cut and mangled in the most barbarous and horrid manner.'[24]

It was evident that the boy was connected to her death; he was, after all, the only person who had been with the girl on the day. At a crowded coroner's hearing, he denied his guilt for some time until he was questioned further, and eventually broke down and confessed. Before committing him to jail, however, where he would wait four months before any trial took place, the justice of the peace took care to ensure that the boy understood the implications of what he had confessed to; he was told the danger he would be in should he be found guilty, and then left alone in a room with food and drink for some hours. When he was finally brought before the magistrate a second time he did not retract his confession, but he repeated something he had said all along: 'The Devil put me upon committing the deed.' His confession records that Susanna had been sulky and had 'befouled' her bed, so he took her into the yard with the intention of killing her with a reaping hook. Realising that this would not do the trick, he:

took hold of the girl's left hand and cut her wrist and cut her all around and the bone with his knife, and then he threw her down and cut her to the bone above the elbow of the same arm. That after this he set his foot upon her stomach and cut her right arm about and to the bone at the wrist and above the elbow. Then he thought that she still would not die, and therefore he took the hook and cut her left thigh to the bone, and, observing she was not yet dead, his next care was to conceal the body. For this purpose he filled a pail with water at a ditch and washed the blood that was spilt on the ground, and made the dunghill as smooth as he could. Afterwards he

William York, aged Ten Years, murdering Susan Mahew, aged Five Years.

2. *This etching of the murder appears in the 1825 edition of the* Newgate Calendar. *Reproduced by permission of the British Library.*

washed the knife and hook and carried them into the house, hid the child's clothes in an old chamber, and then came down and got his breakfast.[25]

John Cutting and the Justice of the Peace witnessed this terrible confession, and it was put into writing together with the results of the coroner's inquiry. The document was then handed over to the commission of jail delivery, and William was detained in the jail at Eye until the crown court assembled later that summer.

The assizes of Bury St Edmunds were held twice a year at the Shire Hall, near the town's medieval centre. The arrival of the judges, together with their train of lawyers and servants, was met by a grand pageant of celebrated local dignitaries. The chief justice leading on 5 August 1748 was Sir John Willes, an unpopular figure even among his own superiors.[26] His naked ambition and indiscreet involvements drew criticism from others, including the writer and politician Horace Walpole who related a disapproving story about Willes: 'An official once came to tell Willes that there was grave talk of one of his maidservants being with child. Willes barked, "What is that to me?" and the grave official replied, "Oh, but they say it is by your Lordship." "And what is that to you?" was the stark reply.'[27]

Judge Willes' own misdemeanours, however, were no moral barrier to him wearing the cap of judgement that day when he sentenced ten-year-old William York. It is not known how many batches of cases there were on the day's business, but almost certainly the murder case of five-year-old Susanna Mayhew would have drawn many local people to the courtroom. This was an assize town that had seen many infamous trials. In 1645 eighteen women had been hanged for witchcraft, and in one of the last possession cases of the seventeenth century, two women had been executed in 1662.

The Crown chamber was a large room of two stories, the judges sitting with the high sheriff and local justices on an elevated podium at the front. Immediately behind and above them was a large window: the only source of light in the room that allowed the justices to see the face of the accused. The jurors were sworn in. The twelve men were drawn from the middle ranks of village and town society, such as yeomen and artisans.[28] Women, servants and the poor were disqualified from serving as they were not property owners. Once the clerk of arraignment had publicly asked the crier to announce the business of the court, the trial began.

A Child's Status in Court

Like an adult on trial for murder at this time, William would have been responsible for his own defence. Being so young he would not have been sworn in, but the jury would have taken his plea as testimony. He could have called witnesses, his little sisters for example, but because they were children they could not be sworn in either, although the jury would have considered anything they might have said in his defence. Underpinning the credibility of a witness were two simple questions: did they have the capacity for moral judgement and understanding; and if so, could they be relied upon to tell the truth? Children, madmen and idiots were not considered competent to testify, their oaths holding no weight because of their 'want of skill or discernment'.[29]

A child's unsworn testimony could be heard in court. Sir Matthew Hale decreed it so, though only if it was 'fortified with concurrent evidence ... as in cases of rape, buggery, witchcraft, and such crimes, which are practised upon children.'[30] Yet in the infamous case of the two Suffolk witches whom Hale tried in

1662, he declared the children they had supposedly bewitched to be too young to give evidence.[31] Clearly there was doubt over the credibility of a child's word. If they were not required to testify under oath, and were not therefore bound by the rules of the court, it was believed that they could lie with impunity. Fourteen-year-old James Lindsay was sent to the gallows for witchcraft in Scotland in 1697 after an eleven-year-old girl, who clearly suffered from epilepsy, accused him of all kinds of devilry.[32] And at one trial in Pendle Forest in Lancashire, a child accused her mother of witchcraft and gave evidence that resulted in her execution.[33] For the most part, though, if a child did tell the truth at a hearing, their evidence simply had less credibility than that of an adult and therefore less chance of being believed.

There was, however, a category of crime where children's testimony appears, perhaps unexpectedly, to have been given serious recognition. Children in sexual abuse cases were sworn in and their testimony taken, and there were instances where evidence of what the child told his or her mother was accepted as evidence in court.[34] In one case, a ten-year-old girl gave evidence against a young apprentice working for her mother. The little girl told the court what he had done to her, and on the basis of this, along with the fact that she had contracted his venereal disease, the apprentice was found guilty and sentenced to death.[35] By the second half of the eighteenth century, Sir William Blackstone (who for ten years sat on the King's Bench division of the high court) stated that:

An infant, though disabled from doing so many acts of his own account, may yet act effectually, as an agent, for one who may have chosen to appoint him as such. He cannot be a juror, but may be a witness, in cases of even the greatest moment, civil and criminal, and though of very tender years, provided the court be satisfied of his intelligence, and knowledge of an obligation of an oath.[36]

The oaths administered in a criminal court during this time included a statement that spoke of the avoidance of malice, hatred, evil, will, greed, favour or affection.[37] Establishing whether or not a child understood the meaning of an oath was achieved by a religious test, one that was also taken by non-Christians. The test made belief in heaven and hell, God and the Devil the necessary condition for an understanding of the oath's meaning, because the focus was on the consequences of lying, and the idea that perjury would be punished by eternal damnation. In one example, an eleven-year-old girl was allowed to be sworn in and to give evidence at the Old Bailey, when in answer to the judge's question, 'What becomes of persons who do not tell the truth after they depart this life?', she replied 'they go to the wicked man', by which she meant 'the devil'.[38]

Young William York appears to have kept silent at his trial and called no evidence in his defence. While the judge deemed this to be due to his ignorance and stupidity, it was just as likely because of the fact that he was only ten years old and illiterate.[39] In any case, his confession meant that he did not stand a chance of a verdict other than guilty. In his letter to the King on this case, Judge Willes wrote:

> I told the jury that notwithstanding his age, considering the circumstances of the case, if they had no reason to disbelieve the evidence they ought to find the boy guilty of wilful murder; for all the law books agree that *Malitia Supplet Aetatem*.[40]

Malice supersedes age, and the boy had shown 'sufficient malice and cunning' for the jury to agree with the judge's direction. The fact that William had hidden the body of five-year-old Susanna in a dung heap was proof to them that he knew his act was evil. They returned a guilty verdict of wilful murder for which he was given the sentence of death. Twenty years later, a King's Bench judge, Sir Michael Foster, wrote at some length about this case in his book *Crown Law*. He was certain that the boy had been 'a proper subject for capital punishment, and ought to suffer; for it would be of very dangerous consequence to have it thought, that children may commit such atrocious crimes with impunity'.[41]

But at the time of William York's trial, Lord Justice Willes could find no recent precedent in the law books for an actual hanging in such a case. William's sentence was temporarily respited while the judge returned to London and discussed the case with colleagues at Serjeants' Inn.[42] It was not unusual for judges to consult lawyers on matters of law, but it was not common to involve so many other judges when considering a sentence. The history of cases where children had stood trial for murder was unwritten, and examples were rare; no wonder Willes was uncertain about the boy's punishment: 'I could find but two instances of infants who had been hanged so very young as this boy is, and the last of them was in the Reign of King Henry the Seventh.'[43] The written opinion of Sir Matthew Hale was his only guide, but as this had been penned more than a century earlier, he sought further opinion. This took time, and William waited in jail under the sentence of death for another six months, receiving three respites on technical grounds, until finally they all agreed that he showed no penitence or remorse, and that the facts dictated that he should be publicly executed. Had it not been for the fact that the majesty of the law depended as much upon mercy as condemnation, the boy might well have gone to the gallows.

It is known from contemporary reports that crowds gathered at the trial, and the judge will have been aware of their feelings and opinions about the case. Since nineteen villagers petitioned for the boy's mercy, it was evident that there was considerable sympathy for him. Roger North reflected on how his brother, the judge Sir Francis North, negotiated the difficulties of trials held in the public eye:

> He was infinitely scrutinous in capital cases, but never more puzzled than when a popular cry was at the heels of a business; for then he had his jury to deal with, and if he did not tread upon eggs, they would conclude sinistrously, and be apt to find against his opinion.[44]

Lord Chief Justice Willes had to demonstrate to the good people of Suffolk the quality of justice delivered in the King's Court. It was important to demonstrate strict adherence to the law, while at the same time leaving the way open for the King to show mercy. The special nature of this case made such a display all the more critical, for it reinforced the sense of legitimacy upon which the rule of law depended. So although the singular role that judges had in the eighteenth-century trial gave them immense power over its outcome, respect for the law relied upon consensual judgements being arrived at between Crown and jury. In this case Willes had achieved an opinion consistent with his own, but he had also to respond to those who were keen for the boy to be shown clemency. The appellants pleaded for the 'very poor ignorant child', but the judge said he could reprieve him no more without the King's direction.[45] Eventually, the pardon was granted on condition that William be sent into the navy.[46]

The case was important legally because it led to the fullest discussion that had ever taken place of the rules that applied at that time to the criminal liability of children. The common law governing these rules had no authorised written version; unlike, say, the texts of statutes enacted by Parliament. As shown earlier in this chapter, similar cases reported in the medieval Year Books had been written up, and other jurists had developed the law over time by incorporating the decisions reached by other courts. However, following precedent in these types of cases was not easy; there appear to be no examples to draw upon between the medieval cases and those of the eighteenth century. Foster's discussion of this case helped establish the modern legal position of a child on trial for murder.

The Devil's Absence in Law

One further aspect of this case marked it out as modern, namely the attitudes to the child's insistent claim that the 'devil put me upon it'. The judge and jury apparently discarded this. But if the boy had killed Susanna, and from his detailed confession there is little reason to doubt that he had, the prosecution still had to prove that he knew it was wrong. Those trying the case had the evidence of concealment and lying, but what if it was to be believed that the devil had put him up to it? It is not so remote a possibility that William believed himself to be maddened through possession, or at least felt that his being was given over to an act he would not normally have committed. In the psychology of William's day, madness was narrowly defined. Generally, it was thought to involve a total loss of the mind, an absence of the ability to reason.[47]

William's concealment of his crime would, under this definition, be seen as evidence that his mind was intact. His description that the devil put him up to murder is more akin to earlier views of madness explained as possession by forces from 'outside'. The capital offence of witchcraft had been abolished in England in 1735 (thirteen years prior to this case) but, for some, insanity was still regarded as evil provoked by the devil. The English legal philosopher Jeremy Bentham, born in the year of this trial, spoke of his youth as a time when he was haunted by spirits and fear of the supernatural: 'This subject of ghosts has been among the torments of my life, the devil was everywhere in it and in me too.'[48] It is surely understandable, if not legitimate, that a child would use the language of possession to mean that he had indeed been maddened by the devil, and that this would amount to more than a simple excuse. Such a description fitted the religious psychology of the day; a belief system that, in part, stood in for powerful, overwhelming emotions. Later, scientific theories of madness might have confirmed William's description, defining it as 'homicidal monomania' deriving not from the beyond, but from the body.[49]

In a later case of a child murdering a little girl, a 'gentleman in black' was mentioned as an invisible hand guiding the dark deeds of the killer. Elizabeth Morton was fifteen years old when she was hanged on Gallows Hill, Nottingham on 8 April 1763. She was a servant employed in the parish of Walkeringham by farmer John Oliver. In August 1762, Mrs Oliver found one of her children hidden under some straw in a barn, 'struggling in the agonies of death, the blood gushing from its mouth, nose and eyes'.[50] The child recovered and accused Elizabeth. The servant was immediately suspected of having strangled the family's two-year-old daughter Mary, who had been found dead in her cradle months earlier.

Elizabeth confessed to the crime, but said she had been incited to commit it by a gentleman in black who came to bed with her and told her she must murder two of her master's children. She could not feel easy, she said, until she had done as he directed. Despite the fact that the report in the *Annual Register* suggested she was an 'idiot' (which would have been grounds for a pardon), she was executed a month later. The *Register* gives a poignant description of the illiterate girl on the way to the gallows:

> Her little chip hat was torn to pieces by the high wind which was blowing. Even when standing in a plank across a cart and with the halter round her neck she seemed as little concerned as the thousands who had come to see her execution. Her features and person were attractive rather than repulsive. She was stoutly built and tall, considering her age.[51]

According to the same report in the *Register*, her body was removed and dissected before burial in a village near her home. Neither infancy nor idiocy saved Elizabeth Morton from the gallows, yet, on the face of it, there appear to have been grounds for either defence to have prevailed. By the time of this trial, and that of William York, the idea of insanity as demonic possession was on the wane, as indeed was belief in witchcraft.[52] Although Sir Matthew Hale had declared his belief in witchcraft more than a century earlier, and had sent two women to their deaths 'because the scriptures affirm it', it is likely that those sitting in judgement of Elizabeth would have sought to distance themselves from the superstitious beliefs of their forefathers.

By the late eighteenth century, society's elite viewed supernatural beliefs with disdain, in order to separate enlightened gentlemen from the deluded rabble of the unenlightened poor. According to historian Roy Porter:

> The repeal of witchcraft legislation was an expression of deeper shifts in the elite outlooks, often represented as a joyous emancipation from dated dogmas repugnant to modernisers anxious to bury the past and to build a better future.

The Enlightenment proclaimed *sapere aude*, and one of the truths it dared to know was that witchcraft, magic and all their supernatural trappings were false or foolish phantasms.[53]

The law as it stood at the time had no way of recognising a child's insanity or feeblemindedness, as scientific explanations of children's cognitive development were still a long way off.[54]

A Child's Comprehension of the Trial

Elizabeth and William confessed to their crimes, but whether they really understood their full meaning is doubtful. In some cases a confession was not always proffered so easily. A report in the *Criminal Recorder* in 1807 shows fifteen-year-old Richard Faulkner being tricked into a declaration of guilt. The case, published by two evangelical lawyers, said that the boy 'manifested a most depraved and vindictive disposition'. He had beaten a twelve-year-old boy to death, and was so 'shockingly depraved and hardened, that after condemnation, he repeatedly clenched his fist, and threatened to murder the clergyman who attended the gaol or anyone who dared to approach him'. His jailers came up with a novel idea to scare him into contrition. They dressed up a boy of the same age to make him look like the murdered boy and at nightfall he was led into Faulkner's cell, where the miscreant lay chained by his hands and feet in total darkness:

> ... he started, and seemed so completely terrified, that he trembled every limb, cold drops of sweat profusely falling from him; and even, almost momentarily, in such a dreadful state of agitation, that he entreated the clergyman to continue with him; and from that instant, became so contrite and penitent

as he had been before callous and insensible. In this transition he remained until his execution on Monday morning July 13th 1807, having fully confessed his crime, and implored, by fervent prayer, the forgiveness of heaven.[55]

There was no recorded protest at this hanging, and no jurors recommended mercy on account of his youth. The jury might have been strengthened in their resolve to find Faulkner guilty because of his demeanour at the time of the trial. A child's bearing or conduct in court could influence jurors' opinion of him. Faulkner's lack of contrition, together with his initial deceit about what he had done, had the legal status of objective evidence, but it also had a powerful moral content. Lying was sinful; it described not only behaviour but also character. A child's lie, especially over such a brutal slaying of another child, was no doubt perceived as all the more wilful and disturbing. Certainly there was a consensus of disapproval about this lad, and a belief that he should die for his hideous crime.[56]

At fifteen years old, Richard Faulkner and Elizabeth Morton were fully responsible in law. The doctrine of *doli incapax* was a legal presumption that children below the age of fourteen years were incapable of criminal intent. In any criminal case involving children over seven, the Crown had the burden of rebutting this presumption, which it did in William York's case on the evidence that he concealed his victim's body. But there is an example of a child killing in this period where the doctrine appears to have operated according to its intended purpose, namely that of protecting young children from liability to be punished. Unfortunately, however, only scant detail of the case survives today. Anne Stimson, Mary Bosworth and Mary Male, aged ten, nine and eight respectively, were tried at Huntingdon Lent Assizes in 1778 for the murder of Sarah Bright, aged three. The *Annual*

Register for that year carries a very brief report:

> The manner in which they committed this act was by fixing three pins at the end of a stick, which they thrust into the child's body, which lacerated the private parts and soon turned to a mortification of which she languished for a few days and then died.[57]

After the trial, the jury found that the girls were *non capax doli* – incapable of understanding the nature of their act – and they were acquitted.[58] Was it because they were girls that they went free? The nature of what they did to the child is an echo of much later crimes such as that committed by the killers of two-year-old James Bulger in 1993. Or are we to believe that, on occasion at least, society and the courts of the past proved more lenient than their twentieth-century counterparts?

Age Without Mercy

Among the cases of child-by-child murder for which there is evidence, this example of acquittal is the exception for the period. The sentence of death is the strongest form of condemnation a society can inflict. Its justification is retribution and deterrence, and although child murderers were, and still are, extremely rare, it is precisely their exceptional nature that was sometimes used to justify the severest punishment. Writing about the William York case, Lord Justice Sir Michael Foster said:

> There are many crimes of the most heinous nature, such as in the present case the murder of young children, poisoning parents or masters, burning houses, which children are very

capable of committing; and which they may in some circumstances be under strong temptations to commit, and therefore,
though the taking away the life of a boy of ten years old may
favour of cruelty, yet the example of this boy's punishment
may be a means of deterring other children from like offences,
and as the sparing this boy, *merely on account of his age*, will
probably have quite the contrary tendency, in justice to the
publik, the law ought to take its course; unless there remaineth
any doubt touching his guilt.[59]

Fortunately this view did not prevail and York, as we know, was
spared the ultimate punishment because he was only ten years
old. When Foster was writing in 1776, 220 offences were punishable in England by death. In London alone there were five times
as many hangings in the second half of the century as there had
been in the first, and 90 per cent of those suffering the penalty
were under 21.[60] The idea of exemplary punishment, particularly
for serious offences, was at its height. Elizabeth Mason was executed for poisoning her mistress when she was only fourteen.[61]
Violent offences against property were a particular target for
the capital laws, and the young were not always spared. In 1791,
teenager John Mead was executed for setting fire to his master's
house, and a few weeks later another boy of sixteen was brought
to the gallows for a similar offence.[62] At fourteen, Robert Cox
screamed and cried incessantly when he came within sight of the
gallows, his anguish being all the more terrible as it is likely that
he was innocent of the violent robbery for which he had been
sentenced.[63]

The medieval cruelty of incarcerating small children was long
gone; it belonged to an era when the law was uncertain about
how to deal with criminals of such a young age. But were we to
end this chapter where it began, in the central provinces of Italy,

we would find that full criminal responsibility did not begin there at seven years, as it did here, but at fourteen.[64] And while England was still sending teenagers to the gallows, the Duchy of Tuscany had abolished capital punishment altogether by 1786. It would be misleading to suggest that the law tightened the noose around the neck of every young criminal that came into contact with it; severe punishments were by no means as widespread as is sometimes thought.[65] Yet hangings of children did occur, even at a time when cultural sensibilities were prevailing against it. Was this because the example of a child brutally slaying another was so extreme that it could easily ignite a call for retribution?

Chapter Two

'DABBLING IN A YOUNG MURDERER'S BLOOD'

*Last year I was called out of town, to hang a little boy for killing with
malice aforethought. [He] was the youngest fellow-creature I ever handled
in the way of our business; and a beautiful child he was too, as you may
have seen by the papers, with a straight nose, large blue eyes and golden
hair ... [The crowd] saw the stripling lifted fainting on to the gallows, his
smooth cheeks of the colour of wood-ashes, his limbs trembling, and his
bosom heaving sigh after sigh as if his body and soul were parting without
my help. It was not a downright murder; for there was scarce any life
to take out of him. When I began to pull the cap ... over his baby face,
he pressed his small hands together (his arms you know were corded fast
to his body) and gave me a beseeching look; just as a calf will lick
the butcher's hand. But cattle do not speak: this creature muttered,
'Pray, sir, don't hurt me.'*
EDWARD GIBBON WAKEFIELD, 1832[1]

John Any Bird Bell was fourteen when he was hanged outside
Maidstone jail on 1 August 1831. The crime for which he was
punished was one of the first child killings in history to achieve
national notoriety. *The Times* reported that 10,000 people came
to watch his execution, which at the time was more than the entire
population of Canterbury.[2] They arrived early in the morning;
groups of people drew up on carts and gathered in expectation
around the large courtyard of the sprawling jail. Within a couple

of hours the yard was heaving; those who could not see the scaffold stage lifted themselves onto carriages, huddled at nearby windows or squeezed further into the tightening throng. A moveable wooden drop had been erected outside the prison entrance, the first of its kind in the county, and specially constructed for this unusual hanging. Up until this August day Kent citizens, like those in London and elsewhere, had always enjoyed a carnival-like parade to the site of execution, where the final agonies of a gallows victim were preceded by plentiful stops for alcohol and merriment.[3] But from this day on, scaffold entertainment was viewed quite differently in this corner of England. It was thought barbarous and indelicate to take pleasure in such a solemn event, and this case in particular cried out for decency in death.

John Bell's punishment was the last in English history given to one so young. Although the execution took place in the third decade of the nineteenth century, it was a penalty that belonged to a very different era, and many at the time believed that it should never have taken place. The jury who tried him did not want his execution, the bereaved father of the child he killed almost certainly did not either, and judging by *The Times'* report of the crowd that day grieving for the lad as he confronted the gallows, thousands of others were unhappy about it too.

The High Court judge Sir Justice Gaselee had, three days earlier, issued his unpopular sentence in the crowded Shire Hall where the assizes for the county were held. Sitting in the centre of the court, elevated on a throne carved in oak, the eminent judge looked down to the dock where the young boy stood, and told him:

> Although one shudders at the idea of having to pronounce sentence of death on a person of your age, and although one should be extremely happy to pay every attention to the

humane recommendations of the Jury on your behalf; when I consider the nature of the offence – an offence against the law of God and man – and that we are told by the divine law, that 'whosoever sheddeth man's blood, by man shall his blood be shed', I am afraid that I cannot give way to their feelings, on this occasion; but must cause the sentence to be executed.[4]

The jury of twelve local men had taken only minutes to return their guilty verdict, but they had pleaded that the boy be spared the death penalty because of his youth and because of the 'profligate and unnatural manner in which he had been brought up'. The judge's refusal of mercy appeared to have occasioned little surprise. Known for his ill-temper, Justice Gaselee 'brooked no contradiction', according to Charles Dickens who made him the model for Mr Justice Stareleigh in *The Pickwick Papers*. Fond of a lunch of mutton chops and several glasses of sherry, he was portly, short, and capable of napping silently through a meandering trial. Alexander Pope's remark that 'The hungry judges soon the sentence sign/And wretches hang that jury-men may dine' was perhaps a fitting description in his case.[5] His pronouncement of the boy's sentence was noted for its want of feeling and betrayed a quality common to others in the profession at this time; judges were a peculiarly unfeeling lot. The humiliating chastisements of their schooling, along with the cool disciplinary environment of their home life, tended to leave them with profound emotional shortcomings. The ease with which they appeared to administer disciplinary violence (every three days, for over a decade, someone died on the scaffold) was, according to the historian Vic Gatrell, because 'such men thought of themselves as created in the image of a punitive, flagellant God, as the disciplines of school spilt over into those applied to children and servants in the home'.[6] Their experience of corporal punishment in childhood, though by no means peculiar to men of their background, meant that they, together with politicians, were uniquely positioned for its effects to be continued in the unforgiving punishments of the state.

Judges had no sentiment about hanging and resisted its abolition; they were a conservative elite who defended their power to punish those whom they believed were deserving of it. In 1800 one judge refused to lift the death sentence for a ten-year-old boy who had stolen notes from a post office because he believed the boy had 'art and contrivance beyond his years'.[7] The crowd in the courtroom were horrified at the sentence for one so young, and had it not been for their cries of protest the King's mercy might never have been sought. Judges in this period had wide powers of discretion, and in the John Bell case, Justice Gaselee could have appealed to the King on the child's behalf in favour of an alternative punishment, since the Royal Prerogative rarely ran counter to the recommendations of a senior judge.

But Gaselee showed no empathy for the boy who looked so much the child as he stood draped in a pale smock surrounded by the grandeur of the Shire Hall. Facing this diminutive figure in the courtroom, the knighted judge could scarcely have regarded Bell as of the same species. The enormous social difference between the offender and himself created a gap that could never be bridged by empathy; and yet, by the 1830s, the qualities of sympathy and fellow-feeling had become defining characteristics for any individual who considered himself part of a new, enlightened world. The identity of the emerging middle class was in large part shaped by a sense of itself as a civilising force.[8] The humanitarian sensibilities of the period which were marked by the movement to abolish slavery, as well as efforts to curb the brutal excesses of child labour through the Factory Acts, were also characterised by a new sensitivity to violent punishments and physical suffering.[9]

Christians were encouraged to walk in the shoes of their fellow man. 'Sympathy', according to the Enlightenment philosopher David Hume, is 'that propensity we have to receive by communication [the] inclinations and sentiments of [others], however different from, or even contrary to, our own'.[10]

Gaselee, however, belonged to a class of gentlemen described by the radical politician William Cobbett as 'the most cruel, the most unfeeling, the most brutally insolent' of all God's creatures; the chances of him recognising John Bell's humanity were remote indeed. Most of those sentenced to death were poor, and young John Bell was no exception. His father was an out-of-work agricultural labourer, his mother and the three children spent their days grubbing woods for firewood, and they would have been lucky to earn more than £18 a year. Sir Justice Gaselee, on the other hand, earned £8,000 per annum, his father had been an eminent surgeon, and his son Stephen had taken the usual route to the Bar.[11] But it wasn't just character and status that were at play in Justice Gaselee's conduct during the trial; he also had an image of himself as God's legal representative on earth.

In an era when crime and sin were linked as one, an offence against the law was effectively a reproach to the Christian religion. 'Christianity is part and parcel of the Law of England', wrote the distinguished seventeenth-century legal scholar and lord chief justice, William Hale.[12] A contemporary and friend of Hale's, the Bishop of Salisbury Gilbert Burnett, believed: 'We owe to human society and to the safety and order of the world our endeavours to put a stop to the wickedness of men; which a good man may do with great inward tenderness to the souls of those whom he persecutes.'[13] The 'good man' to whom Burnett referred was every judge charged with the task of administering the laws of a Christian country, and he could send men, women or children to the gallows with a clear conscience.

John Bell's sentence of death was not the first of the morning's business on 1 August 1831; another young man had been condemned to death by the judge only hours before.[14] This was justice eighteenth-century-style, and it continued to hold sway, though mostly only for violent crime, right up to the beginning of the reform era in 1832. Gaselee's experience of the law had been fashioned by the long tradition of exemplary punishment, the chief purpose of which was to provide a terrifying lesson to those considering crime. In one case at the end of the eighteenth century the actual offence was robbery, but because the judge believed that the thieves intended to murder their victim, he sentenced them to be hanged. Joseph Wood and Thomas Underwood were both aged fourteen when they were executed at Newgate on 6 July 1791. The *Newgate Calendar* reported the case:

> Though of this tender age yet they were convicted as old and daring depredators, so often had they already been arraigned at the bar, where they were condemned, that the judge declared, notwithstanding their appearance (they were short, dirty, ill-visaged boys) it was necessary for public safety, to cut them off, that in order other boys might learn, that inured to wickedness their tender age would not save them from an ignominious fate.[15]

Salutary terror was so important an element in ideas of punishment that children were routinely taken to watch hangings by way of moral instruction. For a vulnerable child the effect could be devastating. One sixteen-year-old boy in Bristol was so disturbed by what he saw on a scaffold that he killed himself the same day. The lesson of the scaffold appeared in children's books: 'Every good boy was to ride in his coach, and be a lord mayor; and every bad boy was to be hung, or eaten by lions', one author recalled of his boyhood reading. A Methodist schoolmaster in Reading was so convinced of the persuasive power of the gallows that he took his class to watch, and a school holiday was allowed so that children could see a girl hanged at Horsham in 1824.[16] In the fictional *The History of the Fairchild Family: or The Child's Manual: Being a collection of stories calculated to show the importance and effect of a religious education* (1818), the middle-class Mr Fairchild reads his children prayers, gives them pious speeches and beatings and then, to punish them further, takes them to see the gibbeted body of a murderer:

> The body of a man hung in chains; [it] had not yet fallen to pieces, although it had hung there some years. It had on a blue coat, a silk handkerchief round the neck, with shoes and stockings, and every other part of the dress still entire; but the face of the corpse was so shocking, that the children could not look upon it. 'Oh! Let us go, papa!' cried the children, 'Not yet,' said their father, 'I must tell you the history of the wretched man before we go from this place'.[17]

The book was published in several editions, and right up until the end of the nineteenth century readers recalled how its images and message had haunted them throughout childhood. In a similar vein, a collection of poems called *The Affectionate Parent's Gift and the Good Child's Reward* shows a father taking his children to the condemned cells at Newgate where they were told that the chilling cries they heard came from 'poor men, who doomed to die upon the coming day, were venting frantic fears of grief, and kneeling down to pray'.[18]

Adult memories show the hold that execution had over the minds of children. The penal reformer, Samuel Romilly, recalls having nightmares as a child about the images of cruelty and murder that he found in the gallows broadsides – the woodcuts and pamphlets sold to the scaffold crowds:

> The prints, which I found in the lives of the martyrs and the *Newgate Calendar*, have cost me many sleepless nights. My dreams too were disturbed by the hideous images which haunted my imagination by day. I thought myself present at executions, murders and scenes of blood; and I have often lain in bed agitated by my terrors, equally afraid of remaining awake in the dark, and of falling asleep to encounter the horrors of my dreams.[19]

Similar impressions tormented the barrister William Ballantine. Stories of criminal cruelties were told to him as a child by his nurse: 'The relation ... of any horrible crime used to produce a most painful effect upon me.'[20] The publisher Charles Knight remembers being taken to see two gibbeted bodies when he was four: 'The chains rattled; the iron plates scarcely held the gibbet together; the rags of the highway man displayed their horrible skeletons. That was a holiday sight for a schoolboy sixty years ago.'[21]

As far as Sir Justice Gaselee was concerned, the exemplary punishment given to John Bell had its justification – hanging being an enactment of the divine will of God. 'Whosoever sheddeth a man's blood, by man shall his blood be shed', he told Bell as he sentenced him; the execution, in effect, being sanctioned by a religious sense of public justice.[22] In the mind of his Lordship, Bell's offence was against 'the law of God and Man', and he must pay the price and pray to his redeemer, 'who is willing to receive a repentant sinner even at the last hour ... in another world [where] you will receive forgiveness which it is my duty to deny you in this'. The Kent county magistrates, most of whom were

clergymen, were in a similar vein, and it fell to them to orches-
trate the details of John Bell's execution.[23]

Careful attention had to be given to how this punishment
would be carried out. The manner of the young felon's demise
would have to reflect a higher feeling than gaiety. The mood
across the country was changing towards capital punishment;
the entertainments shown at hangings in the past were now
beginning to be seen as belonging to an unenlightened age. Many
genteel Christians showed revulsion towards the crowds who
came to watch hangings. The problem, as these religiously refined
people saw it, was that the spectacle was not attended by the right
amount of solemnity. Far from being chastened by the salutary
effects of execution, it was believed that crowds were cheapened
by it. One cleric complained that the witnesses to a hanging he
attended were silent at the moment of death, but afterwards
erupted into 'the most incongruous sounds of low jesting and
indecent ribaldry. The brief silence originated in the morbid
curiosity of the crowd to catch the unexpected words of the hero
of the moment.'[24]

John Bell's death was to be no occasion for laughter. The high
spirits that had previously been shown beneath the old gallows at
Penenden Heath, just on the edge of Maidstone town, were now
considered by local dignitaries to be 'detrimental to the proper
feelings of the sufferers, and outrageous to decency'.[25] The magistrates ordered that a scaffold be built over the entrance lodge
of Maidstone jail, and that it should be carefully arranged for its
small victim. The gibbet on which the boy was to be tied had to
be lowered so that he was at the right distance for the trapdoor
which was levered open. To adjust only the rope would be risky;
if lengthened, it could sever the head; too short, and it might slip
under the lad's jaw, making his end all the more painful and pro-
longed. The sheriff discussed the details with the hangman who

had arrived by stagecoach from London the night before. It was William Calcraft's first execution at Maidstone, and he had been in the job as the country's official hangman for only two years. He had bungled other hangings during his brief office, misjudging the drop that would bring about a quick death.[26]

But execution was not an exact science. On the day itself, one of the ties of the beam was not loosened in time so there was a pause before the boy dropped, seconds in which his mind must have been maddened with mortal terror. The assembled crowd were overcome by what they saw. Local reports told of women, and men too, weeping as the youngster was led towards the platform. What they made of what followed can only be guessed at; the disfiguring of a child's body by what Dickens called 'the hideous apparatus of death'. Finally, as a mark of the boy's infamy, his body was taken away for medical dissection.

The shocking thing about this hanging was that it took place at a time when many were saying that neither reason nor Christianity gave us the right to 'shed the blood of another'. There was a move away from the barbarous state of affairs where deterrence was exercised through terror, towards a more restrained form of discipline with clear rational aims.

The thinking of the Italian aristocrat and penal reformer Cesare Beccaria was influencing parliamentarians and lawyers like Sir Samuel Romilly and the philosopher Jeremy Bentham. They all argued that the effectiveness of any punishment was marked more by its restraint than its excesses, which, it might be expected, is how the hanging of a child might have been seen. Romilly played a leading role in getting England's most severe capital laws repealed in the early nineteenth century.[27] At one time there were 200 offences on the statutes for which both young and old could be executed; though in fact, for children, the sentence of death only rarely resulted in execution. From the beginning of the 1800s to the time of John Bell's hanging in 1831, 103 children were sentenced to death at the Old Bailey, but none suffered the final penalty.[28] Murder, however, was different. While it was expected that youth should be spared the punishment of death, murder was a rare crime among children, and it was not beyond the bounds of the most severe reaction.

Hanging was now used only sparingly for this most heinous of crimes; however, the calculated cruelty of John Bell's savage attack no doubt added to the sense among some that his punishment was just. The London broadsheet in which his story appeared etched the image of the crime vividly, and one dramatic report said: 'Its horrifying detail had never been equalled.' According to the *Newgate Calendar*: 'Few cases had ever produced a greater degree of interest ... but the circumstances of the bloody tragedy in which he [Bell] was the chief actor show him to be fully deserving the fate which befell him', and this because of, not in spite of, his tender age.[29]

The indictment read out at the Kent summer assizes on 26 July 1831 recorded that John Any Bird Bell, 'not having the fear of God before his eyes but being moved and seduced by the instigation of the devil', had 'wilfully and with malice and aforethought' given Richard Taylor 'one mortal wound of the length of four inches and of the depth of three, penetrating into the windpipe from which the lad had bled to death'.[30] The details, though gruesome, are important. They take us to the heart of this story and tell us something about the feelings it evoked among those involved, and among those who read, or listened to, the tale as it was recounted.

The Sound of Loss

One Friday in early March 1831, thirteen-year-old Richard Taylor set off from his home in Strood, a tiny village in Kent, to the small town of Aylesford about five miles away.[31] It was a journey of over two hours, and the lad had been making it on foot, across fields and along turnpike-roads for many weeks. The purpose of his trip was to collect parish poor relief, which the family had come to depend upon after their father had succumbed to illness. He arrived safely at his destination around eleven o'clock, and walked along the main street, past the handsome thirteenth-century church, and joined the queue of dishevelled people waiting outside the overseer's office where the relief was being administered. Mr Cutbath, the man in charge, recalled giving the boy some coins from the piles laid out along the committee room table and seeing him carefully conceal the money in his glove before starting his journey home.

On previous occasions when Richard had gone to fetch the weekly allowance he had returned home around three o'clock, but this March day he failed to appear and with every passing hour his father grew anxious. Friends and neighbours began a search. They set off on foot and on horseback, trailing carts along roads and lanes; they travelled across fields, through bridleways and over hunting-gates, they battered their way through coppices and hedgerows, but they found nothing. Two boys who had been seen with the missing lad were questioned, but all they offered was confirmation that they had walked with the boy for a short distance, and that he had then left them to go home and had not been seen since. The two boys were John Bell and his younger brother James.

The search for the lost child continued for over two months. A bellringer was hired to announce the loss to the public, and hand-bills were posted up across the county alerting the residents of nearby towns and villages to the disappearance and offering a reward for information. The boy's father was convinced his son was dead but the constable charged with the investigation was hopeful that he was still alive, and simply lost somewhere in the dense woodland between the towns of Rochester and Maidstone. He widened the search, covering nearly 200 square miles, and in the final two days of his efforts he took with him John Bell and his ten-year-old brother James to retrace the footsteps of the missing lad on the last day he had been seen alive. The constable would later say in court that at this stage the boys were not under any suspicion; in fact, he would say, 'they joined in the hunt cheerfully', guiding him into the Great Delce Wood then, distracted, rummaging playfully, looking for bird's nests and other creatures hidden in the undergrowth. The hunt yielded nothing.

Finally, one morning in May, a local farm-worker stumbled upon something odd as he walked through the wood on his way to check haystacks in a nearby field. At first he jumped back startled, later saying, 'I didn't know what it was, but then I saw it was a human being in a bad state, and it looked as if he'd been dead a very long time'. The labourer ran towards the road where two men were working and he shouted to them: 'Had the lost boy ever been found, because I think I've found him?' They realised the body was that of the missing child when one of the workmen recognised his clothes: a sou'wester made of canvas, a blue handkerchief with white spots, a blue waistcoat and jacket, and in his small clenched hand an empty woollen glove. The corpse had lain hidden in the wood beneath a small hazel tree for over two months.

The Rochester constable was informed and the news was broken to Richard's father. The ailing man was accompanied to identify his dead child, but the boy, whose delicate features had once been intimately recognisable, had become an object his parent could no longer set eyes upon. 'I stayed there as long as my constitution would admit', he told the inquest between sobs of grief, 'but I could not wait 'til the body was removed'. The corpse was placed into a rough wooden coffin and carried to St Margaret's Parish Poorhouse, where it lay overnight for the inspection of the local surgeon, Edward Seaton, and his assistant.

The autopsy was a hazardous task; 'I have nearly lost my life dissecting a body far less gone', Seaton told the inquest. A clear opening in the windpipe on the left side of the neck was identified, and both doctors agreed that it could only have been by made by a cutting instrument. There was also blood on the top of the boy's shirt and inside his jacket; it was a deep, dark red, leading them to conclude that a major artery had been severed. When they reported their findings to the county coroner the following day, he returned a verdict of 'wilful Murder against some person or persons unknown', adding that he hoped further inquiries would uncover the truth about this case.

Crimes and Misdemeanours

Details of how Richard Taylor met his death, and who was responsible, might never have come to light had it not been for a navy arrest officer serving on His Majesty's ship *Warrior*, which was moored nearby at Chatham. It was Henry Lewington's job to scour the Kent countryside for missing seamen. He was a local man and knew the area well. On the morning of 4 March, he had walked a little way with the Taylor boy on his journey to get poor relief. Later the same day, Lewington saw him again, this time in the company of two other youngsters whom he recognised as some boys from the Chatham area known as John and James Bell, both sons of a local labourer. It was months later, though, when he heard that the body of a boy had been discovered in the wood not far from the common, that he remembered seeing the three playmates together and became suspicious.

Kent had its fair share of crime at this time. Only weeks before the Bell case, there had been a robbery of the Maidstone coach on its way back from London.[32] Witnesses said that a group of young men, one of whom was said to be as young as thirteen, had jumped in front of the coach just before it entered Rochester. They had seized a box of valuables from the roof, emptied its contents, and thrown it into a nearby field. None of the felons had been found.

The early nineteenth century was a time of fear about criminal activity among the young. The belief, widespread at the time, was that child criminals were populating the streets and alleys of the growing English cities. In London it was said that children as young as seven concealed themselves in the maze of lanes also inhabited by prostitutes, beggars and violent figures from the criminal underworld.[33] And while the urban mythology of the time portrayed the city as a fertile ground for vagrancy and corruption, it was also believed that evil disorder was being sown among the villages and by-lanes of the English countryside.

Less than a year before John Bell's criminal trial, Kent had been the location of one of the most important disturbances in English social history.[34] In 1830, rural workers in the arable counties of the south-east had rebelled against the poor standards of living endured by labourers. Gangs of men, and sometimes women and children, blackened their faces and marched like a menacing storm across the countryside. They destroyed machines and set fire to haystacks in an outbreak of violence that was mirrored across other counties in southern England. The Kent rising was by far the most serious of all those that took place throughout the country, and to those in power it represented the terrifying threat of insurrection. The disturbances began in the spring and continued into the winter, and it seemed as if the revolutionary tide that was sweeping Europe at the time was about to wash up onto the shores of England. The harvest had been poor that year, and labourers were recorded as saying that they would 'rather do anything than encounter such a winter as the last'.[35] Most were desperate and only made their protests out of need but, according to one labourer at the time, 'among the young fellows it's possible that political ideas of further significance were abroad'. The unrest created panic in the capital and Sir Robert Peel, then home secretary, ordered soldiers and artillery to be sent to quell the disturbances and punish the instigators. Out of the conflict, eleven serious criminal cases were tried at the regional assizes, including that of Kent. Of the six who stood trial and were executed, half were teenagers.[36]

It is impossible to tell whether or not the fears about youth and crime were misplaced. This was an age before national statistics, so no measure of the true extent of lawlessness existed. However, the criminal registers for urban districts do give some indication. They show the average age of a child's first foray into criminal activity to have been twelve years, and that in 1847 the young accounted for 61 per cent of those criminally indicted in the Middlesex jurisdiction alone.[37] The link between young people and offending was fuelled by the fact that at the time, one out of every two Englishmen in the population was under 21.[38] The volatile mix of youth, urbanisation, and poverty alongside wealth all added to the cauldron of wickedness that was perceived by many to be rife among the young. One contemporary London commentator described these child criminals as a race apart:

There is a youthful population in the Metropolis devoted to crime, trained to it from infancy, adhering to it from education and circumstance, whose connections prevent the possibility of reformation, and whom no punishment can deter; a race *sui generis*, different from the rest of society, not only in thoughts, habits and manners, but even in appearance, possessing morcover, a language exclusively of their own.[39]

Rural areas were thought to harbour lesser evils, although by 1831 crime in Maidstone was becoming a pressing problem. The recent robbery of the Maidstone coach was not the first; it had happened twice before within the previous year alone. John Bell and his ten year-old brother James were already known as 'street lads', often to be found 'riding a donkey down the Maidstone Road, and in playing pitch and hustle with boys, it is to be feared, as neglected as them'. When the arresting officer tracked them down for questioning about this crime, he found them gambling in the street.

The boys were taken to a firm of solicitors in Rochester and interrogated at length for over six days. In an era before a national police force was established, local magistrates undertook criminal inquiries, a clerk recorded the evidence, and the final indictment was then presented to court. The business of the investigation took place at the offices of Messrs Twopenny and Essell, and every day crowds gathered outside to talk and speculate upon the fate of the two boys. One observer recalled: 'Few cases had ever produced a greater degree of interest in the County of Kent than that of these wretched culprits and their unfortunate victim.'[40]

The magistrates were meticulous in their inquiries. The boys denied knowing anything about how Richard had met his death, and insisted that they had not seen him since he left them to go home after playing. As they spoke their denials, they were unaware that the evidence of the navy officer Henry Lewington indicated them as the chief suspects. Another man had also seen them hitting the Taylor boy and had gone to his rescue. The magistrates knew, however, that none of this was proof of their involvement in the actual killing. What appeared sinister could just have been playful mischief, and there was nothing to prove that the boys had set eyes on the deceased after the incident of bullying. The suggestion of violence, however, did arouse their misgivings and they continued to question the boys until, on the fifth day, a development occurred which shocked not only the magistrates and the presiding police officer, but the entire local community.

Ten-year-old James Bell was feeling increasingly uncomfortable at his detention. The pressure was marked in his behaviour which was restless and agitated; eventually, he called the clerk and asked if he could speak to one of the magistrates alone. The Reverend Davies, one of the four clergymen investigating the case, took the child aside into a separate room. James, now convulsing with emotion, could hardly contain himself and blurted out what he knew: 'S'elp me God, Sir, he told me, 'e did it with little Taylor's own knife.' On hearing this, the magistrate marched him into the next room, and told the boy to repeat in the hearing of everyone what he had just said. His elder brother turned pale on hearing this betrayal and, perhaps out of relief, he immediately confessed to the murder.

As the magistrates listened to John Bell's account of how he had come to kill Richard Taylor, the inquiry clerk took his brother James to perform a tormenting, indeed disturbing, task. The body of the dead boy had been buried in the parish of St Margaret's church, where James was taken now. He was led to the graveside, where diggers had been busy overnight disinterring the remains of the murder victim, and were now lifting the lid of the coffin. Frightened out of his wits, James was lowered into the open grave

3. *John Any Bird Bell, aged fourteen years, and his brother James Bell, whose age is given as between ten and twelve years, from* A Narrative of the Facts Relative to The Murder of Richard Faulkner Taylor *(Rochester, Kent, 1831). Reproduced by permission of the British Library.*

and made to search the 'putrid corpse' for the knife that had been given to the deceased by his father, and for the glove that the money had been hidden in. There is no record to tell us how the boy felt about his awful search, but part of its purpose must surely have been vindictive. Now that his brother had confessed to the crime, it was likely that James would be acquitted of any charges, so why not make him pay for his part in it by forcing him to do something that would be certain to shake his very core?

Finally, on 21 May, three months after the Taylor boy's disappearance, John Bell was indicted for his murder and taken off to Maidstone prison to await trial. On the way to his incarceration the boy and his minder, the jail delivery officer Mr Pattison, went past a pond now dried by the heat of an early summer. The boy stopped, saying: 'There's where I washed my hand and the knife after committing the crime.' This spot was about 100 paces from where the body had been found. Bell then took the officer to the small opening in the wood: 'That's the way to the place where I killed the poor boy; he is better off than me – don't you think, Sir?' At this point, the details of that afternoon poured out as if the scene, like a stage, was suddenly lit for the drama to be enacted again. He told Mr Pattison that he had pretended to the little lad that they were lost, 'he then fell on the ground crying, I sprang at him and cut his throat'. Breathlessly Bell continued, 'I forced the money outta the hand, it were in a little bag', then, after confirming its contents to the officer he added the solemn comment: 'I know I'll be hanged, I hope Jem [his brother] is brought, it might be a warning to him to behave in the future.' He then showed the officer the place where he had run out of the wood after stabbing the boy, and said he had had the bloody knife in his open hand. Pattison later told the trial that the boy asked not to be chained in irons while they journeyed to the prison: 'He said he knew he should suffer, he would tell the truth and would not attempt to escape.' Indeed, the officer pointed out, 'the boy's behaviour while in custody was very good indeed'.

An Act of Greed and Depravity?

John Bell committed his murder in an atmosphere already heightened by fear. Although his offence was not one of rebellion, it was an extreme example of social indiscipline and it added to the trepidation felt about youth and crime.[41] There was anxiety over the moral prospects of future generations. Britain was changing rapidly and the transformation was unsettling, not least to the property-owning classes of this newly industrialised nation. They were concerned with protecting their wealth and property, as was shown in their enthusiasm for a reformed and expanded police force, but they were just as troubled by what crime symbolised for the particular model of humanity they wished to promote.

The spectacle of the criminal child, especially one who kills, lent itself to deeper concerns about a child's propensity for evil. How far might a child go, unrestrained by the discipline of a religious morality? The secularising pressures of commercialism were already making themselves felt in the late eighteenth and early nineteenth centuries.[42] There was widespread belief that although commercial society had brought greater wealth, it had also unleashed a torrent of greed.[43] Well-to-do parents belonging to the new middle class had to guard continually against their own children's corrupt nature, particularly if they subscribed to the beliefs of evangelicals such as Hannah More, which many did.[44] She thought that children came into the world with 'a corrupt nature, and evil disposition, which it should be the great end of education to rectify'.[45]

In 1816, the *Report of the Society for Investigating the Causes of the Alarming Increase of Juvenile Delinquency in the Metropolis*, compiled and written by some of the philanthropist members of this society, suggested a range of causes behind the increase in crime, but at the heart of their findings was the powerful suggestion that the poor and their children were at fault for desiring things they could not have.[46] It is unsurprising, then, that in cases of crimes committed for material gain, especially those involving murder, the need to restore an ethical balance became all the more insistent.

John Any Bird Bell was accused by Reverend Winter, the clergyman who attended him in prison, of committing his crime because of a 'love of money'. He said that Bell had fallen prey to his own covetousness and desire. These 'wretched passions' had become his master, according to the reverend, rather than the 'Heavenly Deity whose rules we ought to serve'. The judge believed that the only motive for the crime 'was the desire to possess yourself of the paltry sum of nine shillings', and a newspaper report of the case was appalled that 'the sole instigation to this foul deed, was the desire of possessing nine shillings!' There was little need for newspapers to moralise excessively when they told this tale, on the face of it; the characters of the perpetrator and the victim were so contrasting that they said it all.

The families of the two boys were both poor, but by the end of the account in the *Newgate Calendar* the reader is in no doubt as to where his or her sympathies should lie. Richard Taylor was only a year younger than his attacker, but he is represented as a child, a 'little fellow', possessing a 'peculiar intelligence and an amiable disposition'. On the day of the murder, he had said goodbye to his father wearing a sou'wester with a handkerchief tied round his neck for warmth. On the March morning when his son was about to leave, the concerned parent went to great trouble to

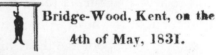

The Trial and execution of

John Any Bell aged 14

For the **Murder** of Richard Taylor at Bridge-Wood, Kent, on the 4th of May, 1831.

4. The contemporary pamphlet containing this etching about the case would have achieved widespread sales in 1831.
Reproduced by permission of the St Bride's Foundation.

The Trial and execution of

John Any Bell aged 14

For the **Murder** of Bridge-Wood, Kent, on the
Richard Taylor at 4th of May, 1831.

At eight o'clock in the morning the court sat and long before that hour every part was crowded to the most inconvenient degree; so anxious was every person to witness the trial of John Any Bird Bell, for the Murder of Richard Faulkner Taylor.

James Any Bird Bell, is about 14 years of age, and was indicted for the Murder of J. R. Taylor on the 4th, of March, at Bridge-wood, in the County of Kent, by cutting his throat. The prisoner manifested not the slightest concern on appearing at the bar.

Mr. Walsh conducted the prosecution The prisoner had no Council.

Robert Taylor—was the father of the deceased in the month of March last he resided at Stroud, in the parish of Aylesford. For some time before that period he had been in the habit of receiving 9s. weekly from the parish, he generally sent his son and daughter to receive it. On Friday the 4th of March went alone. His dress on that day was, what by fishermen is called a south water. I gave him a bag to bring the money home in. Before he started he asked me for my knife, to cut a bow & Arrow with, which I gave him. I never saw my son alive again. He was 13 years of age. Nor heard of him till the 11th of May, & in consequence of information I received on that day." Here the witness fainted away—the prisoner looking at him with the utmost indifference, watching the progress of the means used to recover him, as if he was a mere spectator, his face only a little flushed. The witness resumed—" I went that day to Bridge-wood, I there saw the body"—Here the witness fainted, & was carried out of court.

The Sister of the deceased was then called, a child of seven years of age. Her evidence went to show that on a former day, when she was passing the wood with her brother, the prisoner endeavoured to entice him into the wood.

The father again examined—"When I got into the wood, I saw the body; that body was the body of my son Richard, I recognized it by the dress, and a mark on the body, of a bunch of currants, with which the boy was born. I afterwards saw a knife in the hands of Patterson, which was the one I had lent him, & the gloves which were my sons. The body was in a state shocking to look at, the features of the face were not visible, but the hair was perfect, the trunk of the body was perfectly sound, but the thighs & legs were consumed by worms. I had described the marks previous to going to the wood. I have no doubt but it was the body of my son. When found the glove on the right hand was turned down to the wrist.

George Cutbard examined—I was assistant overseer in March las., on the 4th I gave R Taylor 3 half-crowns 1s and 6d. I put the money in the boys bag myself. His sister was not with him.

Henry Lewington—I am a warrant officer on board his Majesties ship Warrior, on the 4th of March, I saw the deceased on the road in company with the prisoner & his brother, near the Bell public house. I afterwards heard of the loss of the boy, and told his father what I had seen of him, I met the prisoner on Tuesday, & asked if he had seen young Taylor, and the prisoner replied, that he parted with him in the turnip field and that he went towards Master Hawkes's, I recollect the 11th of May, when the body was found; I went to see it, & recognized it emmediately. The prisoner here interrupted the witness, and said that the witness told him he came with pistols to blow his fathers brains out. He explained—that he had a case of pistols when he took the prisoner into custody—

Several other witnesses corroborated the above statements fully proving his guilt. The Jury returned a virdict of Guilty. DEATH. The Judge passed the sentance, and on his ordering his body for detection the prisoner shed one tear

At twelve o'clock the prisoner was brought up to prison in his place at the bar. His behaviour was a firm composed and he retired to the usual convenient seat in effort into the hour, till the Chaplin by his importunate measure brought him to a due sense of the needs of his when he acknowledged the justness of his sentence, and after taking the prayer, for a few minutes, was handed into custody. He wept the first shed during the whole drop at his devotion.

He confessed that when Taylor was aware of his intention, he fell upon his knees and begged to be spared, offered him the money, his knife, etc. and any thing for his life, but he would have him as long as he lived, but this repeated one last, before he received of the said good people and warning by me, Lord have mercy

A COPY OF VERSES,

Written by Himself.

COME children and parents too, and listen to these lines,
Which I have penned within my cell, where I suffer for my crimes.
And from my fate a warning take, and keep from evil ways,
Or if you will pursue you it and it will cut short your days.

Of others I seen guilty been, though my years they are but few,
And now I am condemned to die for a murder it is true,
I knew Taylor had to post all through a lonely spot,
And from the Parish for his father nine shillings he had got,

Of which I thought to rob him, the truth I now unfold,
But he the main remaster with strange stout and bold,
I took with my my knife to do this dreadful fact,
And stationed him close to the hedge with directions how to act.

To see no one was coming with out in interview,
While I did murder young Taylor, for which ever many a one,
As for my down I and, and laid it low amidst the left side,
Poor wounded my hands all in a good sloat along for the road side,

I made my brother swear, he the secret never would tell,
But God above he knew the act, and it is know full well,
When nine weeks were gone by, I thought the deed once was would know,
At some bed then the body found, yet I was still in woe,

But God who gives less murder pass without a punishment,
Caused heard to discover it as through the wood he went,
For which I was brought to trial, and sentenced to go way,
To die in misery morning upon the fatal tree.

Now all ye youths both high and low by me a warning take,
And if you know you're doing ill, give bad ways pray forsake,
Or else like me too late you'll feel distress and woe severe,
Will overtake you in your wickedness and stop your cut course.

Printed and Sold by J. QUICK,
41. Bowling Green Lane, Clerkenwell,

5. *The gallows broadside in full.*
Reproduced by permission of the St Bride's Foundation.

show the boy how best to hide the money. He instructed him to conceal it in a tiny bag which he held in one of his hand mittens. Doing this, Richard said: 'There, father, nobody can tell I have got any money.' He also asked if he could borrow his father's knife, though there was no suggestion that he was asking out of fear or even from a need for protection. Apparently, he liked to use the knife to fashion a bow and arrow, or to peel and eat turnips lying loose in fields along the way. It was a brown buckhorn-handled knife with one blade; as he handed it to the boy, and perhaps to discourage him from using it on crops in the fields, his father gave him a penny so that he might buy a cake. Then, as if by way of reassurance, young Richard said, 'I shall not be gone long'. He was a small lad according to his father, 'a delicate little creature, but very sharp and active'. He waved goodbye and managed to secure a ride on a neighbour's cart some of the way towards a local spot called Kit's Coty, named after the Neolithic burial stones that are visible to this day near the old turn-off to Aylesford.

John Bell, on the other hand, at least if the account in the *Newgate Calendar* is to be believed, had set out that morning with malice in mind. He knew that Richard regularly travelled to Aylesford to collect his father's money, because they had met on the road several times previously. Bell was with his ten-year-old brother James on the day, whose statement, as we know, would eventually incriminate the older boy. The *Newgate Calendar* told its readers that the statement demonstrated a 'remarkable degree of depravity' in each of the boys. It said that there was plenty of evidence of malice and forethought in the crime committed; John and his brother knew their victim well and had played with him a number of times. They also knew that on his return journey from Aylesford he would be carrying money for his sick father. They lay in wait for him on the pathway. According to contemporary reports, John was a bad sort with a reputation for theft:

... small articles from shops in the neighbourhood, sometimes breaking the windows for the purpose, and in one instance daringly throwing down and breaking a glass jar at the very door of the house at which it had been stolen, after emptying its contents. There could be no doubt but that a pursuit of such conduct would ultimately lead to more desperate acts of violence.[47]

The curate of the parish had tried to teach him at Sunday school, but John had kicked him and was expelled for misconduct. However, Bell's biggest problem, in the eyes of the *Maidstone Journal*, was that which was 'very prevalent among [other] children in the lower walks of life; a passion for gambling: pitch and hustle being his favourite game, and doubtless this propensity was the cause of his end'.

The corruptive power of gambling had been commented on in the eighteenth century. Henry Fielding believed it to be one of the greatest evils arising from the desire of the poor for luxury:

> This vice is more dangerous, as it is deceitful, and, contrary to every other Species of Luxury, flatters its Votaries with the Hopes of increasing their Wealth; so that Avarice itself is so far from securing us from its Temptations, that it often betrays the more thoughtless and giddy Part of Mankind into them.[48]

The Society for Investigating the Causes of the Alarming Increase of Juvenile Delinquency in the Metropolis also counted gambling as one of the most important reasons for crime. They insisted that it exerted a baleful influence on the young, and argued that it gave them a taste for crime that could easily slip into more malign levels of depravity. A contemporary pamphlet on the John Bell case remarked on him sharing his 'own wicked inclinations' with other boys:

It is to be wished that his dreadful fate may operate as a solemn warning to his surviving companions in guilt; for they may rest assured, that if they continue in the same course, however they may indulge in the hope of escape, that the stern hand of justice, as in this instance, will at length overtake them ...[49]

The Rage of Poverty

Reports of this story were perhaps as prone as some of today's newspapers to exaggerating certain facts for particular rhetorical purposes. One edition of the *Newgate Calendar* published by two nineteenth-century lawyers, Andrew Knapp and William Baldwin, was of the view that hanging was 'indispensably necessary [because] offences highly injurious to the community should be punished with forfeiture of life'. They considered it to be an important lesson to those 'moved with the sordid passion of acquiring wealth by violence'.[50] Yet there is little evidence that Bell squandered his stolen shillings on gambling. Witness statements record various attempts being made to change the larger coins – three half-crowns – once in a draper's shop, and again at the butcher's shop along the main street in Rochester. But records show that he purchased pies, apples, pastry, bread and cheese. The only overwhelming appetite in this case appears to be not gaming, but hunger. All the children, including the dead boy, spent hours during the day trying to secure free food, usually by eating turnips from the surrounding fields. In the Bell household, supper was often a 'sleeper' (dormouse). These were poor times for land labourers. Their rural way of life, once modestly prosperous, had become impoverished because of high wheat prices, low wages, and the beginnings of a revolution in agriculture. The labourers of other European countries at this time had been raised in status and prosperity, but their English counterparts were poor with little dignity and dim horizons.[51] In his account of his early-nineteenth-century tour of southern England, William Cobbett described the grinding poverty of the field labourer thus: 'Their dwellings are little better than pig-beds, and their looks indicate that their food is not nearly equal to that of a pig. These wretched hovels are stuck upon little beds of ground … it seems as if they have been swept off the fields by a hurricane.'[52]

Bell's father had lived in a cottage in Essex, but was displaced by the agricultural enclosures that were occurring with devastating rapidity at this time. Any privileges he may have enjoyed, such as grazing rights or access to free fuel, were immediately lost to an unstoppable process beyond his control. He moved to Kent to begin a new life, but the lot of a casual labourer was little better. We cannot know how this might have affected the Bell family, but the idea that his son's crime was motivated solely out of a 'greedy thirst of gain' certainly appears to be an inadequate explanation.

Lives lived at the level of brute subsistence produce indignities that are difficult to imagine. Speaking to the huge crowd gathered in the prison chapel for a service that was held for the condemned boy, the chaplain said:

> Though we might and ought to revolt at the thought of our committing so foul a crime as murder, we cannot foretell what might be our doings … those who had been guilty of this crime, were once probably as innocent of it, and as free from all thoughts of it as ourselves.

It was through the preacher's words that those gathered in the chapel, and those who read his remarks in the newspaper, tried to make sense of an act that was otherwise senseless. In his sermon, Reverend Winter speculated about how the boys could have brought themselves to do such a thing (though James, John's brother, did not take an active part in the murder; he was a knowing accessory to it but was not made to stand trial). He suggests that unexceptional feelings of envy or hurt had turned into malice. He told the tightly packed crowd that the boys had 'met with temptations such as we did – they were opposed and insulted in some shape or other, and then unkind or spiteful feelings, like leaven, began to spread in their bosoms'. In this evangelical message, the Bell child was not spoken of as if he were different from anyone else; and while this was because the clergyman saw the boy as just another manifestation of universal human depravity and the sinful state of mankind, it also happened to be a view that invited the congregation to understand and identify with the plight of his fallen innocence.

The Sins of the Father

Although the religion of the day could point to mankind's supposed propensity for sin as a probable cause of this terrible crime, others saw its cause in more earthly terms. *The Times* spoke of the 'barbarous manner' in which Bell was brought up, and the jury alluded to his background when they urged the judge to be merciful. The problem of the Bell parents first emerged publicly on the final day of the magistrates' investigation into the crime. An angry crowd had gathered outside the offices of Twopenny and Essell. Bell's mother and father had to be given protection as they left the hearing because, as one of the magistrates indicated, 'we have learned that the populace outside are so indignant against you, as to make it unsafe for you to go alone'.

Reverend Brown, the chairman of the inquiry, poured pious scorn on the Bell parents, telling them that two of their children could only have become involved in such a crime because of their failure to 'properly train them up to virtue'. He continued: 'Horrible, indeed, must be your reflections, when you lie down tonight on your pillows, and think to what a situation you have brought your own children. They have been taken into schools where every attention has been paid to their morals but their conduct has been so bad at those schools, that for fear of contaminating the other children, they have been dismissed from them.' Another magistrate and clergyman who claimed acquaintance with the circumstances of John Bell's life spoke of the father's violent temper and foul language. Bell senior, however, was outraged by the accusations, and attempted to gain credit for being a good example to his children by making declarations of his impeccable piety, insisting that he attended church regularly, sang in the choir every Sunday, and followed God's teachings through the scriptures.

He was also fond of correction, it seems, a euphemism for inflicting corporal punishment. The nineteenth century may not have been what the historian Laurence Stone called 'the great flogging age', but the evangelical revival in this period did favour harsh forms of punishment by way of moral instruction.[53] It was a form of admonishment that was by no means rare.[54] *The Maidstone Journal* approved of Mr Bell's method for disciplining his children, but conceded that this was sometimes carried out 'unsparingly'. In his book *Father and Son*, the writer Edmund Gosse, describing his evangelical upbringing in the nineteenth century, recalls how a caning from his father at the age of six instilled in him a murderous rage that lingered for quite some time.[55] 'Parents should consider well the path of duty they owe their children', came the warning of the prison chaplain on the morning before John Bell's hanging, 'they were bound to set them a suitable example ... they ought always to restrain every

rising symptom of unkindness ... to discourage the first tendencies towards cruelty, the very earliest indications of a revengeful,
unfeeling disposition'. But what if cruelty was the habitual means
by which James Bell senior had brought up his child?

He was keen to present himself as a responsible parent who
rarely stayed drinking at the Blue Bell Inn later than ten o'clock.
He had declaimed his virtues to the magistrates of the grand jury
not by examples of acts of tenderness or affection towards his
children, but by his abilities as a worshipper and workman. 'You
may be a very ingenious workman,' one of the jurors replied, 'but
you are not a moral man; you must be aware that you are not. Ask
your own conscience.' James Bell was a man whose self-image was
at odds with his behaviour, and he was not about to undo this
image by disturbing the depths of his conscience. According to
him, the blame for his boy's behaviour lay not in too many beatings but too few, and while he was satisfied that he gave correct
discipline to his children they had, he said, proved, 'perverse and
intractable'. On the eve of his son's execution when, together with
his two other children, they visited the condemned boy in his cell,
instead of comforting his child moments before death he chastised him, saying: 'See what your misconduct and disobedience
has brought us to. I have lived for sixty years, and never was taken
before a Magistrate, and now by your disobedience this dreadful
thing has come upon us.'

He also charged his daughter with 'being exceedingly insolent
on all occasions', and he described his other son James as 'a sullen, ill-tempered, spiteful rascal'. His wife, too, was singled out
for rebuke. Mr Bell complained that, although he was constantly
punishing his children for their disobedience, his wife was 'over
indulgent, and concealed their faults when she could'. On her
last visit to her son she held him in her arms and cried. A poignant newspaper extract notes: 'The mother frequently called the

unhappy youth her "tender hearted boy". An expression so little supported by the boy's conduct naturally excited surprise, and she was asked why she so denominated him. She replied she could not tell, but that he was her darling son.'

A Cruel Repentance

Whatever reasons there may have been for Bell's act of murder, the large congregation that gathered in the chapel the day before his death was warned against any tender feelings they might have for him: 'Here is an assassin of only fourteen years – for hours beforehand he contemplates a suitable spot for internment, but from fear of discovery, at last fixes upon the centre of a wood, where human footsteps were seldom heard: there an innocent unoffending little victim, younger than himself, is decoyed, and there meets his death.' On the eve of the boy's execution, however, the father of the dead boy visited him. He came, it was said, 'to offer forgiveness', and the chaplain said afterwards that the condemned child had been 'greatly affected by this'.

Reverend John Winter had been the chaplain for Maidstone jail for more than ten years. He would have seen countless inmates during that time, but this case must have made a deep impression on him. One sensitive prison cleric wrote that a condemned prisoner was always someone upon whom one's thoughts 'perpetually dwelt', and this would surely have been reminiscent of how Reverend Winter felt about his young charge.[56] He had attended John Bell in his cell from the day of his arrest on 21 May 1831 throughout the trial, and right up until the day of his execution on 1 August. It was not his business to say whether John Bell should hang or not, neither was he there only to dispense moral instruction; he was there to give the doomed boy some spiritual consolation, and there is some evidence that John was moved by the 'affectionate' tone of the churchman. At one stage, the lad had said he had never felt any horror or remorse for what he had done; he had daily passed the spot where he had killed poor Richard, but it hardly ever entered his mind.

Reverend Winter tried to bring the horror of Bell's crime home to him by awakening his own moral sense to a feeling of shame for what he had done. In this sense, the priest was doing what any modern counsellor might attempt today – he was help-ing the child to acknowledge the savage crime he had committed and feel some humanity for his victim. Although the modern approach aims at rehabilitation, it is no less moral in its purpose. The problem, however, was that in 1831 this boy had no chance of redeeming his life on earth since both church and state had sanctioned his execution. The chaplain's mission was to save John Bell's soul from eternal damnation, and in this the boy had to be helped away from an attitude of denial towards one of admis-sion and guilt. Had the reverend been more fervently evangelical, he might have told his charge: 'God denies you forgiveness, and before you lies the abyss,' especially given the nature of the crime. But Reverend Winter favoured a more moderate language of Christian atonement, though in the end it was just as committed to suffering. He hoped that Bell would understand his own guilt, and suffer spiritually for the boy he had killed. The chaplain must have had some success, as John Bell 'cried considerably' while lis-tening to the preacher read the 51st Psalm. But it is just as likely that the boy was weeping at the horror of his imminent suffering at the gallows.

On the morning of his execution, the condemned child awoke to the presence of the praying chaplain. At eleven o'clock the prison bell began to toll, and a steady hush descended upon the vast crowd that had been assembling since dawn. By this time

Bell was distraught and was helped by the prison chaplain to the drop, where the prison governor and under-sheriff watched the executioner pinion his arms before fixing the noose around his head. The lad was then asked if he had anything to say, and it was reported that he replied in a quiet voice: 'Pray for a poor boy! Pray for me!'

The body was taken down and removed to Rochester for medical dissection. Since the Murder Act of 1752, judges had used their discretionary powers to hang those who had committed the 'horrid crime of murder', and to make examples of such felons by having their bodies dissected. When Judge Gaselee told John Bell that he was to be 'hanged by the neck until dead and afterwards his body be taken to be anatomised and dissected', the boy collapsed in tears, the image of his own mutilation no doubt adding further terror to his punishment.

The childish appearance of this gallows victim may have been the reason why so many wept that day. Perhaps the murmuring crowd saw something of their own children in his soft, frightened features. Yet despite his having been recommended for mercy, there was no recorded protest or defiance against the learned judge's rejection of clemency; perhaps there was resignation to the outcome, and a sense that justice must take its course. Journalists on the local paper deferred modestly to the power of Justice Gaselee's judgement, convinced that there was 'no doubt that what appeared to be the best possible course was adopted'. Although the same newspaper said that John Bell's crime appeared 'the more revolting from the extremely tender age of the murderer', this was also, paradoxically, the basis of sympathy for him.

After the Bell case in 1831, no child below sixteen years of age was ever again sent to the gallows. One important reason for this was the changing sensibilities of the nineteenth century. Among the characteristics of the new penal reform agenda was the emphasis on feeling rather than reason in its rhetoric for change. In this era of Romantic sensibility, 'benevolence was enlightenment itself: the heart spoke to the mind; the mind was guided by the heart.'[57] Children committing crimes were increasingly served by this revolution in sensibilities, which brought in its wake the idea of the 'Romantic child'. The change had begun with Rousseau's book on education and childhood, *Emile*, published in 1762. Dickens' novel *Oliver Twist*, published in 1838, was the first novel in the English language with a child as its central character. For Dickens, childhood sufferings were the sign and token of all others. His novels return continually to the plight of threatened or abused children, as if all the horrors of the nineteenth-century world resided there. Dickens was influential in creating a public image of the child as both 'pitiable' (*Oliver Twist*) and 'fresh from God'. His child characters were, as one author put it, 'the embodiment of a force for innate goodness which could rescue embittered adults'.[58] With this image of the child so firmly established in the mind of the public, it would have been inconceivable to see a child suffer at the gallows and for his body to be then broken apart by doctors. By the time of *Oliver Twist*, hanging was considered an intolerable punishment for a child, even one who had committed the ultimate crime of murder.

Only four years after the execution of John Bell, the judge who had sentenced him, Sir Justice Gaselee, was unfortunate enough to be confronted with another case of child murder at the Midlands assize court held in Derby during the summer of 1835. This time the eminent judge, who could not have been unaware of the changing atmosphere around him, was moved to seek a very different punishment to the one he had meted out to John Bell.

Chapter Three

A MORTAL BLOW

Increase of crime, and consequent necessity for Punishment, have been produced by the neglect and mismanagement of those who have had charge of the Children of the Poor.
CAPTAIN EDWARD PELHAM BRENTON, 1834

Unlike the case of John Bell, the story of William Wild, who had killed two infant children, never found its way to the London streets. The genteel readers of *The Times* saw it in the columns of the assize reports, but at no time was it published in the broadsheets peddled on the streets of the capital. Yet after almost two centuries it is possible to trace the events of this child's life at the time of his trial, and to follow his hazardous journey across the seas to the other side of the world, where his story took a further dispiriting turn. Deep in the Archive Offices of Tasmania there is a lengthy and detailed conduct record for William Wild, and within its parchment pages the copperplate writing is plain to see, the elegant hand having unwittingly placed on record a harrowing personal account of the convict system of an empire.

In 1835, however, William could have no idea that he would appear on this huge historical stage; his experience of the power of others began when he lost his freedom having just turned thirteen.[1] His mother had sent him to become a servant for Josiah

Smith and his wife and family, who had a small farm in the parish of Church Broughton in Derbyshire. They had three children; John aged seven, Elizabeth aged three, and Martha who was eighteen months old. Philanthropy, which was already doing so much publicly for the 'poor little white slaves in our cotton factories', made little impact on the private world of slave labour.[2] Children in rural communities were often employed as farm servants, and could usually be found and hired at statute or pleasure fairs that took place in rural towns up and down the country. Although not indentured slaves, the difference was, in part, only one of ownership. In a government report on the employment of women and children in agriculture, one nine-year-old girl gave an affecting description of her onerous work as a farm hand:

> I was employed in driving bullocks to field and fetching them in again; cleaning out their houses, and bedding them up; washing potatoes and boiling them for pigs; milking; in the field leading horses or bullocks to the plough. Then I was employed in mixing lime to spread, digging potatoes, pulling turnips, and anything that came to hand like a boy. I reaped a little, loaded packhorses and went out with the horses for furze. I got up at five or six, except on market mornings twice a week, and then at three. I went to bed at half past nine, I worked more in the fields than in the house.[3]

Wild's life on the Smith farm was similar. He fetched cows, fed the pigs and ran errands, but according to each of the accounts available on this case, he had been at work for only two weeks when he ran away to his mother, who immediately sent him back.

William clearly laboured at the farm against his will, but in this respect he was no different from other poor children of the time, who from the age of ten or earlier were required to work for their living. Had he gone to nearby Derby and worked in one of the silk mills, he would have laboured alongside boys and girls much younger than himself, some running up to 30 miles a day in the long rooms, fixing and unfixing the ends of silken thread onto machines that were then twisted and eventually woven into garments.[4]

On the day of the murder, the Smith children's grandmother paid them a visit. She punished Wild for not keeping the house clean, taunting him with the insult that he was 'an indifferent maiden', and adding that 'if she had such a maiden as he, she would knock his head off'. The insult drove deep into the boy, as will become clear. The farmer's wife joined in with the reprimands, asking her servant to clean the fire irons, but he ignored her. She ordered him to do other errands such as cleaning out the pigs, and then complained that they were not done properly. William insisted that the work had been done 'as the master had asked me to', but her husband was not around to settle the row as he was away at a cattle fair in Derby.

Later in the afternoon, Mrs Smith asked the boy to fetch her two youngest children who were playing in a nearby field. Wild, clearly angry, shouted, 'I'm no maiden'. He nonetheless went as instructed, returning half an hour later to tell his mistress that she should bring them instead, because 'they cry their hearts out when I try to'. Not finding them in the place he had told her, she went along a nearby pathway, through a gate; and then, walking towards the cattle pond, she caught sight of a child's body. A neighbour soon heard her anguished cries: 'She was screaming her child's name Bessy over and over again.' It was not long before nearby villagers came running to her aid. A group of them then found a second child, also drowned, in the same watery pit. Among the helpers was William, who followed the bodies of the little girls as they were carried back to the farmhouse where the mother, in grief, and believing that her daughters could be revived, despatched the boy for the doctor.

He went off, but only pretended to call on the doctor, and returned much later to tell those gathered at the farm that the physician was unable to come. Still not under suspicion, but disturbed by the tumultuous events, William was told to go home to his mother.

The following day an inquest was convened at a tavern in the village, where a number of people came forward to give their evidence to the coroner and his jury. One said that William Wild had described the children as 'floating about in the water like blind puppies'. Another insisted that he had told him that the children had 'swum about like fishes and he had tried to get them out with a stick'. Several of them swore that they had seen the lad walking each of the Smith children towards their place of death. Confronted with the compelling testimony of these adult witnesses, the coroner ordered the parish constable to arrest William and bring him to the hearing. He did not take long to find the boy at the end of the village playing marbles in the street, seemingly unaware that he was the sole suspect in a case of double murder.

The unofficial cross-examination in the inn was, by contemporary standards, extraordinary. At one point, the tearful boy was told to kneel down. 'I have a very serious question to ask you,' the constable told him, 'and I expect you to tell the whole truth in the presence of God.' The lad was put under a great deal of pressure, and was bombarded with leading questions to which he gave confusing and contradictory replies. At first he insisted that it was an accident. He said he'd taken the children to the bank of the pit, and put them down while he went to pluck flowers to give to them. When he returned, he saw that they had gone nearer to the bank of the pit. Running towards them, he stumbled over Bessy and caught his foot on the other child, and they both fell in.

According to *The Times,* when questioned further the boy twice told those present that he had committed the murder, 'through spite to the Smiths for having brought him back when he ran away, and for having insulted him'. (A reference to the 'ill-tempered maiden' remark.) The *Derby Mercury* reported that the local constable had also asked William if his employers had done anything to him, to which the boy had answered that the grandmother had 'fallen out with him, hit him, and called him an idle rascal'. 'Thou didst it for spite?' the constable asked him, and the boy replied that he had. The lengthy interrogation eventually produced a confession, and the verdict of 'wilful murder' was returned, with William being immediately committed to trial at the next assizes.

Trial and Retribution

Draped in his official robes, Judge Sir Stephen Gaselee left his lodgings in St Mary's Gate, Derby, and stepped into his waiting carriage. Drawn by a fine pair of bay horses and attended by footmen in liveries of blue and crimson, he was taken the small distance to the assize court where a crowd was waiting to hear the trial of the thirteen-year-old killer they'd read so much about. Public curiosity about the case had been building ever since the coroner's inquest two months earlier, so that on the day of the hearing, according to a local news report, the court was 'crowded to suffocation', even though the Midland assize circuit was held in town, twenty miles or so from the crime's rural location. Making his way to the bench, the judge might well have been forgiven the sullen temper for which he was renowned. Only four years since John Bell's hanging, the prospect of trying another child murderer could not have been something he looked forward to.

An officer in the Derby courtroom called silence as the judge was ushered in. He nodded solemnly to the bar and took his seat at the bench. As the indictment was read out, a deepening murmur spread round the gallery and each of the barristers turned their eyes upon the small thirteen-year-old boy in front of them. Had he wilfully and deliberately murdered Martha Smith, aged eighteen months, and her sister Elizabeth, who was three? Throughout the day-long trial, the lad stood impassively as sixteen witnesses gave their evidence and underwent cross-examination. His stepfather was the only person to speak in his defence, testifying to the boy's good character and saying that he had cared for his siblings very well. William remained silent but a confession statement, put together at the time of the inquest, was read out on his behalf. The defence counsel rose to object: 'It should not be admitted as evidence, my Lord, it was extracted from the prisoner under circumstances calculated to produce an undue influence on his mind.' The irascible judge frowned at this interjection, but promised to refer the matter to fellow justices for their opinion. Meanwhile, he ordered the trial to continue.

The examination of the witnesses resumed until, finally, Justice Gaselee gave his summary. After only a few minutes' deliberation, the Crown jury returned a guilty verdict. According to *The Times*, William had 'manifested a total absence of all sense of the awful situation in which he was placed and seemed quite indifferent to the proceedings taking place, until the learned Judge placed the black cap upon his head, and proceeded to pass sentence of death upon him, when he cried a great deal and continued to do so until he was removed from the bar'.[5]

From a modern standpoint it appears surprising that the doubt over the boy's confession did not halt the trial proceedings. In fact, evidence obtained in this way tends to lead to a trial's collapse today. William was told that there would be a stay of execution to allow the judge to consult his colleagues on a technical matter of law, but it is doubtful that he understood what it all meant. The proceedings of the court were incomprehensible to many of the illiterate and impoverished adults who were accused of crime, so it is unsurprising that the boy behaved as if none of the events unfolding had anything to do with him. He could not read or write, and although he was assigned a barrister it is unlikely he was helped in any way with an understanding of court procedure.

William's fate was not decided upon for many weeks, during which time he was kept in Vernon Gate prison in Derby. This huge building, with 25-foot walls and two Martello towers, dominated the growing manufacturing town, and was emblematic of the moral authority of the new middle class. The gradual move away from the scaffold towards incarceration was driven by the political aims and necessities of rapid industrialisation. The practice of punishment could no longer be based upon the public spectacles favoured by the *ancien régime* in which the power of the sovereign was inscribed on the body of every hung criminal. It was considered more humane to incarcerate prisoners and regiment their days with scripture and discipline.[6] Vernon Gate prison opened in 1824 and was designed along lines similar to Jeremy Bentham's 'Panopticon', a prison layout in which a circular cell block was built around a centrally placed observation tower. The enormous entrance gates of Vernon Gate prison can still be seen today, but the condemned prisoner's cell in which William Wild awaited his execution has long since gone. He languished there for over three months before learning that he would not, after all, face death. Only four years earlier, Justice Gaselee had executed John Bell, believing that it would set an example to others. This time, although he had terrified William Wild with the sentence of death, even he could not bring himself to ensure that it was carried out.

Perhaps he now realised what the reformers and philosophers Beccaria and Bentham had argued all along: that execution as an exemplary punishment had failed as a deterrent against crime. Doubtless, though, he never read these philosophers' writings, and besides, hanging was still the public's favoured punishment for murder.[7] Is it possible that he was moved by the prevailing humanitarian voices of the time? Quaker activism, and its belief in mercy rather than vengeance, would have made little impact on a judge who was more persuaded by the principles of retribution. But he might have read or heard of the powerful propagandist against capital punishment, Edward Gibbon Wakefield, who chose to write a fictional account of the John Bell hanging by way of an attack on that punishment's cruelty. Published in 1832, a year after the execution, it was a unique broadside because it made use of empathy as a narrative device in its message. Writing in the guise of the hangman, he gives a vivid account of the hanging that is made all the more forceful because of the way in which it engages the reader's feelings. At the point where John Bell is about to have his neck placed in the noose, he says to his executioner: "'Pray, sir, don't hurt me.' "My dear," answered I, "you should have spoken to my master: I'm only the journeyman and must do as I'm bid." This made him cry, which seemed a relief to him; and I do think I should have cried, myself, if I had not heard shouts from the crowd: poor lamb! Shame! Murderer! "Quick", said the sheriff; "ready", said I; the reverend chaplain gave me the wink: the drop fell: one kick, and he swayed to and fro, dead as the feelings of an English judge.'[8]

Whatever the effect of this poignant polemic, the pamphlet is bound to have found its way into the haunts of lawyers and justices around the Inns of Court. It certainly made an impression on the heart of public opinion, which was already moving away from the ideas of justice that Gaselee had once held dear.

This was the reform era in which the oligarchic system of eighteenth-century government was being transformed, and execution as an instrument of social control was losing its central position in the criminal justice system. As one historian pointed out, 'you might plausibly kill 56 per cent of the capitally convicted in 1785, but you could not sustain that proportion of deaths in the 1820s without outrage'.[9] Conditional pardons were becoming the punishment of choice. In the four-year period between the date of John Bell's execution and that of William Wild's sentence, 97 per cent of capital convictions given at the Old Bailey in London were commuted to transportation.[10] As home secretary in 1835, the Whig reformer Lord John Russell was responsible for repealing the capital law and reducing the number of offences that were punishable by hanging, and it was to Lord Russell that Justice Gaselee wrote his letter of appeal on the William Wild case.

His words express a change of mood: 'I have thought it my duty to reprieve the convict, and to request your Lordship to apply to His Majesty to grant him his most gracious pardon, on account of his being transported for life.' The letter goes on to plead the child's ignorance and want of religious instruction which, he said, had been remedied by the 'humane exertions' of the prison chaplain: 'He has been taught to read his Bible, and to be duly sensible of the enormity of his crimes and the awful situation in which he is placed.'[11] If Judge Gaselee did have a tender conscience about executing John Bell four years earlier, it will have been a relief to recommend transportation for William Wild.

A Sea of Troubles

Arriving on board the convict hulk *Euryalus* which was moored at Chatham in Kent, news of this felon's appalling atrocity travelled with him.[12] His offence record baldly stated what he had done: 'Drowning two children Elizabeth and Martha Smith.' His jailers might well have been disgusted by the young boy's actions, but it appears that he told them it was partly an accident: 'I was playing with them by the side of a pond, the littlest fell in and I shoved the other in for fear it should tell.' Perhaps he had convinced himself that his actions had been unintentional; there was, after all, an air of adolescent impulse to the murders, but whatever had been in his mind at the time, he was oblivious to the bewildering aftermath. As a country boy with no previous convictions, he had little or no knowledge of what exactly his sentence held in store for him.

At the time of Wild's imprisonment on the holding ship *Euryalus*, it was widely believed that, as an alternative form of punishment, transportation was only just less horrific than death; indeed, many did not survive the confinement. It was winter when William was taken on board and he had to wait many months before he was finally shipped out. The dark cells below deck offered little protection against the sharp east wind that swept across the Medway. A number of the confined boys knew each other from the London streets, but William had come from a tiny rural parish in Derbyshire and knew no one; he was alone, and he would never set eyes on his mother or family again.

Subject to the same discipline as the other inmates, he was put to work, given minimal exercise, and suffered the nagging reproaches of a religious education. The violence that had been his own undoing, he would now see in others. Except that, whereas his actions had perhaps been the outcome of a sudden murderous rage, there was a calculated cruelty to the inhumanity on board the *Euryalus*. As well as the beatings and whippings that were routinely given by the guards, chilling acts of intimidation were also carried out by fellow prisoners. In one attack, a boy describes how his eyes were pricked with needles, 'just as I was awaking – they took the needle, held my eyes up … as I laid in the corner of my cell in my hammock, and jagged the needle three or four times in each eye'. He was left partially blind by the assault.[13]

When the hulks came under official inquiry in 1835, the year of Wild's incarceration, Thomas Dexter, an ex-convict, told the parliamentary committee: 'Frequently when I have seen it in a newspaper that a judge has sentenced a boy out of mercy to him to the hulks, I have made the observation that if it was a child of mine, I would rather see him dead at my feet than see him sent to that place.'[14]

Dexter had worked in the hospital for juvenile convicts where ill and beaten prisoners were received from the *Euryalus*. He was called to the committee and questioned about his experience:

'When these boys were ill in the convict hospital, did you see any signs of their being sensible of the offences which they had committed?'

'In very few instances …'

'Did many of them die when you were in that hospital?'

'Many.'

'What was the oldest boy that you recollect in that hospital?'

'Seventeen.'

'And the youngest?'

'Six years and seven months.'

'Do you know what he was convicted of?'

'I understood for some robbery at Birmingham, from the Warwick Assizes.'

'Was that boy reformed?'

'He died very shortly after he came in; and he was so young that he had hardly any religious or moral impressions on his mind.'

Dexter also referred to the severe physical bullying which took place between rival groups of boys, where victims had their limbs broken and others suffered starvation because they were forced to give up their rations to others.[15] According to his testimony, the convict hospital had a number of young prisoners who had harmed themselves in order to escape the ordeal of the ships. A retired Royal Navy captain, Edward Pelham Brenton, launched a scathing attack on the *Euryalus* in his controversial publication, *Observations on the Training and Education of the Children of Great Britain*:

Who would have believed the existence of such a ship, and for such a purpose, as the *Euryalus* at Chatham: 417 boys, between the ages of nine and sixteen, confined as convicts for seven years, each to cost from £70 to £100 – a floating Bastille; children in iron cages, who should have been in a nursery garden; children pining in misery, where the stench was intolerable … and while unfortunate girls are starving for want of needle-work, these boys are confined in dungeons, making shirts for convicts … I denounce this system as atrociously extravagant, cruel and vindictive, and I challenge any man to come forward and justify it.[16]

This was the voice of someone seeking to reform the hulks, but even if the captain had exaggerated the conditions for the purpose

6. *A prison hulk in Portsmouth harbour with the convicts going on board.*
Plate from Shipping and Craft *by E. W. Cooke, 1829*
© *National Maritime Museum, Greenwich, London.*

of his campaign, Wild's time on board the *Euryalus* would not have been easy. The boys were herded together in cramped and unwholesome conditions, they had a meagre diet, sanitation was poor, and infectious diseases were rife.[17] Yet, although discipline on the hulk was chaotic, William managed to receive a reasonable conduct report and after five months, and now aged fourteen, he was ready to be officially transported.[18]

In the first half of the nineteenth century, parliamentary debates on penal transportation were underpinned by opposing ideas of punishment. The reformatory ideals of one side came up against the old guard, who wanted to stress the punishment aspect of transportation and its desired deterrent effects.[19] Those who favoured change wanted to emphasise transportation not as punishment, at least not for certain offences, but as an opportunity for a new life as a migrant to the colonies. The idea was that by removing the young criminal from his fellow offenders, he could be given a chance to reform and make a new start.

The child would serve time until he secured a 'ticket-of-leave', enabling him to begin his life afresh. There is no doubt that for some children this more benign experience was a real possibility, and it was certainly imagined as such. One boy interviewed on the *Euryalus* said he had no regrets about his sentence. He had a brother at the bay whom he heard was 'at his trade and doing well'.[20] However, for those like William whose sentence was for life, the overwhelming feeling could only have been one of dread. Thirteen thousand child convicts were transported in the first half of the nineteenth century, and as one distinguished civil servant at the colonial office put it, many of them were as good as 'doomed'. Every boy sentenced to transportation, he said, 'bid a long farewell to the hopes of visiting his native home, of seeing his parents, or of rejoining his companions. These are the hopes and pleasures which his crimes have forfeited. He is being sent to a place where every hardship and degradation awaits him and where his suffering will be severe.'[21]

On 24 April 1836 William was taken alongside the *Lord Lyndoch*, which was moored at Sheerness in Kent. Not long after he boarded, the ship set sail for the 15,000-mile journey across the ocean to the other side of the world. Once the vessel hit open seas, the irons that shackled him were struck off and the gruelling four-month journey was under way. At this time, the system of transportation was almost half a century old. The dangers of the early years had been largely overcome and the prospect of being shipwrecked or lost was almost non-existent. Nonetheless, suffering and sometimes death did still occur; only the previous year the transport ship *Neva* had gone down off King Island with 225 people on board, and the year before that a fifteen-year-old boy had reported seventeen deaths from disease on his ship.[22] However, apart from these incidents, by the mid-1830s only 1 per cent of the total number of transported prisoners lost their lives.

But just as for any seaman, going to sea was a risky venture, and so it was for the child convict herded below deck in violent storms. One description picks up the journey from Rio:

> We were constantly meeting with squalls of wind, rain, lightning and heavy rolling seas, so that for many days we could not sit at table, but were obliged to hold fast to boxes on the floor and had all our crockery ware almost broken to pieces, besides shipping many seas into the cabin and living in a state of darkness from the cabin windows being stopped up by deadlights – I never was so melancholy in my life before. Not a single comfort either for the body or mind – the provisions, infamous – the water, stinking – our livestock destroyed by the cold and wet, and every person with a gloomy countenance.[23]

The gloom is likely to have continued, for in this equatorial region raging storms were frequently followed by periods of calm that all seamen know as the doldrums, where the winds disappear and the sea becomes uncannily still. This would have been a moment in the voyage where the pounding rays of the sun were made worse by poor ventilation in the areas that housed the wooden berths. Dehydration, dysentery and hunger were the most pressing problems faced by the surgeon superintendent on board, and often, hidden from him, a boy could find himself the object of unwanted sexual attention from an adult convict. One vicar to Van Diemen's Land (now Tasmania), the Reverend William Ullathorne, spoke of boys on ship being huddled together and indulging in 'a great deal of evil', which was obviously sexual in nature because he also felt it wise to caution them against mixing with the men on board.[24]

It appears from the report of the ship's surgeon on the *Lord Lyndoch* that William tolerated the 120-day voyage quite well.

However, surgeons were always anxious to minimise the problems of their cargo so as to cause little or no trouble for the island's governor and its officials. The lad was reported to be in sound health and although small for his age, he had a large oval face and a good complexion. His appearance, young and fresh, must have been striking in the circumstances.[25] What must this fresh-faced boy have thought of his predicament?

Disembarking at the penal settlement of Port Arthur, William was linked together with the other boys to be taken a further 60 miles across the bay to the special colony for juveniles. Point Puer was just over two years old when this group of youngsters arrived there. In its brief history it received 2,000 boys, all part of the growing number of offenders that Britain had no home for. It was a prison for boys between the ages of nine and eighteen. Many of them were what would now be called repeat offenders, some quite hardened, and at the time William arrived there were 271 inmates. Situated on the rocky outermost edge of the island, it was said that the odd visitor there could see boys 'climbing among the rocks and hiding or disappearing from sight like land-crabs in the West Indies'.[26] The first thing that William may have noticed as he journeyed across the bay from Port Arthur was the cliffs. The writer and historian of the convict system Robert Hughes knows them well, and offers a dramatic description: 'When the clouds march in from the Tasman Sea and the rainsqualls lash the prismatic stone, these cliffs can look like the adamantine gates of Hell itself. Geology had conspired with Lieutenant-Governor Arthur to give the prisoners of the crown a moral fright as their ships hauled in.'[27] Once the shackled band of young convicts had reached the barracks, they each received a uniform of jacket, trousers, waistcoat and cap. Then a corporal took them to their mess with twelve to a room, and they were each given a hammock and blanket for the nights ahead.

It was intended that Point Puer should house only boys because adult convicts, with whom they were normally housed, were thought to have a malign and corrupting influence. The settlement did also have a reforming aim; under strict supervision, boys kept there were to learn a trade and be given religious education. Some achieved this and went on to develop the skills of carpentry, gardening or blacksmithing, but not all benefited; much depended on the nature of the child's offence and his good behaviour. William was sent to work in labouring gangs where, judging from his record, he mostly sawed and carted timber for furniture, firewood and buildings. To begin with the regime, though strict, was tolerable. He got up at sunrise, rolled away his bedding, and stood with the other boys for morning prayers. After a wash and breakfast, work began and continued until midday when the bell brought them in to a meal of soup, brined beef and potatoes, turnip or cabbage. The menu never varied, except on Sundays when a pudding of raisins was provided. When work had finished at 5 pm they received the rudiments of a basic education, mostly consisting of scripture recital.[28]

What happened as the weeks and months continued is known because of records that were left behind by the convict system. It seems extraordinary now, at a time when this history is so firmly part of Australia's national identity, that it took until the end of the twentieth century for the archive to be brought to life. Up until then very little had been written about the feelings and experiences of the men, women and children who were transported; and while some parts of the archive are complete, others are absent or have been destroyed either deliberately or through the hazards of time. Remarkably, William's conduct record survived. Reading it we can see that only a few months after his arrival, a creeping fatalism began to overtake him. At the outset, he resisted what perhaps he only gradually realised were going to be the repetitive, everyday disciplines of his future existence. Over the years prisoners would come and go, and some were lucky enough to take on trades, but William's capital crime left him with a life sentence, and it must eventually have dawned upon him that this was a life from which there was no release.

He had arrived on Van Diemen's Land two years after Point Puer had been set up. The colony did attempt to employ reformatory techniques at this time, but the means were crude and unrelenting. Charles O'Hara Booth was in overall command of the convict settlements on the peninsula, and he had a reputation for tough justice. Boys were routinely subjected to physical and mental punishments. Booth's friend Lieutenant William Knight was in charge of Point Puer during Wild's detention, and under his command the number of punishments doubled.[29] An investigation into boys' convict records during this time shows a regime where beatings and physical deprivations were used for a wide number of minor breaches in discipline.[30] William Wild's convict record certainly bears this out.

Less than two months after his arrival at Point Puer, he was punished for misconduct during a religious service, and was placed in solitary confinement where he was fed only bread and water for two days.[31] O'Hara placed a high value on this sort of punishment because it was 'much dreaded' and it had great power over the minds of convicts, making them easier to subdue. Wild's conduct record is full of petty challenges to the system, small to twenty-first-century eyes, but serious by the rigorous standards of the colony's staff. For 'talking', 'idling' and 'wilfully destroying his shirt', William was left alone in a darkened cell for days. On the first occasion he tried to run away, and was given fifteen lashes on the breech (lower buttocks and back). According to the record, hardly a month went by without William being punished for something.

In April 1837 he was moved to Port Arthur, where his conduct seemed to get worse. Each time he misbehaved, he was punished and given more strenuous labour. He was put in the chain gang with adult offenders, but was reprimanded again for trying to escape. Later he was sent to Launceston, a small town on the northern coast of the island, but his work there was nothing more than hard slave labour in chains. The record shows that Wild made numerous pathetic attempts at escape, but he was always seized by the authorities who returned him to the chain gangs. His last recorded offence was refusing to work, for which he was lashed 25 times.

Wild never gained the freedom he was striving for. He spent a total of six years on Van Diemen's Land, until he died in 1842 aged 21. No cause of death is given on his record. Before he died he was severely reprimanded for 'idleness', and for not wanting to work. More likely he was exhausted through illness. Like many other convicts whose lives ended while they were still serving their sentence, he would have been buried in an unmarked grave on the Isle of the Dead, just off the tip of Point Puer. Evidence indicated that if an individual defied the penal system of the colony, for whatever reason, it would methodically crush them with harsher punishments, and elements of this are marked in Wild's record. Even if he had wanted to comply with the demands of his jailers, he may not have been saved from the attention of other prisoners who had their own code of behaviour which, as well as the black economy, also included bullying and intimidation. Wild must have been daunted by a life sentence that appeared to offer no hope, especially when the majority of his juvenile peers, some of whom had worse conduct records, were freed after seven years.

William had travelled a long way from rural Derbyshire where he had committed his awful crime, but the measure of just how devastating his punishment was is shown through comparison with another case of child murder. Astonishingly, the record of this young criminal, Alfred Dancey, also survives. It is interesting to examine the outcome of William's punitive life sentence alongside that of this case where the boy was given a time-limited sentence. The circumstances of the crime were different to Wild's, but it had been a violent killing. The contrasting sentences that each boy received affected their futures quite differently, and the two experiences show how the competing views, of transportation as tough punishment on the one hand, and reformatory aspirations on the other, operated in practice.

A Tale of Luck

Alfred Dancey was fourteen years old when he was indicted for murder on Christmas Eve 1849.[32] The boy had been playing with another friend of the same age on a road just outside the Gloucestershire village of Bedminster. Three older teenagers walking nearby began taunting them and calling them names. Dancey's friend pulled out a knife and threatened the older group, one of whom began to struggle with the boy to get the knife off him. Dancey shouted to let his friend go. He then drew a pistol and warned that he would shoot, but just as the older boy was getting up, Dancey fired his fatal shot.

The trial was held four months later at Gloucester assizes. The defence pleaded that the boy had acted in the heat of the moment and had not meant to kill the young man. The jury agreed, and returned a verdict of manslaughter. When issuing his sentence of ten years' transportation, the judge indicated to Dancey that it would remove him from the 'bad company' he had been keeping in Bristol. The judge's remarks reflected the idea of transportation as being not simply a punitive solution to crime, but a reforming possibility too.

The treatment that Wild and Dancey received after they were transported could not have been more different. This was not entirely due to their differing sentences; the boys' backgrounds were different too. The illiterate Wild was fatherless from a young age, though he did have a stepfather who spoke well of him at the trial. His mother, on the other hand, was described in a jailer's report as a 'most vicious character [who] has made [the boy] subservient to her vicious purposes'.[33] Whether this was true or not, Wild's background was less secure than that of Alfred Dancey who could read and write, had a father who worked at a local mill, and who lived at home with his mother, brother and sister.[34] These differing family circumstances may also have affected the boys' attitudes. There is plenty of evidence to show that character and good behaviour counted a great deal when serving time in a penal colony.[35] Those who behaved well avoided the more severe aspects of the penal regime, and went directly into assigned service where they could learn a craft or trade. However, it was also the case that when Dancey arrived in Hobart in 1852, sixteen years after William Wild, the reformatory model in which boys were given skills and education was more established, and Dancey, even with a conviction for a violent crime such as manslaughter, was in a good position to benefit from it.

Dancey arrived on Van Diemen's Land in 1852, three years after Point Puer was closed down. It is almost certain, though the records do not confirm it, that for the two years prior to his transportation, Dancey was imprisoned in Parkhurst prison, as the *Euryalus* had been finally abandoned in 1846. In 1838 Parkhurst was changed from a military hospital into the first dedicated prison for juvenile offenders. It later became a holding establishment for boys, like Dancey, who had committed serious crimes and were destined to be transported. His convict record says nothing of his behaviour in prison, but on his arrival at the prison barracks in Hobart he was given the classification of 'Pass Holder' for two years. This suggests that his behaviour had been favourable, as the pass granted him privileges including greater freedom of movement. A month after his arrival, he was assigned to a settler on Hamilton Island to work as a labourer. Later the same year he was granted a ticket-of-leave for good behaviour, with the note that he must serve two years for a conditional pardon. The only note of misconduct on his record was for being out after hours, for which he was simply given a warning. Dancey received his pardon in 1855 having served only half his sentence. He was nineteen. His name does not appear in the death or marriage records for Tasmania, so it is not possible to know for certain what became of him. At the time when he was freed, there was a large migration out of Tasmania to Victoria in the gold rush, and it was not unusual for ex-convicts to alter their name and join it. On the other hand he may, like others did, have looked forward to returning home to be reunited with his family.

Two years after Dancey's pardon, transportation came to an end. This was not so much due to the virtues of prison or reformatory school life back home in England, but more because of opposition to the system from the colonial authorities in Australia. It was no longer acceptable to the territories to receive uneducated children with dubious morals. Colonists, 'increasingly proud of their land', did not want to jeopardise its social stability. In the harsh words of one English chaplain, the colony refused to 'keep an open cesspool for the criminal sewage of England'.[36]

Once boys like Wild and Dancey could no longer be sent to a colony on the other side of the world, the home-grown option of prison was increasingly used. Thanks to the efforts of past reformers, the early 1800s had been marked by the construction of elaborate new penal institutions. As well as housing adult inmates, it was hoped that these prisons would deal with one of the century's biggest problems – juvenile crime. Where once it was considered just and reasonable to execute a child; then, instead, to wrench him from everything and everyone he had known, to send him to the punishments of a faraway island; now it was thought humane to put him in a solitary cell, clothe him in uniform, and press correction upon him with doses of scripture and hard labour.[37] Surely, children involved in murder would bear the worst of such a system.

Chapter Four

DANGEROUS MISCHIEF

It is expedient in the interests of public justice, and for the purpose of example and deterrence, that notorious offenders should receive punishment before being admitted to the advantages of these [reform] institutions.
ROYAL COMMISSION ON REFORMATORIES, 1884

What shall we do with the child criminal? We say, do not send him to prison, if you would not hinder the advance of civilisation and humanity.
ELIZABETH SURR, 1881

If transportation had once been considered the next best punishment to execution, by the mid-nineteenth century, prison was by far the favoured option. But just as the experience of transportation could be brutal, jail was by no means a benign environment. Ever since the great prison reformer John Howard had carried his lantern into the dungeons of English prisons in the 1770s, the conditions of filth and corruption had gradually improved and new jails were built. But as places of punishment for children, they were dismal and their bitter regime of moral correction was failing, with greater numbers returning to jail for further offences. Some politicians and writers at the time thought that these austere institutions were unsuitable for children, and it was from this group that the idea of reforming young criminals in separate establishments began to emerge.

The fate of a child who committed murder was much improved by the philanthropic, sometimes Utopian, campaigns of this period. But for more pessimistic voices, the behaviour of such a child was a sign of the propensity for evil inherent in human nature, for which prison punishment was the only solution. The softening of heart that the nation was experiencing regarding children generally could, in equal measure, harden when it came to the child criminal. Even Dickens, who had built his literary reputation on the strength of his feelings for children, and always had their sufferings at heart, was ruthlessly unsentimental about the criminal child. On a journalistic foray into Newgate prison, he described a group of prisoners, all of them under fourteen:

> The whole number, without exception we believe, had been committed for trial on charges of pocket-picking; and fourteen such villainous little faces we never beheld. There was not one redeeming feature among them – not a glance of honesty – not a wink expressive of anything but the gallows and the hulks in the whole collection. As to anything like shame or contrition, that was entirely out of the question. They were evidently quite gratified at being thought worth the trouble of looking at; their idea appeared to be that we had come to see Newgate as a grand affair, and they were an indispensable part of the show.[1]

For others, like the redoubtable campaigner Mary Carpenter, such children, no matter how 'vicious and degraded', were 'capable of being made useful members of society'. There was, she believed, 'an indestructible germ of a divine nature in these unhappy little beings'.[2] Anxieties about youth crime were at fever pitch in the early nineteenth century, with the dislocations caused by mass migration to cities. The tensions between these two moral outlooks were to characterise the debate about what should be done with the criminal child, and the story of how children who kill were treated belongs to this context. They had committed the worst crime imaginable, and at such a young age. Did this expose them to the harshest iniquities of prison life such as that given to adults, or were they spared for simple moral instruction instead? How did they fare in a climate that was benevolent on the one hand and punitive on the other?

Stunted Little Men

By the 1850s, the treatment of a child who had killed became entwined with that of those who fell into the category of 'juvenile offender'. Youth and crime had been linked through the ages, but this was the time in which the foundations were laid for the construction of a whole new juvenile justice system that still operates in a broadly similar way today.[3] This new system evolved in the middle years of the century, but some of its contours had been established earlier. At the start of the 1800s, social investigators who tried to seek out the causes of crime did so with almost scientific precision. Their systematic categorisation of these causes led, inevitably, to generalised descriptions of criminals. The social backgrounds of the juveniles in their studies revealed a sorry picture of 'temptation, ignorance and destitution sufficient to account for almost any extent of vice and crime'.[4]

The remarkable growth of city populations in the nineteenth century created numerous miseries. The urban world of the poor was often a vortex of violence, prostitution and lawlessness with children growing up into the ways of the adults around them.

Generations of young people, for whom the endearments of parental love were alien, knew little of the comforts that were afforded to the well-to-do child. A child of the slums had to grow up quickly, and from a very young age displayed adult mannerisms and a familiarity with the adult world. Standards of propriety, so important to the genteel Victorian, were of no consequence to the criminal or destitute. Children from these backgrounds were roughly-hewn and could often be angry, violent and disagreeable in their mannerisms and speech. The Victorian middle class identity, on the other hand, tried to base itself on a shared set of cultural manners and refinements. Its children's literature and child guidance manuals nurtured 'self-control and fine sympathies', not least because sound moral character conferred considerable social benefit.[5] While good middle-class children submitted to the authority of their parents and especially the Church, young urban rebels, described as 'street Arabs' or 'ownerless dogs', were seen by the comfortably-off as observing no moral code.[6] Theirs was a childhood that every well-to-do nineteenth-century family wished to avoid, one based not on innocence but experience, and where the child, governed by its own will, became resistant to the habits of virtue. Such a child was, according to one description, 'a little stunted man already – he knows much and a great deal too much of what is called life – he can take care of his own immediate interests. He is self-reliant, he has long directed or misdirected his own actions and he has so little trust in those about him, that he submits to no control and asks for no protection.'[7]

When Dickens wrote of children as 'idols of the heart and of household; they are angels of God in disguise', he clearly did not have child criminals in mind.[8] In his optimism he was creating a new sensibility of childhood, one that marked a separation between child and adult, a distinction long blurred by the enforced labour of the young. But the existence of the criminal child marked a social difference between children, in which the poor were thought not to inhabit the same moral universe as the well-heeled. It became a crusade for some Christian reformers to shine light onto souls lost to the degradations of poverty: 'It is to our low neighbourhoods, and to the neglected children roaming the streets, that we must look, if we could check the current of crime ... It is in the dwelling-place of the poor that the zealous must labour for the dissemination of Christian principles ... This is the fountainhead of crime, and it is here that the evil must be grappled with.'[9]

In 1851, Mary Carpenter was one of those reformers. She described children who were skirting the edges of crime as 'perishing', and those who had fallen into it as 'dangerous'.[10] Her simple descriptions were to provide an evaluative moral framework where none had previously existed. Yet in many respects the child killer defied Carpenter's categorisation. Their offence was unusual and horrifying, but it was not, for the most part, committed by hardened or 'dangerous' criminals. Even John Bell's 'wrong doings', which featured heavily in the commentary on his case, did not amount to what could be described as a serious criminal record. But there were perhaps ways in which most of the children who appear in this book did fit the description of 'perishing', not because they were on the fringes of criminal activity, but because they were vulnerable, as vagrants were, and almost all them were poor. Some had troubled home lives, and others found themselves confused by the responsibilities of the adult world. It is perhaps unsurprising, but worth noting, that among the cases featured in this book, a significant number of them include murders by children charged with full-time responsibility for other children who were not family members. William Wild, from the previous chapter, had been visceral in his response to the childcare aspect of his duties: 'I am no maiden', he had shouted, his youthful masculine identity clearly humiliated by the task.

There were other implied distinctions in Carpenter's descriptions that were also relevant to child murders, and these were of a more profound nature. They centred upon the idea of reform and reclamation for child criminals, an enlightened outlook far removed from the evangelicals' emphasis on sin, guilt and atonement. Mary Carpenter's Unitarian religion committed her to 'a strong faith in the immortality of the human soul, the universal and parental government of God, and the equal value in His sight of each one of these poor perishing young creatures with the most exalted of our race'.[11]

The victims of neglect, or the 'perishing' class of criminals as Carpenter called them, were hopeful subjects for redemption as they had not become habituated to criminal behaviour, but even the 'dangerous' classes, the category which might have encompassed child killers, were also considered redeemable if not always immediately compliant.[12] A belief in the equality of souls was part of Unitarian teaching, as was a vision of humanity as essentially good and inherently perfectible. Unlike the Calvinist variety of Protestantism, the Unitarians saw no innate depravity in the human soul; according to them everyone had access to the goodness of God, and a rational religious education was the best means of reaching it. Unitarianism included a reformist political attitude, and an enlightened commitment to education. This was the foundation of Carpenter's idealism and it drove her, unusually for a single woman, into a public world where she encountered visions of humankind less generous than her own.[13]

The first government attempt to deal with the issue of young offenders came in 1847. Nearly half of convicted criminals were under 21; the problem of juvenile offenders had become so pressing that a House of Lords Select Committee was set up, and every judge in the land was consulted for their views on how best to treat them. The majority favoured extreme forms of penal discipline that included imprisonment, hard labour and whipping. On the new idea of reformatories for young offenders, the high court judge Lord Denman expressed a commonly held view:

> I greatly dread the effect of giving them the benefits and privileges which they could never have hoped but from the commission of crimes. I owe myself extremely jealous of the gratuitous instruction of the young felon in a trade, merely because he is a felon, and of the displacement of the honest from employment by his success in thus obtaining it ... I hold the only legitimate end of punishment to be to deter from crime; but I think I perceive in some of the theories of benevolent men such a mode of administering the criminal law as to encourage instead of deterring.[14]

At a glance, attitudes towards the punishment of young criminals in Victorian England could easily be characterised as an opposition between the two contrasting moral views of Mary Carpenter and the eminent Lord Denman, echoes of which can be heard in today's debates on youth crime. These views, however, were at the extreme ends of the arguments over the treatment of young offenders, but the middle ground was still much closer to the punitive inclinations of the judge than to the sentiments of the radical reformer. The idea that all crimes needed prison punishment, no matter how small or young the offender, would continue, and this was reflected in the sentence received by child murderers.

Child's Play

In 1855 two nine-year-old Liverpool boys, John Breen and Alfred Fitz, were sentenced to an adult jail, which the judge told them was 'a great mercy' as they had been indicted for the murder of a seven-year-old boy.[15] One lawyer who became involved in the case said it was 'the most affecting and terrible story' he had ever heard in a court of justice. The boys had been playing in the brickfields on the edge of the city, near one of the great canals linking Liverpool to the major industrial areas of the country. It was summer, and hordes of young children roamed as if feral across the quarries and wastelands, away from the cramped cubby-holes of the 'courts', or dwellings, which were notorious for their terrible overcrowding.

Like most urban centres of the period, Liverpool was a city of contrasts. As one of the world's major ports it had seen enormous commercial success, gilding the lives of many, but it was also home to the largest poorhouse in the country. England's first public medical officer described it as the unhealthiest city of all those he had visited. The mortality rate was higher than that of the other large cities and its population, in terms of sheer density, was greater than those of Manchester, Leeds and London.[16] The famine migration from Ireland in the 1840s had swelled the ranks of the growing population, adding to the crowded conditions near the waterfront where many of the unfortunate inhabitants worked. The Victorian clergyman and writer Silas Hocking knew these communities well, and he painted a vivid picture of the children and their neighbourhoods:

> On the western side of Scotland Road – that is to say, between
> it and the docks – there is a regular network of streets, inhab-
> ited mostly by the lowest class of the Liverpool poor. And

those who have occasion to penetrate their dark and filthy recesses are generally thankful when they find themselves safe out again. In the winter those streets and courts are kept comparatively clean by the heavy rains; but in the summer the air fairly reeks with the stench of decayed fish, rotting vegetables, and every other conceivable kind of filth ... The children that seem to swarm in this neighbourhood are nearly all of a pale, sallow complexion, and of stunted growth. Shoes and stockings and underclothing are luxuries that they never know, and one good meal a day is almost more than they dare hope for. Cuffs and kicks they reckon upon every day of their lives; and in this they are rarely disappointed.[17]

Breen, Fitz and their companions had broken free from the dark hovels of home to play in the open spaces at the city boundary. On the fateful summer's day, the game they were playing was called 'cap o' the beak', and involved one child jumping over the back of another where a cap was placed; a clear leap meant you were the winner. On this occasion the younger boy had achieved victory, but Fitz accused him of cheating. They quarrelled and the exchange must have been violent, because a woman nearby tried to intervene and was told to mind her own business. Fitz then picked up a brick and threw it at his playmate, who immediately fell to the ground with blood pouring from his head. As he lay there, Fitz went over to him, took up the brick again, and repeated the attack. Convulsed by this blow the boy uttered something faintly, and then lay still. 'Let's throw him into the water or we'll cop it', Fitz apparently said. Little John Breen agreed, and they both carried their lifeless friend to the canal and threw him in while the other boys watched and did nothing.

The drowned boy was never reported missing. Even though one of the young witnesses told his parents what he'd seen, they chose not to tell anyone, neither a policeman nor a magistrate, and they made only cursory efforts to find the dead boy's father. This was a closed world into which no lawmaker was ever invited. Quite apart from the crimes of poverty, there were the melancholy acts of violence brought on by drink. According to a House of Lords committee, drunkenness in Liverpool was the highest in Britain with one in every twenty of the population being apprehended for its effects. Mistrust of the authorities was widespread, and for all the blunt and often violent exchanges between members of this community, it was fiercely self-protective.[18]

Five days passed before a policeman found James Fleeson's body floating in Stanley Dock. It would not have taken long for the corpse to drift into the Liverpool to Leeds canal, but amid the crowded activity on the waterfront it had simply gone unnoticed. News of the shocking discovery circulated quickly and eventually reached the dead boy's father. He had never officially reported his child missing, but within the crowded slums word had spread.

At the South Lancashire assizes held on Wednesday, 23 August, the two nine-year-olds, barely visible over the dock, stood trial for the murder of James Fleeson. The prosecuting lawyer told the jury: 'If it could be shown that they knew they were doing wrong and committing an act which would lead to death then [you] must return a verdict of guilty, even of wilful murder, and however painful it might be to do so, bearing in mind the awful sentence which would follow such a verdict, still [you] must leave to other people the responsibility of dealing with the punishment for that offence.' In its wisdom, the jury returned a verdict of manslaughter with a recommendation of mercy for both boys.

The defence had managed to create reasonable doubt about whether the boys really intended to kill their friend. Judge Baron Platt delivered his sentence: 'Certainly, you did not mean to kill this boy when you threw him into the water. The greatest mercy

I can show you is to send you to prison for twelve months.' This penalty seems generous in the light of such a serious crime, but appears less so when put against a case he had tried earlier the same day. A middle-aged man, who had dragged his wife by the hair into the street and beaten her to death, was given a similar sentence.[19]

The judge's expectation was that the boys would receive schooling and moral instruction as if the new reforming ethos had made prison, nineteenth-century-style, as benign as any well-run school: 'I will make sure you keep out of more mischief by having you a little instructed before you get out of prison again. You will have a schoolmaster and a chaplain and you will be taught how to get your own living.'[20] In reality, however, there was a marked punitive element to the disciplinary system the boys were about to experience.

The Prison's Cradle

The house of correction that they were sent to was Walton prison in Liverpool, the same destination as the 40-year-old man who had killed his wife. Built in 1849, it was organised according to the so-called 'separate system', a new model for English prisons, the most important element of which was total isolation of the prisoner from any sensory input whatsoever other than the chaplain's nagging voice.[21]

Walton had 1,300 single cells where convicts were housed alone. The two nine-year-old boys had come from the worst, most overcrowded conditions in the country, but had enjoyed roving with the pack of children they'd grown up with, and now they found themselves alone in their cells, spending most of the day in silence. There is no surviving record of the boys' experience in prison, but as there was a degree of uniformity to the regime under the new separate system, the young criminals would doubtless have been stripped of their names on arrival, and then given a number before being put into uniforms.[22] It is possible that they were also given head masks to wear, in order to prevent eye contact or communication of any kind when they exercised in lines with the other inmates. The mask was an unsettling weapon in the prison armoury; it was worn like a cap, with a long peak that fell over the face. A number of magistrates, chaplains and governors thought that its use was inhumane, and by the end of the 1850s it was abandoned. One of the rationales for this system was to ensure that hardened offenders had no malign influence over other prisoners, but the other perceived advantage was the effect that it had upon the mind. In their isolation, prisoners were supposed to reflect on their crimes and repent, but the effect could be far more chilling than that, even for adults, as the Reverend John Clay, chaplain to the House of Correction in Preston, describes:

> [A] few months in the solitary cell renders a prisoner strangely impressible [sic]. The chaplain can then make the brawny navvy cry like a child; he can work on his feelings in almost any way he pleases; he can, so to speak, photograph his thoughts, wishes and opinions on his patient's mind, and fill his mouth with his own phrases and language.[23]

At the time Breen and Fitz arrived at Liverpool jail, the building was only six years old, but it was criticised in the local press for being 'exceedingly dark and gloomy'. Mary Carpenter had visited the year after it opened and saw two small boys 'crying bitterly in dark cells; one, the officer said, was usually unruly and hardened and the other was being punished for beating another child as they went up the stairs! Solitary confinement and a bread and water diet are generally found sufficient punishment; flogging is resorted to very rarely for insubordination. Handcuffs and irons have not been used here for many years except on going to trial.'[24]

The records provide no indication of whether there was a special juvenile department of the prison, which often depended upon there being sufficient numbers to make it economical, but as there were 990 'juveniles' imprisoned in the year the two boys went there, it is likely that special arrangements were made to keep them from the adult inmates. In most other respects, their regime and treatment was the same as that of the older prisoners. They slept on plank beds and were fed a meagre diet, which they ate alone inside their cell. Each cell was no more than eleven feet by seven and was provided with a small table, a stool and a writing desk. The inmates were allowed a Bible, prayer and hymn books, and, for schooling purposes, a slate and pencil. They were separate from one another at all times, even during periods of religious education when they would sit in specially constructed wooden compartments that shielded them from each other and made them face towards the chaplain in front. Generally, children were excused from hard labour, but they were employed in workshops making shoes or doing carpentry, and they sometimes did manual work on the buildings or in the grounds. They were also put to work inside their cells.

All physically fit boys were subjected to daily drills and exercise that their military-trained masters used to instil discipline.[25] Corporal punishments such as whipping were used, as was solitary confinement. At Parkhurst, the first prison dedicated to holding young prisoners, they also had a more severe punishment of sending children to the 'Black Hole', a windowless underground cell with only a small grille to allow fresh air to circulate. In

Liverpool jail they used the 'dreaded' treadwheel. This pointless labour had prisoners standing in boxes like upright coffins with the bottom open, allowing inmates to move a wheel with their feet while they stared at the wall in front of them. The prison chaplain admitted that this contraption could only be used with 'the most vigilant and careful safeguards, [otherwise] the tendency to inflict the most serious consequences, and even irreparable injury, is so great as to excite the most painful anxiety'.[26]

By the mid-nineteenth century, there was already evidence that adults were experiencing psychological disorders as a result of this new separate system of prison discipline, and many attempted suicide. The prison chaplain at Reading jail thought that such extreme systems were certainly going to be injurious to children, while Mary Carpenter was outraged at its use, believing it to be an assault upon the true spirit of childhood:

> The child is placed in a condition perfectly discordant with his nature. The exercise of his buoyant animal spirits is severely visited as a prison offence: he must not even raise his voice in those loud and joyous sounds which seem a necessity of his nature; all exercise of his social feelings is cut off, no voice of tenderness is heard, and the spirited boy who will be softened to tears by the gentle reproof of his teacher, vents his energy in ingenious attempts at mischief in the prison cell.[27]

Given the number of young prisoners who were returning to prison – 66 per cent in Liverpool, with more than a quarter having been imprisoned four times or more – it is possible that for some offenders at least, prison held no particular fear.[28] Certainly this was the view of some members of Parliament, even those who did not favour imprisonment of the young. One politician thought that the new system 'provided such comparative comforts, that in many cases the prison becomes a real home to the criminal', while the permanent undersecretary at the Home Office, Sir Godfrey Lushington, opined: 'Unlike their elders, they [juveniles] are accustomed to be ordered about; they do not mind discomfort and hardship. They have no anxiety for their family being impoverished, and no power of looking forward or realising the after effects of imprisonment.'[29]

There were also reformatory school officials who believed that children benefited from a prison term because it was an improvement on their home life, and increased their chances of reforming. John Trevarthen of Redhill Reformatory considered that a child's home circumstances 'have been a thousand times more contaminating than any prison can possibly be, and I should think that the wholesome effect of the prison treatment upon him very much enhances the chances of our doing him good.'[30]

Yet there were many children for whom imprisonment was a devastating experience. A fifteen-year-old inmate at Birmingham borough jail, Edward Andrews, committed suicide by hanging himself from his cell window. Like Liverpool, it was built on the model of the separate system. Prisoners were isolated from one another and the regime was harsh. Petty offences were punished with long stretches of solitary confinement and arduous hours on the hand crank, which involved turning a handle attached to a set of cogs that pushed a paddle through sand. There was no product from this labour, and the prisoner, alone in his cell, turned the hand crank all day. Edward Andrews had refused to work (or more likely had been unable to), so he was strait-jacketed, beaten and fed on bread and water. The night before he died, the prison schoolmaster had seen him in a state of exhaustion, looking 'very deathly and reeling with weakness'. His death created a public outcry and a commission of inquiry was set up, but no changes were made to the prison regime.[31]

One child who became an emblem for those who wanted to bring this kind of punishment to an end was the frightened figure witnessed by Oscar Wilde while in Reading jail. Wilde recalls the look on the child's face, 'like a white wedge of sheer terror. There was in his eyes the terror of a hunted animal. The next morning I heard him at breakfast-time crying, and calling to be let out. His cry was for his parents.' Wilde discovered later that this child was on remand. In a letter to the *Daily Chronicle*, he wrote:

> Judges and magistrates, an entirely ignorant class as a rule, often remand children for a week, and then perhaps remit whatever sentences they are entitled to pass. They call this 'not sending a child to prison'. It is, of course, a stupid view on their part. To a little child, whether he is in prison on remand or after conviction is not a subtlety of social position he can comprehend. To him the horrible thing is to be there at all. In the eyes of humanity it should be a horrible thing to be there at all.[32]

A number of contemporary witnesses of child imprisonment recalled young convicts on remand, bewildered and frightened by the prospect of their incarceration. Among them was the governor of Stafford prison, Major Fulford, who gave evidence to the Carnarvon committee inquiry into prisons:

> I have had them [children] really so small and so tender that I have been obliged to put them in the female hospital to play with the kitten; that is an absolute fact ... and I have had three or four boys in whose cases we have been obliged to light their gas, and leave the door of their cells open by night.[33]

The irony of the nineteenth-century 'invention' of the juvenile delinquent was that more children faced imprisonment in that century than in the previous one.[34] With the development of the institutional framework of the juvenile justice system, greater numbers of children were brought within its remit. Magistrates had increased powers of summary jurisdiction together with a greater range of penalties that they could enforce for all kinds of offences, from petty larceny to violent crime. The chaplain of Liverpool jail complained that the proportion of prisoners on short sentences had doubled in ten years, and he doubted the value of such a punishment, saying, 'Can any abiding impression be made on the minds of these in so short a time, and under the opposing influences by which they are here surrounded?'[35]

Moral Limits in the Reform of Punishment

Despite the growing debate over whether prison was the right place to detain young criminals, the need to punish them never disappeared from view, even though in many cases this punishment was only a token measure. The reformatory school movement was pushing hard, and Mary Carpenter was ever the zealous campaigner, but old traditions and fears about child criminals were still strong. The principle of public justice was invoked by many as grounds for the continuation of prison as punishment. It was argued that as a custodial arrangement, the reformatory school was unsuitable because it was mainly educational in its focus, and therefore not fit for the purpose of example and deterrence. Public justice, however, is as much a 'working fiction' as public opinion. It is defined by the most powerful voices, and it suggests, as the historian Vic Gatrell has argued, that 'their high ground is a lot more thickly populated than it is'.[36] As a construct, it is also prey to historical contingencies, such as the changing reality of crime and shifting attitudes towards it. Events like the London garrotting scare in 1862, a series of attacks where the victims' throats were cut, could bring any enlightened argument to an abrupt end and result, as it did, in a more severe penal system.[37]

The reform ideal, however, would not have been so easily at risk were it not for the widely held doubts about the extent to which human behaviour could ever be transformed. Children were slowly gaining a separate legal status from adults, but the fear that small sinners, unchecked, would ripen into greater criminals shadowed Victorian society. There were pessimistic voices such as Thomas Carlyle who described prisoners as 'perverse creatures, sons of indocility'. For him, the idea of reform was a hopeless project:

> The abject, ape, wolf, ox, imp and other diabolic-animal specimens of humanity, who of the very gods could ever have commanded them by love? A collar round the neck, and a cartwhip flourished over the back; these, in a just and steady human hand, were what the gods would have appointed them.[38]

Carlyle was a disenchanted man. Like other Romantic writers of the early nineteenth century such as Wordsworth and Coleridge, in his youth he had welcomed the hopeful beginnings of the French Revolution that were symbolised by the storming of the Bastille in July 1789. But the Terror that came in its wake shattered these hopes, and demonstrated for such writers that human nature was stubbornly resistant to reform and enlightenment. Carlyle may not have had child criminals in mind when expressing his contempt, but in the minds of many, these children were not far from men in their ruthless and deceitful ways. The delinquent was seen as having 'qualities the very reverse of what we should desire to see in childhood; we have beheld them independent, self-reliant, advanced in the knowledge of evil'.[39] For some, such as Mary Carpenter, this was poignant evidence of a lack of childhood, but for others it was exactly this knowingness that made them indistinguishable from adults. According to this latter opinion, child criminals were viewed as deserving of the same punishments as their older counterparts: 'Juvenile Offenders should be treated as all other offenders … they must be hurt so that the idea of pain might be instantly associated with crime in the minds of all evildoers.'[40] This same commentator condemned 'effeminate and diseased sentimentality', which he believed characterised the attitude of the reformers. Another expressed the same revulsion over sentiment, and was contemptuous of 'the belief that juvenile offenders are little errant angels who require little else than fondling'. He was clear that children who committed crimes knew they were doing wrong, and deserved punishment.[41]

The 1854 Youthful Offenders Act reflected the ambivalence that existed over the potential of young criminals to reform. While it accepted the necessity of reformatory treatment for juveniles, there was a final clause in the Act which stipulated that children were to serve a minimum prison sentence as payment for their crime before they could be sent to a reformatory. It was a disappointment for Mary Carpenter, who believed that a punitive environment for a child was utterly useless for reform because 'the heart is not touched'.[42] At the start of the government debate on the reformatory school idea, she had been asked by a select committee member if her system would effect 'due correction', to which she had replied:

We ought in the first place to consider the position of these children in regard to society. I consider that society owes retribution to them as much as they owe it to society, or in fact more, for we are told in the Sacred Volume, that 'to him that knoweth to do good, and doeth it not, to him is sin' ... I believe the child will make better reparation, as I before said, by afterwards sowing the seeds of virtue, than by scattering those of vice, which he would otherwise do.[43]

Others in the reform movement, perhaps more pragmatic than Carpenter, believed that the imprisonment clause in the Act was a small price to pay for what one of them hailed as the 'Magna Carta of juvenile delinquents'. One of them, Matthew Hill, believed that the new law would in time come to be seen as 'a great epoch in the jurisprudence of this country'.[44] By establishing separate institutional arrangements for criminal children, the Act provided an acknowledgement of their different legal status. Yet the punitive element of the law continued to be debated for the rest of the nineteenth century. Later legislation reduced the prison sentence to ten days, but it was not until the Reformatory Schools Act of 1899 that the courts were finally prohibited from combining a reformatory school order with the punishment of a prison sentence.[45]

The Beginning of the End

Victorian society's response to the child criminal was certainly equivocal, but nothing suggests that the unusual crime of children murdering other children led to louder calls for retribution. Fitz and Breen did have to spend a year in circumstances that would concern us today, but while their sentence was undoubtedly harsh, there were examples of other, lesser offences being treated just as harshly. A reformatory school sentence was an option when the Liverpool boys were convicted in 1855, and records show that in the year in which they arrived at Walton prison, nineteen children were sent to the reformatory; the boys, not being among them, were obviously thought to deserve due punishment for their more serious crime. But, as the century progressed, more convicted children were to benefit from the lesser penalty and spend shorter spells in prison. In fact, based on the figures for Liverpool prison, it is evident that had nine-year-old John Breen and Alfred Fitz received their sentence ten years later, they would have had a one in three chance of serving most of it in a reformatory.

The schools were proving themselves as reforming institutions, and more government grants were made available after consolidating legislation was passed in 1866. The motivations behind their expansion were mainly pragmatic. They could contribute to the reduction in reoffending rates, and they were said to be cheaper than prisons. As one MP argued, if only 'from the low motive of economy', it would be 'wise to improve the system'.[46] The virtues of reformatory institutions were rarely argued for on moral grounds. Christian duty was invoked as a reason for taking care of the religious and moral education of criminal children, but punishment was never far from the agenda of reform. A good instance of this is shown by the position of Gladstone. Before his rise through Parliament, in his capacity as treasurer of the Philanthropic Institution, Gladstone supported a reformatory system, but proposed that there should be two kinds of schools: one with a regime for the 'wilfully criminal and vicious' – much like an ordinary prison, but for children only – and the other for education and reform.[47]

By the 1860s, the idea that reforming initiatives should be directed at the young was uncontroversial; children were seen as more suggestible and stood a better chance of being trained out of what was perceived at the time as the malign impulses of their nature. Indeed, at this point when momentum for change was at its strongest, two eight-year-old boys who cruelly murdered a boy of two served the majority of their sentence in a reformatory. This was proof indeed that the punishment of children who murdered other children had come a long way since the execution of John Bell and the transportation of William Wild. For the first time in history, children were treated differently from adults in the criminal justice system and, even more uniquely, a child who committed murder would not face the ultimate punishment. Formally, a child's legal liability for the crime of murder had not changed, but the adult understanding of childhood was on the point of an important transition. Murder was an adult crime, and the child who committed it highlighted concern not so much about the fearsome cruelty of children, but about the failure of parents to transform this and to influence their natures towards virtue.

Chapter Five

REVERSAL OF FORTUNE

The child ... must be placed where the prevailing principle will be,
as far as practicable, carried out, where he will be gradually restored
to the true position of childhood.
MARY CARPENTER, 1853

One of the perceived strengths of the Victorian era was the extent to which the child became an emblem of social good. The historian George Trevelyan, for example, wrote that 'the enlarged sympathy with children was one of the chief contributions made by the Victorian English to real civilisation'.[1] The late-nineteenth-century reformer Gertrude Tuckwell believed that 'among the social questions with which the nation has to deal, there is none so important as the question of children. The wise treatment of this question ... must affect the eventual solution of other social problems.'[2] Of course, law-breakers and vagrants were still viewed in savage terms, described as bestial, 'prowling' like 'wild brutes, preying on society'. Dickens likened the criminal young to 'wild birds, pilfering the crumbs, which fall from the table of the country's wealth'. But increasingly, even these lawless spirits became worthy of protection, their identity as children seen as something important, and a childhood as something they deserved. The Puritan idea in which the heart of every child was full of evil ended in this era, not because of the triumph of any alternative religious doctrine, but rather because of the Victorian ideal of progress, so that by the close of the nineteenth century, children's welfare and happiness became for many a measure of what it meant to be a civilised society.

A particularly disturbing case of child murder in 1861 threatened this new ideal of childhood and had the potential to reignite older beliefs about children and their sinful nature. Confronted by such an unsettling event, it would not have been surprising to find the public clamouring for severe punishment. Instead, the new thinking about children, even criminal children, shaped the moral responses of those involved in the case and affected their judgements, leading them, often against their own ethical inclinations, to conclusions of a more enlightened kind.

This was a crime of 'unspeakable juvenile depravity'. Peter Barratt and James Bradley, both aged eight, had abducted a boy of two-and-a-half, stripped him naked, then beaten him with a stick before weighing his body down with a pair of wooden clogs and flinging him into water to drown. The local *Stockport Advertiser*, not known for sensationalism, gave the story a dramatic headline: 'Diabolical Brutality.'[3] By all accounts it was a cruel and frightening killing. Yet a lengthy editorial in *The Times* was devoted to an explanation of the reasons why 'it would have been absurd and monstrous' for the two eight-year-olds responsible to be treated like adult murderers.[4] What had changed to lead *The Times* to reach such a bold conclusion?

There was little about the crime to lend itself to this response. From the moment the victim's body was discovered, the true scale of the violence used by these young boys began to emerge. On Saturday, 13 April, fourteen local men gathered at the White House Tavern in Hempshaw Lane, Stockport, because a little boy had been found dead the previous day.[5] At first, the inquest jury had little evidence other than the discovery itself, but suspicion was prompted later that afternoon when the Stockport surgeon Thomas Massey delivered his post-mortem report. He found evidence of severe injuries to the deceased's body, with marks of extreme violence to the head and back. In the days that followed, the details of what happened to this vulnerable child began to unfold, revealing a disturbing picture of undisguised cruelty.

Murder in Love Lane

The town of Stockport, just outside Manchester, was described by Frederick Engels in the 1840s as 'one of the duskiest, smokiest holes' he'd ever been to. The dwellings, with their bricks blackened by smoke, stretched out in long rows back-to-back, but an Ordnance Survey map for 1851 also shows the sprawling fields and meadows beyond, edged by a network of footpaths.[6] It was in this open countryside that a local labourer, John Buckley, saw the body of a child laying face down in water. He told the coroner that 'the body was quite naked with the exception of a pair of clogs'. He sent for a policeman, Inspector William Walker, who on arrival was puzzled by the clogs and the dry clothes on the ground nearby, but surmised that the drowning was probably an accident and ordered that the body be removed to the White House Tavern where an inquest jury would investigate.

Before his death, George Burgess was known in the neighbourhood as a 'child of misfortune'. For reasons we cannot know, he did not live with his parents but was nursed by an unmarried woman living in the same area, Higher Hillgate. His father Ralph and mother Hannah were both cotton weavers in one of the town's numerous mills, and they had two other infant children close in age to George. Perhaps the mother found working and nursing three small children too much – we can only guess. It was odd that she made no appearance at the inquest or later at the trial, and that none of the reports mention her. It is not known whether or not she was responsible for the injuries that the little boy had already received in his short life, but his body showed the signs of earlier suffering. His arm had been broken twice, there were scars from a severe scalding, and other burn marks had been made on his small frame. The neighbours of Higher Hillgate must have sensed the child's defencelessness, as by all accounts he was petted and favoured by them; his 'lively, chatty' manner no doubt added poignancy to his sufferings. Hundreds of townspeople and villagers turned out for his funeral, they wept at the horrible manner of his untimely death, and they turned up in equal numbers at the trial to stare in curiosity at his killers.

On the inquest's first day, however, only a few attended, word having not yet got out about the alarming nature of the boy's death. Inside the oak-beamed tavern, George's father stood before the jurors and told them of the last time he had seen his son alive. He visited the boy regularly after work, and on the afternoon of his disappearance his last memory was of George playing with other infants of the same age on a piece of waste ground in the neighbourhood. He said: 'On Thursday night I was told my little boy was lost; I searched for him 'til three in the morning but he was not found.' The next witness, the family nurse, Sarah Anne Warren, described how she had dressed George that morning in a frock fastened with hooks and eyes, and a red flannel waistcoat with a calico shirt. When asked whether it was likely that the boy had undressed himself, she answered no, and insisted that this was 'impossible'.

The evidence of the third witness had a subduing effect on the jurors. Mary Whitehead lived with her husband in Love Lane, which ran alongside the narrow brook where George Burgess was found. Her testimony, like that of the other witnesses, was taken down by a coroner's clerk. The language is not hers; the Stockport dialect is not there, nor her nervousness or hesitancy. But even in the economy of the recorded statement there is a portrait of a brief but chilling scene:

> On the Thursday afternoon, a little before three o'clock, I was standing near my own house when I saw two boys coming from the direction of Hempshaw Lane ... there was a little boy with them, perhaps two years old. They passed me, the larger one having the smaller by the hand. The little one was crying; he was fully dressed except his hat. I asked them where they were going and the bigger one said 'Love Lane', dragging the little one after him; he seemed unwilling to go.[7]

This testimony, together with the surgeon's post-mortem report, provided unwelcome news to the jurors. They heard of the violence done to the boy's body before it suffocated; of heavy bruises to the head, back and bottom, all of them 'produced while the child was still alive'. Finally, they were told that the lad's face 'had been pressed down on to a stone in the water of the brook', by which time he was probably unconscious.

It was a dreadful litany, and the exhausted jurors retired in order to try to refresh themselves with an early supper. Efforts were already being made to track down the two boys identified by the witnesses. The first suspect that the authorities visited was Peter Henry Barratt, who lived with his mother, father and two siblings in Middle Hillgate, lower down the slope on the steep hill of Stockport's valley. Mr Barratt worked as a barber, and he was cutting hair when the police constable arrived to interview his son. There is no record of the interview undertaken by Constable Morley, but on the strength of it the eight-year-old boy was taken to the home of his playmate, James Bradley, where the exchange that followed is recorded in some detail.

James Bradley's father was present in the kitchen when the constable began the interview. He repeated the questions that he had put to Peter Barratt earlier:

'Do you go to school?'

'Sometimes on Sunday,' Peter replied.

'Who did you play with on last Thursday afternoon?'

'With Jemmy Bradley.'

'Where did you go?'

'We went beside the Star Inn.'

'Which way did you go then?'

'Down the narrow lane by the Star Inn, down Hempshaw Lane and up Love Lane.'

'Was there anyone else with you?'

Peter Barrett made no reply, but James Bradley said: 'A little boy we met beside the Star Inn.'

'Did you see anyone in Love Lane?'

'Yes, we saw a woman,' James continued.

'What did she say to you?'

'She just asked where we were going; I told her only down Love Lane.'

Carrying on, he said: 'We went down the lane until we got to a hole with some water in it.'

'What did you do then?'

'Peter began to undress it.' At which point Peter Barrett intervened angrily: 'Thou undressed it as well as me.'

'So you both undressed it?' the constable asked, and they each nodded.

'Then what happened?'

Bradley answered: 'Peter pushed him in the water, and I took my clogs off and went in and took it out again and then Peter said "let's have another".'

'Another what?'

To which Bradley replied: 'Another dip in the water. Peter got a stick out of the hedge and hit it.'

'Thou hit it as well as me,' Peter said immediately.

The policeman asked where they hit the boy and Bradley replied: 'Over the back.'

'Anywhere else?'

'Yes, over the head.'

'Was it in the water then?'

'Yes.'

'How long did you hit it with the stick?'

Bradley answered: ''Til it was dead.'

Barratt said nothing at this point, and when the policeman asked if the little child was 'quite dead before you left it', only James Bradley nodded.

'Then, you left it in the water before you came away?'

'Yes.'

'What did you do with the stick?'

'We hauled it in th' field.'

This interview having concluded, both boys were taken away to a lock-up opposite the courthouse. Originally built in the eighteenth century, the building was at this time used as the county police offices, where prisoners were kept until their cases were heard at the assizes. Bradley and Barratt were imprisoned in one cell built of thick stone that was roughly rectangular in shape and measured ten feet by six, with a small barred window near the arched roof – too high for them to see out. There was a ledge, which served as a bed, and the officers who watched over them gave them food and water.

Three days later they were brought to the White House Tavern for what would be the concluding day of the inquest. Every room was filled with people anxious to get a look at the two extraordinary murderers. Both fathers, 'deeply grieved' at the position their sons were in, sat alongside them as the hearing continued. Witnesses identified the youngsters, and Constable Morley read out the interview statement. Then, turning to Bradley's father, the coroner asked if he had any questions. 'No,' he said, 'the officer stated the conversation correctly – more the pity for me.'

Summing up the evidence, the coroner said the case was one of a 'very painful nature'. Nonetheless, he insisted that the conclusion was clear. From the surgeon's report, the prisoners' statements, and those of the witnesses who had seen the boy being led towards the brook, this was certainly not an accidental drowning: 'No motive for the crime had been proved or suggested,' said the coroner, 'but the prisoners had certainly chosen a very secluded place and had not disclosed what they had done for two days.' All this, he insisted, was evidence of their 'consciousness of guilt', but because of their 'extreme youth' he believed it necessary to explain where the law stood on a child's capacity to commit crime.

At eight years old, Peter Barratt and James Bradley were over the age at which the law deemed them to be without criminal intent. But they would still have protection under the law if it could be shown they were incapable of judging between 'good and evil'. For, as the coroner informed the jurors, it is the *strength* of understanding and judgement, and not age alone, that 'is the true criterion of the capacity of the delinquent to do evil or contract guilt'. If they were satisfied that the prisoners had acted with 'mischievous discretion', they would have to return a verdict of wilful murder, 'for there was nothing in the evidence to reduce it below that offence'. The instructions could not have been clearer; without hesitation, the jurors indicted the two eight-year-old boys for the capital crime, and they were taken away to Chester Castle to await a full criminal trial.

'Babyish mischief'

Today the journey from Stockport to Chester takes about twenty minutes, but in the mid-nineteenth century it took five hours. Bradley and Barratt were taken on the early-morning mail train under police guard, and arrived in Chester as the townspeople were beginning their day. The sight of Chester Castle must have affected their spirits, which up until now had still been lively. If the two of them really were insensible to the enormity of their crime, the view of the Castle's imposing façade would have changed all that. It could not have been more intimidating. The court building had an immense portico held aloft by towering Doric columns. Inside the grand entrance hall to the right were the cells into which the accused were led, and where they remained imprisoned for nearly four months awaiting their trial.

Their experience at Chester summer assizes was in stark contrast to the inquest hearing at Stockport. The environment was different, of course – they were 40 miles away from home – but the main difference was in the attitude of the court. Right from the start, the presiding judge, Sir Charles Compton, set a changed tone. He indicated that this 'very sad' case was 'difficult and distressing' and needed proper time, so he would hear it last. There would be other changes, too, in expressions and sentiment, which indicated the degree of sympathy for children during this period, even for those who had committed the heinous crime of murder.

The first signs of these differences came in the remarks of the defence counsel, Mr Morgan Lloyd. After the prosecution evidence was put to the court, Mr Lloyd rose to give his argument. In the usual manner of a defence barrister he first interrogated witnesses but then, in an 'impassioned plea' on the two boys' behalf, he dwelt at some length on the 'tender years of the prisoners', and suggested the improbability of them having committed such a 'grave offence'. He argued that if the jury 'were of the opinion that the deceased met with his death at the hand of the prisoners, it must have been in childish play'. The reference to childish play was striking, but more surprising still was the warning he gave to the jurors not to rely too much on the interview with the boys that PC Morley had conducted, 'because there was nothing easier than a police officer, like a barrister, to get any answer he pleased by putting leading questions'.

The direction that the judge gave the jury was also unexpected. He was surprisingly frank in expressing his own view of the case. First, he went through the evidence and told them that they had to decide not only if the two boys, Bradley and Barratt, had been the cause of the infant's death, but also whether or not they knew what they were doing and that it would result in death: 'A schoolboy might inflict injuries upon a companion, and those injuries might terminate fatally; still without knowing the consequence of what he was doing, it would not be murder but manslaughter.' Referring to the prisoners actions as 'mere babyish mischief', he also repeated the warning already given by the defence that there were things the children had said which might, to some extent, have been put into their mouths by the policemen; for example 'that they pushed the deceased child into the water, pulled it out again, and let it have another dip. That looked to me very like childish mischief; but the jury must say if the children were of sufficient discretion and knowledge to know what they were doing.'

Obviously, the judge was duty-bound to make clear to the jury what might otherwise have been a confusing point of law. But by referring to their actions as 'babyish mischief', he was signalling his view that the two lads should not be held fully responsible for the crime of murder; his interpretation of the law was as important as his knowledge of it, and he must have known he was guiding the jury in a particular direction. He knew that the boys were guilty; sentencing them, he said: 'I'm afraid you have been very wicked, naughty boys, and I have no doubt you caused the death of this little boy by the brutal way in which you used him.' Yet he declared himself pleased with the jury's verdict of manslaughter, believing that it reflected age as a mitigating factor in such a serious crime. The reaction of the judge was influenced as much by the growing debate about child criminals as it was by compassion for the awful predicament of these two youngsters.

More Sinned Against Than Sinning?

The matter of whether or not it is possible to attribute criminal guilt to children was the topic of much public debate from the mid-nineteenth century. While reformers like Mary Carpenter believed that all children lacked the moral discretion expected of adults and could not therefore be held fully accountable for their crimes, others believed that many of the children committing crimes were worse than adults, and to exempt them from punishment on the grounds of their age would simply be an added incentive for their deeds. In subsequent years, wider knowledge of the appalling social conditions that children were being brought up in changed the general thinking about a child's capacity to tell right from wrong. The legal rule remained the same, but there was, as one conference report reflected, not only a greater desire to consider the young age of a criminal, but more importantly recognition that 'his age, the neglect or vice of his parents, and the depraving circumstances of his childhood should be taken into account'.[8] The case of Peter Barratt and James Bradley brought a dramatic focus to this debate, and led to lengthy commentary in both local and national newspapers.

Initially, it appears as if enlightened ideas about children had little impact on the case. Though not a Tory paper, the *Stockport Advertiser* was declared by its founder and owner James Lomax to be a 'virtuous' paper with veneration for the Christian religion. Lomax's son had been one of the gentlemen jurors at the inquest, and described the two felons as 'average specimens of the little street Arabs who infest all our great towns'.[9] Yet the two eight-year-olds were more respectable than this casual epithet suggested. Stockport's big industry was cotton, but hatting was almost its equivalent in the 1860s, and a firm called Christy's was the largest. The 1861 census returns show James Bradley's 37-year-old father working as a hat washer at Christy's, and his mother as a maidservant in one of the big houses nearby. They were a churchgoing family, of the Congregational denomination, and it seems that they attended services regularly. The other accused boy, Peter Henry Barratt, was the son of a hairdresser and his Irish-born wife, Mary Ann. He had two sisters, Mary, aged three, and Emma, aged six, who was enrolled at the same church school as her brother, but apparently had a better attendance record. Each of the boys' families were, with the exception of Peter's mother, born and bred in Cheshire. Theirs were stable backgrounds, outwardly at least, and any remarks made by newspapers inevitably betrayed assumptions about the conduct of their class.

The *Stockport Advertiser* had to accept that the young murderers had parents, but implied that they might just as well not have had, as they had failed in their moral duty to instil the 'habits of discipline' in their children. The consequences of such neglect were, in the view of the newspaper, catastrophic:

> Every child born into the world is a little savage; and if he does not grow up one, it is because he is brought out, *educated* out of it. 'Cain was Eve's', and the babe of the most amiable and intellectual mother, if allowed to grow up in its natural state, without the humanising advantages of Christian and civilised association, would be as brutish and barbarous as our fathers long ago in the vastnesses of Scandinavia, Germany, or Gaul. These are relevant considerations when commenting on the atrocious acts of the two children Barratt and Bradley.[10]

On the question of whether or not these boys knew what they had done and were responsible for it, the newspapers were as one. *The Times* believed the crime the boys committed was 'as deliberately contrived a proceeding as any murder on the records of the Old Bailey'.[11] Meanwhile, the *Advertiser* was at pains to point out that 'we are not among those who consider a child of only eight years old as irresponsible. On the contrary, we regard the faculties and perception between right and wrong as very lively then, and of maturity and activity to make the boy amenable for his acts.'

Yet both editorials accepted that a child's moral faculties were not equivalent to that of a 'grown man', which, in the words of one, is due to 'training and education'. Although the children had consciences, argued *The Times,* and therefore knew their act was wrong, 'the conscience, like other natural faculties, admits of degrees; it is weak and has not arrived at its proper growth in children, though it has a real existence and a voice within them;

it does not speak with that force and seriousness which justifies us in treating the child as a legally responsible being'.

Both newspapers were keen to attach blame to the boys, but just as keen to exempt them from adult liability. Their commentary indicated a more sophisticated, if contradictory, understanding of the moral capacities of young children, and of the environmental factors which influence them. Although it was accepted that their crime did not arise out of the sinfulness of their particular natures – they were never spoken of as children of the devil, for example – cruelty was, nonetheless, considered to be a feature of our animal nature, so it was therefore logical, in the opinion of these newspapers, to acknowledge the expression of cruelty in the crime the boys had committed. To ignore it, or to suggest that they were somehow not culpable, would have amounted to an acceptance of their innocence when the crime for which they were tried was that of wilful murder. *The Times* said:

> Children's storybooks have stock examples of cruel children spinning like cockchafers around pins for the purpose of guarding the childish mind against tricks of cruelty. This would amount to a testimony to a certain propensity of cruelty in children, and a certain kind of cruelty is, perhaps, a sin of the childish age ... the only conceivable motive that could have led these two children to take a child that could hardly walk to a pool to drown him was the pleasure of witnessing an agony – the death struggle of a human creature. The desperate efforts and contortions of a smaller member of their own species were the same kind of gratification of a cockchafer, but of course, much more exciting in proportion to the greater dignity of the victim.[12]

What these newspapers wanted to do, especially the local ones which were not established as businesses to make a profit, but rather as organs of opinion for the community, was to make a distinction between, as they saw it, 'common sense' and the over-sentimental view of children as innately good. The idea that the original nature of children was innocent, with which people like Mary Carpenter had sympathy, was difficult to reconcile with such a 'barbarous act'.

The innocent child had been the creation of the eighteenth-century philosopher Jean-Jacques Rousseau. His book *Emile* had been widely read in upper- and middle-class circles when it was published in London in 1763, but it influenced moral thinking well beyond the eighteenth century. In *Emile*, Rousseau wrote that childhood was a period defined by the 'sleep of reason', and that children should be free to respond to nature rather than 'reason about things they cannot understand'. As innocents, children could do no harm because they had no proper intention to do so. Mendacity, for example, is 'not natural to children'. They are without guile or deceit and adults should make no attempt 'to give the innocent child the knowledge of good and evil'.[13] He believed that although children appeared to understand such things, they actually did not: 'Their shining, polished brain reflects, as in a mirror, the things you show them, but nothing sinks in. The child remembers the words and the ideas are reflected back; his hearers understand them, but to him they are meaningless.'[14]

Early on in the book, Rousseau addresses the issue of childhood cruelty when he writes of a boy killing a bird in innocence because his capacity to reason between right and wrong is non-existent:

Before the age of reason (early teens), we do good or ill without knowing it, and there is no morality in our actions ... A child wants to overturn everything he sees. He breaks and smashes everything he can reach; he seizes a bird as he seizes a stone, and strangles it without knowing what he is about.[15]

Rousseau was not popular among the established figures of British society. The prison civil servant Sir Edmund du Cane believed: 'The gospel according to Rousseau is largely responsible for the development of a certain breed of sentimental tiger, to whom the atrocities of the French Revolution were principally due.'[16] Rousseau was widely, if perhaps mistakenly, accredited with the idea that man was naturally good and only became corrupted by the development of human society.[17] Opponents like du Cane believed that were it not for the civilising strictures of the Gospel and its Commandments, mankind would be lost to universal chaos and barbarism. Yet paradoxically, the influence of Rousseau is evident in some of the thinking that was expressed in *The Times* editorial. The paper describes children's cruelty as natural, and harmless, it describes the 'delight' children take in the 'agonies of sentient life'. However, it goes on to argue forcefully:

> But it is a totally different thing when this thoughtless delight of children … is transferred from an insect to one of their own species, only differing from themselves in being much younger and much less in size than they are – in being an *infant* when they are no longer such. This is a horrible and inexplicable exaggeration of childish cruelty, an enormity, and a monstrosity.[18]

A child killing another child represented something altogether different from ordinary childish curiosity. And for this reason the murder took on a meaning beyond the act itself, which, though horrible, was nonetheless extremely rare. This crime ended up inhabiting a larger narrative – the editorial continued: 'There is something for old and young to think about, something for statesmen to ponder upon, in the rare and exceptional trial of these two little boys.' Readers were encouraged to read this murder as reflecting the darkened heart of our humanity. While the articles said a great deal about attitudes towards children and childhood, they also conveyed, indeed reinforced, profound beliefs about the nature of humankind in general.

A Crime of Human Nature?

For most nineteenth-century Christians, human beings were inherently wicked: consumed by greed, driven by sensual desires, and possessed of natures indelibly marked by violence. The *Stockport Advertiser* echoed this view and translated the killing of little George Burgess into a universal symbol for the inscrutable and brutish nature of our origins: 'In truth, the most civilised and educated of us are not lifted far above savage life.' Still preoccupied by the tragic turn of the French Revolution and keen to drive home its own conservative message, the paper goes on: 'Let us look to France at the close of the last century to learn what civilised man may become. Let us look to America now. Slitting noses and ears, and mutilations of the most horrible kind are, we are told, practised on both sides by the belligerents on the other side of the Atlantic.'[19]

At the same time, although the idea that man is corrupt by nature is present in the editorials of these newspapers, it was by no means so securely rooted in its original theological conception. Such Christian pessimism still endured, of course; the American novelist Herman Melville may have summed it up best when he wrote that its source came 'from its appeal to Innate

Depravity and Original Sin, from whose visitations, in some shape or other, no deeply thinking mind is always and wholly free'.[20] But by the 1860s the whole Christian doctrine of man's fallen state was already being challenged by the evolutionary ideas of Charles Darwin. He upturned the Biblical account of human history (Creation, Fall, Redemption) with an account that put man, not God, at the centre of the story. Other theories, like that of the influential thinker and writer Herbert Spencer, carried the evolutionary model further.

Spencer's radical idea was that human nature was constantly in a state of flux. He believed that human society was like a complex organism that changed organically, developing new capacities in response to need, and perpetually adapting to ever-changing circumstances.[21] Ideas of progress were central to this thinking.[22] However, underpinning Spencer's evolutionary theory was a Lamarckian belief in the inheritance of acquired characteristics. This idea, derived from the nineteenth-century zoologist Jean-Baptiste Lamarck, suggested that we transmit adaptive behaviour from one generation to the next by a process of learning. Just as new animal species are the result of new conditions acting upon an original form, so too, by analogy, have external social conditions acted upon human behaviour. The biological content of this theory was unproven; the idea of cultural inheritance through, say, education had no real biological mechanism to support it. Nonetheless, the evolutionary model spawned whole new ways of thinking about the ways in which environment and circumstance were seen to influence human behaviour.

The modern science of mankind was having an effect on popular thought, and these newspaper editorials on the Stockport murder show the extent of it. It was understood that if children were brought up in circumstances of cruelty, then it was likely that they would behave in cruel ways. 'It is a very ominous sign', argued *The Times*, 'of the *genius loci* of a neighbourhood where such an idea as this [murder] could enter into any child's head ...'[23] This killing was viewed as the outcome not of evil, but of the ineffective socialisation of the perpetrators. Poverty, poor parenting and the absence of any education are all emphasised as factors in the account of the murder. The *Stockport Advertiser* believed the case to be an illustration of the 'many ills attendant on the neglect and abandonment of poor children',[24] while *The Times* asked:

> Who was taking care of these children? The murdered child, it seems, was given to a nurse to take care of, the parents being at work all day in the mills. Is this the way of nursing at Stockport? Again, who was in charge of the two little murderers? One of them, on being asked by the policeman whether he went to any school, said 'Yes, sometimes on Sunday'. The whole affair shows a very neglected state of the childish population there, and the want of some remedy to meet the bad effects of our manufacturing system in taking away the parents from the home and family and transferring them to the Mill.[25]

Bad parenting and lack of education had been associated with crime before, but by the second half of the nineteenth century they were being viewed in very different terms. These deficiencies had traditionally been put down to the moral failings of individuals.[26] Increasingly, however, the idea of public virtue and social wellbeing was reflected in calls to improve the lives of the poor. *The Times* pointed to the need for changes in the manufacturing system because the long hours spent in the Stockport mills, where the typical working day was fourteen hours or more, were having a devastating effect on family life. Their call reflected growing pressure from the group of middle-class reformers that consisted of radical liberals and liberal conservatives, who were driven by an ideology of improvement.[27]

If the voice of *The Times* wanted to stress the criminal responsibility of the two eight-year-old boys who had committed the murder, it was never in order to seek vengeance. They wanted this crime, for all its shocking aspects, to have a positive outcome. Reactionary ideas of blanket retribution were, by the late Victorian period, inconsistent with growing sympathy for children. Also, such ideas ran counter to new beliefs about the importance of mass education and its role in crime prevention. The party political inclinations of newspapers like *The Times* were changeable, but by 1850 it had largely become the organ of 'respectable reform', and its audience was a growing middle class that championed many causes of liberal reform precisely because order and political consent depended upon it.[28] Education was important in this respect because it was seen to exert a civilising influence on human behaviour. For some, the utility of reform and education was simply considered the best hope, especially in the case of criminals, where it was favoured 'in despair of any other solution'.[29]

Reform as Redemption

Great cries of approval went up in the courtroom of Chester Castle when the judge told Peter Barratt and James Bradley that they were going to a place that would give them a chance for education and work. Some members of the public wept. The boys were going to be sent to prison for one month before spending the rest of their five-year sentence at a reformatory school. The judge told them it would be 'an opportunity of becoming good boys, for there you will have a chance of being brought up in the way you should be, and I doubt not but that in time when you have come to understand the nature of the crime you have committed you will repent of what you have done.'[30] At this James Bradley began to cry, while his friend, clearly wondering what the whole business meant, tried to make a joke; and then suddenly, as if absorbing the reality of it all, also broke into sobs.

The nearest reformatory was the Bradwall School for Boys, just outside Sandbach in Cheshire. Set up in 1855, the Home Office file for the school shows no record of Peter Barratt – the boys were probably separated, as reports indicate that they had begun to quarrel and fight with one another. The record for James Bradley, though, begins six months after his ordeal began; at this stage he could neither read nor write, and he was measured at just under four feet tall. He was the youngest in a school of 60 boys, the rest of whom were all over eleven. But he was lucky to be in one of the most enlightened institutions of its kind in the country.

Bradwall was built by George William Latham, a kindly lord of the manor at Bradwall Hall. He owned the entire 2,000 acres of land that included the small village of the same name. As a result of his philanthropic efforts, Latham had secured enough voluntary subscriptions from wealthy donors to finance the school for difficult boys.[31] The basis of the reformatory school model, of which Bradwall was one of the most successful examples, was a belief in the practical value of work and training together with the discipline of a sound moral education. The children were taught to read and write, and were allowed generous periods of recreation. The idea, as the reformatory schools' champion Mary Carpenter had first envisaged it, was that these schools would provide everything that family life did not for these children; a loving, disciplined environment, with the school manager as the parental figure at the centre. This role, which she herself had earnestly taken on when she set up a reformatory school in Bristol, was to be 'entered on with no light sense of its responsibilities, and with no light feeling of its exalted nature'.[32]

George Latham was the overall manager of Bradwall, but the day-to-day running of the school was down to the superintendent and his wife, who employed three or four teachers. The boys slept in dormitories and were put to work on the land, cultivating it for food and grazing. Corporal punishment was kept to a minimum, and there was a system of rewards for good behaviour. Boys who had proved themselves trustworthy were allowed a day's leave to visit parents, and all children were eligible to receive weekly visits from family members. Not all reformatory schools were run on such an enlightened basis, and there are many grateful letters on file showing thanks from former boys.

Young James Bradley was evidently one of the school's success stories. Satisfied with his progress, George Latham petitioned the Whig home secretary, Sir George Grey, for the boy's early release. The reply, however, was disappointing: 'I am directed to acquaint you', wrote a civil servant on the politician's behalf, 'that having regard to the serious nature of the offence of which this lad was convicted, he thinks it would not be right to remit any portion of the sentence passed upon him by the court.' Despite this, Latham took it upon himself to release the thirteen-year-old boy six months early.

The fate of Peter Henry Barratt is unknown and, judging from the records, neither of the boys returned to their home town of Stockport. Their names do not appear on the 1871 census when those of other family members do, and there is no mention of them on the postal registers. As for their victim George Burgess, his name appears in the burial records for the parish of Christchurch in Lancashire. Written beneath his name and age are three words: 'Under Coroner's Warrant.' This rarely-seen notation is the only indication that the death of this infant was suspicious. Fortunately, the tragedy of his cruel end was not compounded by the vengeful punishment of his killers; they were rescued in a spirit of reform, and given a future.

The Victorians may have been equivocal about child criminals, but their treatment of the two young murderers in this case could not have been wiser or more compassionate. The crime they committed came to symbolise a lost childhood and, at the same time, a warning of just how low human nature could go if left unchecked. The personal circumstances of the two killers and their victim, though by no means desperate, none the less belonged to a pitiful environment of poverty that could brutalise adults and their children alike. It was these conditions in which such a murder could occur. Because of this, they became a target for social reform in the second half of the century, not least through the establishment of mass schooling in 1870, and also more widespread forms of welfare and protection such as the founding of the Societies for the Prevention of Cruelty to Children, firstly in Liverpool in 1883, and the following year in Bristol, Birmingham and London.

By the time Bradley and Barratt were discharged from their reformatory, the idea of evolution was beginning to dominate perspectives on human nature. When Darwin published his study of the origins of human life in 1859 it had an explosive impact on Victorian thought – not only because, for many, it was the beginning of the end of God's place in nature, but also because it provided a secure scientific basis for the idea that certain animal behaviours might also be natural to human beings in a shared evolutionary history. If the 'monstrous evil' perpetrated by child murderers was generally assumed to be a crime in which only adults could be involved, then perhaps its cause originated in a biological flaw of the species. The idea that nature could be the repository of all that is fundamental in humanity, and everything considered to be the most troubling, started with Darwin or, more accurately, with post-Darwinian explorations of humankind. The idea of the child murderer as a clear case of inborn insanity was to become persuasive, and it found favour with lay and expert opinion alike.

Chapter Six

'GRIEVOUSLY VEXED BY THE DEVIL – BUT NOT A DEMONSTRATIVE DEVIL'

To talk about the purity and innocence of a child's mind is a part of that
poetical idealism and willing hypocrisy by which men ignore realities …
in so far as purity exists it testifies to the absence of mind; the impulses
which actually move the child are the selfish impulses of passion. It were
as warrantable to get enthusiastic about the purity and innocence of a
dog's mind. 'A boy,' says Plato, 'is the most vicious of all wild beasts'; or, as
someone else has put it, 'a boy is better unborn than untaught'. By nature
sinful and vicious, man acquires a knowledge of good through evil:
not how evil entered him first, but how good first came out of him,
is the true scientific question.
HENRY MAUDSLEY, 1899

In June 1881 the weather in Cumberland, the old north-western county of England, was cold and grey. Charles Darwin was taking a holiday in the Lake District and was disappointed by the bitter climate. He had also recently been diagnosed with the illness that would kill him the following year. Seventeen miles further north a young girl, Margaret Messenger, had just started work with her first employer, a respectable farming family of three children and their parents, John and Mary Pallister. These ordinary working people, living outside Carlisle in the village of Sprunston, may not have known of Darwin, but his fame and influence was such that even they were to become affected by it, though not in a way that any of them could ever have expected.

The young girl that the Pallisters had taken on as their maidservant was soon to gain notoriety for an unnatural act of murder in their household.[1] Many of those who were to become involved or interested in this distressing story spoke of Margaret Messenger's immorality, describing not a spiritual evil, but a natural one. After Darwin, human attributes such as morality were no longer considered a Christian characteristic of the soul, but a quality that was part of our nature.

The evolution of humans was not the focus of Darwin's *On the Origin of Species* when it was published in 1859, but it came to provide the biological context in which human behaviour was understood. When he published *The Descent of Man* in 1871, and in the following year *The Expressions of the Emotions in Man and Animals*, one of his central themes was how the moral sense possessed by human beings had been acquired naturally through evolution. Beginning with a study of the ways in which animals behave in order to nurture and protect their own offspring, he argued that human morality had developed from the same instincts. One of the effects of this behaviour, he believed, was to control aggression. A species could not turn upon itself with violence if it was to survive:

A tribe including many members who, from possessing in a high degree the spirit of patriotism, fidelity, obedience, courage, and sympathy, were always ready to aid one another, and to sacrifice themselves for the common good, would be victorious over other tribes and this would be natural selection.[2]

Darwin argued that the intelligence of mankind had allowed this primitive morality to develop and become articulated in more sophisticated ways. Those who followed in his footsteps would describe how important language was in this development, enabling human beings to acquire mastery in their mental capacities, to think and reflect upon their actions and motives, and to confer approval on themselves and others. In other words, over the course of human history, mankind had acquired judgement and conscience. It was suggested, implausibly as it turned out, that the moral sense had become wired into our biology. This way of thinking influenced a range of scientific disciplines, including the mental sciences of psychiatry and psychology. The child and its development became the centrepiece of new ideas about how human beings acquire consciousness and communication, and of how behavioural traits are passed on through generations. Darwin even used observations of his own children as evidence for his work on emotional expressions, arguing that these were similar in both humans and animals, and therefore must be considered innate and the result of the unlearned responses of the nervous system.

But the morality that Darwin believed was innate to the social instincts of our species was missing in the thirteen-year-old who was about to begin employment on the Pallister farm in Cumberland. Margaret Messenger had been in her job for only three weeks when she murdered one of the family's children. This was a crime believed by many at the time to be so unnatural, and so inimical to what it meant to be human, that they were relieved to find a scientific explanation for her actions. Even though evil was no longer embodied in the devil it still had meaning for most people, and one renowned psychiatrist of the day maintained that evil could emerge from our biology. Writing in 1867 on the subject of insanity in early life, Henry Maudsley argued that:

The impulse which springs up out of deranged feeling and is fed by it, is sometimes homicidal: an instance occurs from time to time in which a child drowns, hangs, or otherwise kills another child, with an amazing coolness and insensibility, and from no other motive than a liking to do it; and there have been a few cases recorded in which more than one murder has been done in this way by the same child. The question of hereditary taint is in reality the important question in those cases, as it is in all cases of insanity in early life.[3]

Maudsley was one of the most eminent doctors of the Victorian era. Acerbic and critical, he had a distinguished career that began at the age of 24 when he became medical superintendent of the Manchester Royal Lunatic Asylum. In 1862, he arrived in London to make his fortune, and ran a lucrative private practice while editing the *Journal of Mental Science*. He went on to become professor of medical jurisprudence at University College London, and achieved public fame with his numerous works outlining his theories on the biological basis of insanity.[4] The evolutionary models of both Darwin and Herbert Spencer influenced his ideas. Human beings' common ancestry with animals was evoked by Maudsley to suggest that both species also shared aspects of a sensory system, and mental pathologies in mankind appeared to conform, or at least were analogous, to behaviours observed in lower animals.[5]

He was interested in the extreme behaviours of infancy and childhood as possible illustrations of this idea. Children's lack of physical and mental control – for example, an infant's jerky movement and a child's extreme egotism – were all extensions of the behaviours of an earlier primitive species:

In the insanity of the young child we meet with passion in all its naked deformity and in all its exaggerated exhibition. The instincts, appetites, or passions, call them as we may, manifest themselves in unblushing, extreme, and perverted action; the veil of control which discipline may have fashioned is rent; it is like the animal, and reveals its animal nature with as little shamefacedness as the monkey indulges its passions in the face of all the world.[6]

Among the examples which he used to develop his scientific theories of abnormal mental development in humans was that of a murderous child. Citing the case of an eleven-year-old girl who enticed two tiny children to a village well only to push both of them to their deaths, he said that this was a case in point of a destructive impulse that could become murderous in instances of inborn insanity. According to Maudsley, the affected child can give no account of itself and neither does it have any particular awareness of the aim or purpose of its act; any crime he or she commits is motiveless.[7] It was precisely this quality of purposeless action that suggested to those involved in the Margaret Messenger case that hers might be an example of inborn insanity.

A Crime Without Motive?

After she was hired as a maidservant in that damp June of 1881, Margaret Messenger went about her work quite happily; if she was sad or distressed about her new position, it did not show. 'The girl never complained to me,' her employer later said in court, 'I had servants do the same work before. They were always about the same age ... she seemed happy and contented.' Three weeks after her arrival on the farm, the Pallisters' middle child, two-year-old John Mark, was found drowned in the well belonging to the house. The inquest into his death returned an open verdict and the boy was buried.[8] The household returned to normal as best it could; the demands of the summer season must have weighed heavily upon the family. Then one Saturday in early July, the farmer and his wife went off to the market in Carlisle, leaving the two children in the charge of their young servant. Although taking care of the children was not Margaret's main duty, she was occasionally called upon to do it. She appeared fond of them, and they liked her. Sometimes she teased the five-year-old, Maggie, but apparently meant nothing malicious by it.

When her employers returned to the farm later that afternoon, they were given the terrible news that their baby Elizabeth was dead. Doctors who examined the infant's body said that she had been smothered in a spot of wet and boggy ground.[9] According to the testimony of George Haffen, a young worker on the farm, he had been labouring in a field above the house when he heard the family's baby screaming; paying no heed as it had cried many times before, he went on with his work, but half an hour later he heard the 'nurse', as he referred to Margaret Messenger, shouting to him: 'George you must come.' He continued: 'I ran to the gate and she said, "There is a man run away with our little Elsie".' He went on to tell the jury: 'I didn't believe her at first, but she said he was tall with no whiskers and she pointed to the orchard near the well where I went to look for him.' Discovering no one, he returned to the farm to find the house and yard empty. Assuming that nothing was amiss and that the baby had been found safe and well, he went on with his work. It was only later that he saw Margaret Messenger coming from the direction of the well towards the house 'carrying the baby in her arms'. The child was covered in mud and her mouth was full of wet soil. George recalled: 'I fetched the neighbour, Mrs Story, who washed the child and cleaned the dirt from its mouth, but she were dead.'

Margaret lied when she was accused by the neighbour, Mrs Story, of knowing something about the infant's death. Yet she told the police superintendent who had been called to the crime that she had fallen asleep momentarily and the baby had crawled into the puddle of water. She was eventually taken into custody at the citadel in Carlisle, home to the county's criminal court, where three months later, at the autumn session of Cumberland and Westmoreland assizes, she would stand trial for the murder of six-month-old Elizabeth Pallister.

Inside the west tower in court number one, the circular, wood-panelled room was crammed with people. They fell silent when the prisoner was brought in. Before them stood a girl whose demeanour was uncannily calm. Journalists spoke of the prisoner's 'composure', which, they said, 'was remarkable for a girl of her age'. They had been unnerved by reports that she had passed the night before her trial peacefully. What was perhaps a lack of understanding of what she had done, they saw as detachment and insensitivity. They took her calm, unperturbed manner as that of a person for whom feeling did not exist, and in whom conscience was absent. How could they know the reality? Instead, their minds were full of excited speculation. The thoughts and emotions of this young girl were hidden to them, but this was no obstacle to their thinking that she showed no remorse for her crime, and they found this troubling.

Opening the proceedings on 2 November 1881, Lord Justice Kay warned the jury that they were about to try one of the most 'mysterious' cases he had ever encountered: 'Its nature is enough to puzzle a moralist, a legislator, judge and jury. Here is a child under fifteen who without any apparent motive, in cold blood, commits a most brutal and barbarous murder.' Appalled by what

Margaret Messenger was accused of, he asked the jury to consider carefully what should be done with the child if her nature
had shown such a propensity for murder. She had pleaded not
guilty to the crime and although she was suspected of killing the
Pallisters' other child, two-year-old John Mark, she was not on
trial for double murder. For all those who followed the case in
the newspapers, and talked of it in shops, taverns and the back
parlours of humble homes, the most perplexing thing about this
'monstrous crime' was the absence of motive.

Violence without purpose or motive was, for scientists like
Maudsley, one of the markers of insanity in early life. He wrote
of the phenomenon in one of the first-ever works on child
psychiatry:

> In the case of homicidal impulse in a young child, the con-
> sciousness of the end or aim of the act must at best be very
> vague or imperfect. It is driven by an impulse of which it can
> give no account to a destructive act, the real nature of which
> it does not appreciate.[10]

This certainly explained the bewilderment that pervaded the
court during the trial of Margaret Messenger. Distraught and
mystified, the dead child's mother told those assembled, 'I had
no occasion to find fault with her nor had she ever made any
complaint to me either about the children or about the work or
anything; she did her work fairly well: I never noticed any peculiarity in her manner, she was an intelligent girl.'[11]

The lead prosecution barrister also declared himself baffled
over the motive for this murder, but said that 'crimes might be
committed where there was no motive whatever, and what to
the jury or I would be no motive for a crime, to another would
be sufficient'. He speculated that when the farm worker George

Haffen had heard the dead child's screams, the prisoner may have 'in consequence of some naughtiness, been seized with a desire to kill the child or, it could have been that she had no cause other than a desire to quit herself of the child in order that she might thereafter lead a more easy life; or, whether it was giving way to some murderous instinct – an instinct of mere cruelty that delights in torturing another, it was impossible for him or them to say'.

He knew the jury were silently asking themselves questions about the girl's motive. They, like everyone else following the case, wanted to know her reasons for committing the crime. But he insisted that they must ignore her supposed motive because the facts alone, and Margaret Messenger's deceit, were evidence enough of her malicious intent. Newspapers, however, continued to speculate. If the crime had no reason, what did that say about the kind of heart this girl had? Surely, as the *Carlisle Patriot* suggested, a murder of this magnitude, committed by one so young, could only have been caused by an evil that had been created by madness. Her behaviour, said the newspaper, 'recalls the Bishop's text, "Grievously vexed by a devil," – but not a demonstrative devil'. The comments were an echo of Maudsley himself, who believed that although science had banished the superstitious identification of disease with the devil, an abnormality that affected the moral sense, or damaged the will, could lead a person to choose evil. A child who was morally errant enough to commit murder, was, in Maudsley's view, 'a truly asocial being. So incorrigibly vicious as it is at so tender an age, so perseveringly set on evil-doing, so utterly incapable of penitence, everybody who has to do with it feels in the end that it is not really responsible for its conduct … it labours under a native incapacity of moral development: it is congenitally conscienceless.'[12]

In the opinion of the *Standard*, a London paper that syndi-
cated articles of local interest to other regional papers and took
a keen interest in this case, Margaret Messenger displayed all
the symptoms recognised by the medical world as 'indicative of
homicidal monomania'. Drawing upon one of the most important psychiatric texts of the time which had been cited extensively
by Maudsley, the editorial said: 'It may be taken for granted that
insanity consists in some actual lesion or disease of the brain,
although the injury might be so slight as to comprehend every
grade of perversion of mind or moral sense.'[13]

An Absence of Morals?

It was initially the French psychiatrist Jean-Etienne Esquirol
who identified a disorder that 'perverted' the moral sense.[14] He
published his book *Des Maladies Mentales* ('Mental Maladies') in
1838, when Darwin's discoveries in the Galapagos Islands were
just beginning to excite scientists in London. The work was translated into English in 1845; it became popular among doctors of
the mind and was widely consulted by thoughtful sections of the
public. Citing it, *The Standard* newspaper opined:

Monsieur Esquirol, from observations of numerous cases
in France and Germany, has come to the conclusion that
many forms of monomania, especially in women, only show
themselves in an unexpected tendency to commit homicide
or incendiarism. Works on medical psychology are full of
instances in which persons unsuspected of insanity have confessed to murderous inclinations.[15]

The French doctor had created the term 'homicidal monomania' to describe how someone could be impelled to carry into action a singular preoccupation with the idea of murder. In one of his case histories, he describes a visit to his Paris clinic by an eight-year-old girl and her stepmother. The intelligent little girl was obsessed by murderous feelings towards her new step-parent. The doctor was disturbed by the case, just as the journalists had been unsettled by Margaret Messenger's apparent equanimity. Esquirol wrote of the child's icy air: 'The coolness, composure and indifference of the child, excited in my mind the most painful emotions.' She had been separated from her real mother when she was young and had since shown unremitting hostility towards her stepmother, who had also recently given birth to her first baby. The woman told Esquirol, 'not a day passes on which she does not strike me. If I stoop down before the fireplace, she strikes me in the back in order to cause me to fall in the fire. She beats me with her fist, sometimes seizes the scissors, knives, or other instruments that fall in her way always accompanying her abusive treatment with the same remark, "I want to kill you".' The girl was eventually removed from the family and fortunately did not manage to achieve her murderous desire, but Esquirol cited the case as an example of how the mind, even in one so young, could become fixated on a wish to kill. An illness of this kind, he believed, 'spares no age, since children from eight to ten years old are not exempt from it ... The act [of murder] accomplished, it seems that the attack is over; and some homicidal monomaniacs seem to be relieved of a state of agitation and anguish, which was exceedingly painful to them. They are composed, and free from regret, remorse or fear. They contemplate their victim with indifference; and some even experience and manifest a kind of satisfaction. The greater part, far from flying, remain near the dead body ... a small number however, retire, conceal the instrument and hide the traces of the murder.'[16]

In the past, descriptions of insanity, especially if they involved crime, focused upon a person's reasoning capacity – in other words, could they understand the difference between right and wrong? In a legal context there were really only two ways in which one could be defined as insane: an 'idiot' was insane because he was not able to reason at all, and a person who was suffering a degree of madness – for example, one who was delusional – might only be partially insane, because he or she still had the ability to reason, but did so only on the basis of false beliefs.[17] Esquirol believed that this latter description of insanity was inadequate. Many of the illnesses he had seen in the asylums that he had visited throughout France could not be neatly classified as disorders of reason. A number of them sprang from the emotional regions of the brain, and often did not affect a person's judgement at all. These emotional states were sometimes characterised by mania or uncontrollable impulses and in his view, new symptom categories were needed for illnesses such as these, that seemed to arise directly from the vulnerable system of the 'passions'.

In Margaret Messenger's case, however, not everyone was convinced that she was innocently insane. Newspapers did not howl for retribution, but neither would some of them accept that a disease, one that apparently affected only the morals of the perpetrator, could excuse such an atrocious crime. They relied on the tried-and-tested definition of insanity as a disease that primarily affected the ability to reason. It was argued that the child had shown a capacity to understand and make judgements; she had, after all, apparently deceived everyone about the first murder and continued with everyday life as though nothing had happened. There was also a conscious purpose and deliberation to both killings, and, being a girl noted for her intelligence, she was certainly not mentally deficient. Indeed, her cleverness was further justification for one newspaper to insist that 'there was not the most faint presumption of insanity'. However, this picture of a purposeful, rational person having full knowledge of the consequences of her acts became less convincing if, as Esquirol and a number of his French colleagues proposed, a person could be thought of as having two halves of themselves, and that one part of the personality – the part that feels – could have a life or function separate from its other, thinking part.

Maudsley believed that it was illogical to judge an insane person by the standards of sanity and reason when 'the observation of abnormal mental states' set a better standard of comparison, because 'the driving impulse by which men are moved to act' comes from 'neurological sensation' rather than reason.[18]

If Margaret Messenger's mental disturbance was due to a diseased nervous system that impelled her to commit a sudden, violent act with no motive, then the conclusion of one newspaper would appear correct: 'We may safely assume that Margaret Messenger was not responsible for her actions when she murdered the two little children ... the presumption of her insanity, and therefore her incapacity to commit crime, is strengthened by her extreme youth.'[19] It must have been a relief to readers that such a disturbing crime was due to a diseased mind. Terrible though the act was, it appeared less so when it was believed that the child responsible was mentally ill. The ideal of childhood innocence, so loaded with the hopes of late Victorian progress, was too reassuring a symbol to be destabilised by murder. But just how accurate was the view that Margaret Messenger was insane?

While her murderous actions may have had no obvious motive, they could hardly be described as sudden. Esquirol believed that impulsive insanity was characterised by a heightened emotional state; an autonomous force of feeling that compelled those affected to do things they might otherwise not have done. Once relieved of this irresistible compulsion, there was an absence of awareness or feeling about what they had done. One medical writer even referred to this state as 'homicidal orgasm'. The 'lesion of will' that Esquirol suggested as the cause of such insanity, and which one of the newspapers seized upon to explain Margaret Messenger's crime, gave the destructive force of inflamed emotion full reign and expression. Such blind impulse could take hold of a person and erupt into unexpected, violent catastrophe. But this was not how either of the Pallister children were killed, and this is known because of what the prisoner herself told two medical doctors who interviewed her.

Proof of Motive – The Evil of Degeneration

Turning the pages of Margaret Messenger's Home Office file, one can find, among the lengthy depositions, plans of the Pallister farm, official letters and personal appeals, and an eleven-page handwritten report by two doctors. These were Dr William Orange, the medical supervisor at Broadmoor Criminal Lunatic Asylum, and Dr MacDougal, the physician at Carlisle jail.[20] They interviewed the child at some length and made a 'careful inquiry into her state of mind'. She confessed to them the murder of two-year-old John Mark, saying that she 'intentionally drowned him'. Continuing their account, they write: 'She tells us that the act was not due to any sudden impulse, but that it had been contemplated by her for some days.' In answer to their question as to what had put into her mind the idea of committing such atrocious acts, Margaret replied that she had read a story in a newspaper of a local woman who was tried and acquitted of the murder of her child. It was this, the doctors point out, 'that suggested to her that she might kill the children entrusted to her without being found out'. Attached to their report is an extract from the *Carlisle Express* giving an account of the trial of Jane Noble.

Like Margaret Messenger, she was a maidservant on a farm in a village outside Carlisle. It was alleged that the 22-year-old gave birth to her illegitimate child, took him to an ashpit on the edge of the farm and suffocated him. The defence barrister, the same lawyer who went on to defend Margaret Messenger, managed to convince the jury that there was sufficient doubt over whether Jane Noble's child was stillborn for them to return a favourable verdict. Margaret must have stumbled across an old copy of this story on the farm while she was working, because the woman's trial was held in March, at least two months before Margaret had joined the Pallister family. Reading it, one can see why she might have recognised something of her own situation. Jane Noble had been doing the same job, on a farm with strangers, and desperate to be relieved of an unwanted burden. The case evidently made a deep impression on Margaret's imagination, but it also showed the extent to which she contrived her crime rather than being overtaken by a sudden impulse.

But what if the symptoms of moral insanity, outlined in their various ways by Maudsley, Esquirol and others, also included the contradictory aspect that although a person could be conscious and deliberate in his or her actions, he or she might still not understand their moral wrongfulness? Margaret Messenger certainly had the idea of murder, and she also knew how to carry it out, but she may well have had no real appreciation of its immoral nature. Was it possible that she fixed upon the idea of killing in the medical sense of a (mono)maniacal pursuit, but failed to grasp its moral meaning? If this was the case, then what kind of derangement was she suffering from?

According to Henry Maudsley, there was a condition that began at puberty in which 'a good deal of moral disorder' was triggered. When girls are affected, he wrote, they have been known to 'kill their employer's child, if they are in service, rather than have the trouble to look after it'.[21] Other doctors noted this 'morbid' condition too. One described the case of a young girl engaged as a nurse who had been responsible for killing more than one child. As in Margaret Messenger's case, there was initially no suspicion of her involvement until the sudden death of the last victim. Accounting for her acts, the girl apparently said that the cries of the infants had 'roused in her unconquerable revulsion, and excited her to such a degree that she lost all control of herself'.[22]

Infanticide was an alarming problem throughout the second half of the nineteenth century. In one 30-year period alone, the murder of children accounted for more than half of all female crime tried at the Old Bailey; the majority of the rest included either the assault or the wounding of infants. One London vicar wrote in horror of what he saw as an epidemic of child murder:

> Bundles are left lying about the streets, which people will not touch, lest the too familiar object – dead body – should be revealed, perchance with a pitch plaster over its mouth, or a woman's garter around its throat. Thus too, the metropolitan canal boats are impeded, as they are tracked along by the number of drowned infants with which they come into contact, and the land is becoming defiled by the blood of her innocence.[23]

This account may seem exaggerated, but it shows something of the extraordinary scale of this 'unnatural act', and it was not always the mothers of children who were committing it.

Infanticide was a social evil that was mostly brought about by the poverty and overcrowding that came in the wake of rapid industrialisation; however, due to some recent developments in medicine at the time, physical causes were also found in the hormonal imbalances that accompany childbirth or lactation.[24] Maudsley, though, was describing what he believed to be a more specific, congenital defect, one that he named 'moral imbecility'.

Those afflicted are, he observed, 'inherently vicious ... they have no trace of affection for their parents or of good feeling for others'. While a good number are especially slow in learning and development, others, he said, are astonishingly clever and astute – not so much weak in intellect, but weak of moral character. Murder of the kind perpetrated by Margaret Messenger could, according to this description, have been the outcome of such a defect. It was possible that she belonged to a class of people who, the psychiatrist believed, were 'congenitally destitute of moral sense, have not the sensibilities to feel and respond to impressions of a moral kind, any more than one who is colour blind has sensibility to certain colours'.[25]

Others in the field of mental sciences shared this view. The psychologist Havelock Ellis wrote an influential book called *The Criminal*; it was among the first study of its kind to take a psychological approach to the perennial problem of criminality. It was based on the belief that there were some individuals for whom the ability to fashion even the most basic of moral intuitions was totally absent. He illustrates this with two cases; one involved a fifteen-year-old boy, 'clearly of abnormal or degenerate character', beating his ten-year-old sister's skull until she died.[26] The other was a case of a twelve-year-old German girl who was sentenced to eight years in prison for murdering a child of three. It appears that Marie Schneider had a history of cruelty. In her statement to the court, she admitted:

Some time ago, playing in the yard, I came behind a child, held his eyes and asked him who I was. I pressed my thumbs deep in his eyes, so that he cried out and had inflamed eyes. I knew that I hurt him, and, in spite of his crying, I did not let go until I was made to. It did not give me special pleasure, but I have not felt sorry.[27]

Ellis describes the girl as being 'intelligent beyond her years'. The evidence given to the court reveals her to have been fully aware of the crime she had committed but, he says, morally she was an 'idiot'.[28]

Maudsley differed with Ellis on the idea that there was a specific criminal type, but they were united in the belief that there are some individuals who are congenitally deprived of a sense of morality. They both shared Darwin's view that the moral sense had been developed through evolution, and like the eminent biologist they relied upon a mixture of natural selection and Lamarckian ideas about the inherited effect of habit and learning in order to explain how moral behaviour was transmitted through the generations. However, Maudsley in particular was less interested in how human nature appeared to progress, and more in trying to discover what might be holding it back – he wrote: 'The wicked are not wicked by deliberate choice of the advantages of wickedness, which are a delusion, or the pleasures, which are a snare, but by the inclination of their natures which makes the evil good to them and the good evil.'[29] The human organism, in other words, begins with the propensity for corruption or disease because of the way in which we have evolved.

In Maudsley's opinion, much could be learned about what goes wrong in human development, or what is abnormal, through studying the normal human infant. To him, infancy was analogous to a state of 'moral idiocy', because the 'fabric of mental organisation' in a baby has not yet been built up. Any defects observed in the adult's brain and sensory system were symptoms of arrested development, rooted in the inheritance of faulty physiological characteristics. According to this view, the individual who inherits this unstable nervous system is bound, as a consequence, to inherit its corresponding mental symptoms. A congenital deficiency in the moral sense is, according to Maudsley, a throwback to an earlier, primitive stage in the organism's development; in other words, the adult has become stuck or arrested at a lower-functioning stage. The concept used to describe this process was degeneration, and in the closing decades of the nineteenth century it became, for some doctors of the mind, the single most important idea that explained the origins of insanity:

> There is the rapid undoing of what has been slowly done through the ages; the disruption and degenerate manifestation of faculties which have been tediously acquired; the resolution of what has been the gain of a long process of evolution; the formless ruin of carefully fashioned form. We are sad witnesses of the operation of a pathological law of dehumanisation in producing dehumanised varieties of humankind.[30]

Degeneration was a concept first used in the 1850s by the French psychiatrist Benedict August Morel, who had observed that many patients in asylums had strange bodily shapes and expressions. From this he inferred that they 'recapitulate in their bodies the pathological organic characteristics of a number of previous generations'.[31] In effect, these patients' perceived strange physical characteristics represented a kind of atavism, a biological reversion from normal development to a primitive or even a pre-human type. To a post-Holocaust generation, the horrific consequences of this concept are all too clear since it was used to justify systematic sterilisation and genocide. But, in the late nineteenth century, psychiatry briefly relied upon the concept of degeneration, because it appeared to fill some gaps in understanding about the role of genetics and biology in neuroscience.

There was in fact, a credible scientific basis in biology to a limited idea of degeneration, which described the way in which some neurological illnesses deteriorate progressively through the generations. However, some doctors gave the concept a much wider role, claiming that it explained many forms of deviant physiology and behaviour. Maudsley, for instance, shaped by the moralistic environment of the Victorian age in which he lived, was quick to see abnormality in any expression of childhood sexuality. He believed that adolescents showed worrying signs of pathological illness in what he saw as their 'licentiousness and promiscuity'. Among the aggravating causes of moral insanity that he identified were factors such as head injury and intestinal worms; but masturbation was also singled out. The idea behind this was that irritations caused by worms, or excitations caused by masturbation, acted negatively upon the 'supreme [nervous] centres to derange them'.[32]

These were the early years of the psychiatric profession. Doctors of the mind were still sometimes referred to by their old name, 'alienists', and the classification and diagnosis of mental illness was rudimentary, sometimes downright absurd. But Maudsley's discussions and lectures on moral insanity came before any descriptions of emotionally dangerous children existed. Few young people were brought into the lunacy system in the nineteenth century – instead, they tended to end up in prison, the workhouse or, later, in reformatories and industrial schools. Such vulnerable children, who were as much a danger to themselves as others, were not characterised as having (twentieth-century) learning difficulties or behavioural disorders, but in their conduct they showed an unmistakable failure to learn or adjust morally and socially. Psychiatry's description of moral imbecility, for all its attendant problems and errors, was the beginning of a classification of such children that others would go on to revise and contest.[33]

A Murder Most Banal

While the crimes that took place on the Pallisters' farm that summer in 1881 were clearly morally outrageous, they were not in themselves evidence of Margaret Messenger's dehumanised or immoral nature. At the time, neighbours, newspaper men and even the police thought that only someone who was inherently wicked could do such a thing, and that she must have some 'strange kink' in her nature. It was compelling to have this confirmed by science, according to which such extreme behaviour was said to be due to an innate inability to form moral intuitions, or a lesion or disease of the brain, or both. But for the doctors on the ground in this case, who had been dispatched by the home secretary Sir William Harcourt with the specific purpose of inquiring into the girl's state of mind, their analysis was a good deal more commonplace. Admittedly Dr McDougal, the surgeon at Carlisle prison, had no particular expertise in mental illness, but his co-author, Dr Orange, was the head doctor at Broadmoor, and they both came to a surprising and unexpected conclusion:

> In our conversations with her we were not able to detect any indication of the existence of insanity, and we do not find in the family history any hereditary tendency to insanity or epilepsy. The letters written during her confinement in prison,

so far as they have been examined by us, are also free from indications of mental unsoundings. The conclusion therefore at which we have arrived is that the girl is not insane; but that she is a child, who although quite aware of the sinfulness of her acts, was yet, by reason of her youth, not capable of fully appreciating their nature and character and consequences to the same extent as would be the case with a person of mature age.[34]

Dr Orange in particular would certainly have been familiar with the prolific writings on Darwinian neuroscience. His counterpart at Bethlem Royal Hospital had written a number of books on the subject. Yet he and his colleague from Carlisle jail make no reference to it. Perhaps they were both of the view that academic science had overstretched the principles of evolutionary biology. What Maudsley and others thought they had identified as the 'moral sense' was not a human faculty in the same way as the sense of smell or vision. Conscience and morality had to be learnt afresh by each individual, and there was simply no proof that either quality emerged from our biology. Whatever opinion he and Dr McDougal harboured about the science of their profession, there was no mark of its influence in their report on the girl. In fact, the document says more about their powers of empathy.

That Margaret Messenger was very emotionally vulnerable was certain, and this clearly affected her moral conduct with tragic consequences. But their document, for all its officialdom, manages to remind us that this was a child, with childish hopes and dreams: 'We gather from her that she much preferred house-work and field-work to taking care of the children during what seemed to her the long and wearisome days when she was left entirely in charge of them.' They write that before committing one of the murders she had been invited to go to a summer fête in a neighbouring village. She was looking forward to it, as most of her days were spent on the farm working, but she was told that she could not go because of her duties to the children: "The change from her life at home, amidst brothers and sisters, to a life amongst strangers; the irksomeness of being left for entire days in a strange place, in charge of strange children; the curtailment of freedom she formerly enjoyed … appear to constitute the circumstances and the motives which led to [her] sad acts.'

The employment position of Margaret Messenger was not unique. It was common for huge numbers of children to take on work like hers. Between 1851 and 1871, the number of nursemaids in England and Wales increased by over 100 per cent.[35] Though this appears to be the only case on record of such a murder, the impulse may have been more widespread. In a commentary on the Messenger case, one newspaper mentioned an unnamed 'eminent doctor', who had written of a nursemaid who had admitted that 'upon the occasion of dressing or undressing the infant confided to her charge, she was seized with an almost uncontrollable desire to murder it'.[36] The lives of these working children were arduous and unrelenting. They could be as young as six or seven, and still be sent to work in positions of responsibility for strangers. As the historian Anna Davin points out, 'the child servant who drudges from morning till night in some house where only one servant is kept is called a "slavey" for obvious reasons'.[37] And it is from a child's point of view that we come to glimpse how near to extremes they often felt. Scrawled into the wall of a nineteenth-century Norfolk vicarage is the following rhyme:

The pay is small
The food is bad
I wonder why
I don't go mad.[38]

Margaret Messenger was certainly not mad by the criteria of the degenerationist school of psychiatry, but she must have been psychologically vulnerable, otherwise she would not have reacted so violently to the burdens imposed upon her. Convicted of murder in November 1881, she had her death sentence commuted and was given penal servitude for life. In a twist of irony, on the same day that she was tried a much older woman, Anne Little, was in court for the attempted double murder of her two children.[39] It was common, in cases of infanticide, for juries to seek any suggestion that a baby had died from natural causes in order to secure an acquittal.[40] A great deal of sympathy was attached to these crimes. In this case, however, the woman's two children were beyond infancy, but her penalty was nevertheless light – only eight months in prison. The same judge who, later in the day's business, would issue fourteen-year-old Margaret Messenger with a life sentence, told Anne Little:

> It is my belief that you were driven to this fearful act by misery, partly by ill-treatment [by the husband] and that you did it – I think you did it – I try to believe you did it in a paroxysm of temporary insanity.[41]

This woman had not entered a plea of insanity – she had no need, as the circumstances of her life elicited sympathy enough. Beaten by her husband and living without means, she had come to the end of her tolerance. As a woman in her forties, she was able to convey her desperation to the lawyer employed on her behalf. She was a victim and had managed to articulate her humiliated status. Margaret Messenger, on the other hand, may not have spoken to her defence directly; she was certainly not questioned in court. Her crime was different, of course, but she was in her own way a victim too, something the judge was not inclined to accept.

Having been declared of sound mind by Home Office doctors, Margaret Messenger went on to serve her life sentence not in an asylum, but in prison – first at Carlisle jail, then more than 200 miles away in Woking. We know from her case records that her first petition for release in 1886 was turned down, not because of any recorded misconduct, but because the Conservative home secretary believed that five years in prison was insufficient punishment. He conceded only that the case could be reconsidered 'after the prisoner had served ten years'.[42] In 1891 she appealed on her own behalf, although her appeal was written in the hand of the prison chaplain, saying that she was 'seriously sorry for the past and anxious to have the opportunity of redeeming her character'.[43] She had been given the blessing of the parents of the murdered children, and the chaplain confirmed that she was 'deeply penitent and fully sensible of the enormity of her crime'. He described her as 'thoughtful, serious and religiously disposed. The period in prison has, I think, specially in her case, proved to be a wholesome season of training. She is neither vindictive nor passionate.'[44]

Her parents, referred to by one newspaper that covered the case as 'good people', also petitioned the home secretary, and pleaded to let them take charge of her: 'We feel satisfied that if once liberated, she can lead a good and useful life, under our parental care and guidance.' In an unequivocal expression of the love they still felt for their daughter, they continued: 'We can assure you that during the ten years she has been imprisoned, no one can tell the mental anguish and suffering, we as sorrowing parents have endured and we are extremely anxious to obtain through you her liberation.'[45]

She was released on licence in 1891. Now aged 23, Margaret Messenger never forgot her terrible crime. For those journalists who had observed her in the dock all those years ago, and saw in her impassive face the mark of inhumanity, a surviving letter to her old friend and warden tells a different story. She asks to be remembered to other inmates and staff: 'I often think of you all, and of all the kindness I received from all at a time when a kind word or even a smile was valued and treasured, I sometimes wonder if it was real, or only a bad dream, but I have only to look at my "Ticket" to realise the truth of it all … but it is a just punishment.' Her 'ticket of leave' for a life sentence was eventually lifted in 1892 when the prison superintendent wrote to the Duchess of Bedford (chosen possibly for her title, useful for any appellant, rather than any distinguished record of prison reform):

> During her thirteen years of freedom she has enjoyed since her liberation she has earned and maintained a character for respectability industry and God fearing ways. Had you known her as I do you would do all in your power to reward her perseverance in the struggle for life, by lifting from her the burden of a 'Ticket of Leave' borne with patience for thirteen years.[46]

Margaret Messenger returned to Howrigg, her home in the village of Thursby, as soon as she was released. It was the place she had grown up in and where she had gone to school. No one seemed perturbed by her presence even though five years previously, when there had been rumours in the newspapers of her early release, the Bishop of Carlisle, who was a high-profile supporter of her case, expressed concern for her safety. But her eventual resettlement appears to have taken place without disruption or comment, and according to the census records from a decade later, she was earning her living at home as a dressmaker. Her mother had died, but her father was still alive, working as a freestone quarryman, and together they shared their modest home with her 21-year-old stonemason brother, George.

It can never be known if the murder of the Pallisters' two children was caused by any mental deficiency in Margaret Messenger; 'backwardness' was certainly never mentioned in her record. In fact the evidence suggests the opposite, although this was at least twenty years before any means of measuring intelligence was available. Her successful rehabilitation, however, would suggest that the immorality that led her to kill was not something fixed in her nature. Heredity had been one of the most contentious themes to arise out of Darwin's work, and it was the most influential, but doctors found no inherited malady in her case. Yet, for lay commentators in the press at least, mental defects that were perceived as biological in origin provided a convincing account for crimes that otherwise seemed unfathomable.

'Wickedness', Darwin had once written, 'is no more man's fault than bodily disease.' It was unsurprising, therefore, that the idea of the child murderer as a clear instance of native depravity has endured, finding favour not only with some nineteenth-century psychiatrists, but also dominating assumptions about child killers right up to the most recent cases on record. The story of Margaret Messenger is perhaps a counterbalance to this. She was vulnerable, desolate, and the persisting pressures of her duties turned out to be, uniquely in her case, triggers for the fatalities that followed. Yet ten years later she had grown into an ordinary, responsible young woman for whom the events of the past, however inescapable, were no obstacle to her successful rehabilitation.

Chapter Seven

A POISONER'S CONSCIENCE

He might know [right and wrong] as a principle of hearsay,
but not as a controlling principle of his mind.
DR FREDERICK DUESBURY

Moral insanity is only the self-delusion of hardened conscience.
JUDGE BARON ROLFE, 1847

The extraordinary thing about Margaret Messenger's case was that although lawyers, journalists and doctors questioned her mental state, a plea of insanity was never entered at her trial. Her youth was probably the reason. Insanity defences were usually submitted where a defendant faced death if convicted, and although she had been given the death sentence, by 1881 her young age guaranteed her a reprieve. The Home Office did call for an inquiry into her sanity, but this was only done later in order to determine whether she would live out her sentence in a lunatic asylum or a prison.

There was little incentive for lawyers at this time to rely on the insanity plea. It was still controversial in the courtroom, and its chances of success were uncertain. There had been two attacks on monarchs and one celebrated assassination attempt on the prime minister since 1800, all three of which had resulted in acquittal on grounds of insanity.[1] Judges, politicians and the public were beginning to suspect that defendants saw it, in some cases at least, as a mere excuse for murder. One famous trial in 1847 shows the extent of this controversy. It was the first trial on record in which a young boy was tested in court over his sanity.[2] The crime alone – he had poisoned his grandfather – was enough to capture the interest of the popular press, but the proceedings of the trial at the Old Bailey in London also set doctor against judge, and psychiatry against ordinary medicine, in a case that made history in the annals of medical jurisprudence.

Lawyers for twelve-year-old William Newton Allnutt, a boy of 'diminutive appearance', argued that the boy's 'not guilty' plea on mental grounds was justified by the fact that although he knew his act was wrong, he did not *feel* it to be so, because he was suffering from a form of insanity that affected his 'moral sentiments' only. In other words, there was a split between his knowing self and his feeling self, a description that did not go down well with either the judge or the jury. In fact, so enraged was the trial judge by the defence offered that he referred to it dismissively as 'idle sophistry' serious enough to warrant his detailed and lengthy rebuttal. He ranked the medical term 'moral insanity' as describing little more than 'moral depravity not only perfectly consistent with legal responsibility, but such as legal responsibility is expressly invented to restrain'.[3] It was all very well for psychiatrists to argue over how mental illnesses should be described, but to bring their ideas into the courtroom was another matter. Moral insanity, whether described as irresistible impulse, lesion of the will or homicidal monomania, put its proponents on a dangerous collision with the law.

A Victorian Delusion

Judges thought that a clear line had been drawn under this issue after the case of Daniel McNaughtan four years earlier. The Scottish wood-turner had shot and killed Sir Robert Peel's private secretary on a cold January night, thinking that he was the prime minister. Acquitted on the grounds of insanity, McNaughtan was sent to Bethlem hospital, but not without a national outcry.[4] Queen Victoria expressed her concern over the 'not guilty' verdict, as did *The Times*, which called in exasperation upon philosophers to explain, 'for the edification of commonplace people like ourselves, where sanity ends and madness begins and what are the outward and palpable signs of the one or the other'.[5]

The jurors who had attended the McNaughtan trial in 1843 could be forgiven for thinking that madness was always evident in the visible behaviour of the afflicted person; this was, after all, the common-sense view. The mad were those who, to any ordinary observer, behaved differently from the rest of us, or so it was believed; they rambled incoherently, rocked back and forth, or raged distractedly like wild beasts. But at this trial, jurors were presented with medical testimony that offered them new perspectives on insanity, in which the divide was not between the mad and the sane, but between the conscious and the unconscious. The idea that the mind was a unified entity capable of knowing itself was one of the most basic tenets of culpable behaviour. Jurors were being asked to accept that there could be mental states in which a person, such as in McNaughtan's case, who was in all respects thoughtful and aware could suddenly become agitated and extreme as if he were someone else. Today, doctors might identify this as a symptom of schizophrenia, but in the early nineteenth century such a term, along with knowledge of all the complex behaviours it now describes, did not exist.

McNaughtan had been suffering from delusional paranoia in the lead-up to the crime; he was convinced that the Tory party was threatening him. The prosecution accepted that he was delusional about this one subject, but believed that in all other areas of his life he was a perfectly rational and intelligent being, and therefore capable of understanding that his act was unlawful. The defence, however, offered innovative medical opinions to demonstrate that forms of insanity had been discovered in which reasoning ability could coexist with unreasonable acts. As far as McNaughtan was concerned, he believed that he was doing the right thing by killing the man he was sure was threatening him, namely Sir Robert Peel: 'The Tories in my native city have compelled me to do this,' he declared in a statement. 'They follow and persecute me wherever I go, and have entirely destroyed my peace of mind.' In the grip of such a delusion, it was no wonder he could not resist acting to protect himself.

Delusion was not an entirely unfamiliar state to the legal world – it was even referred to as 'partial insanity' for over three centuries – but it was the particular definition that psychiatrists were now giving to it that really caused the controversy.[6] The jury were being told by the defence that McNaughtan's illness was a kind of partial insanity that can lead to an 'aberration of the moral senses and affections, which may render the wretched patient incapable of resisting the delusion, and lead him to commit crimes for which morally he cannot be held responsible'.[7]

The arguments of the defence relied heavily upon the thinking of Jean-Etienne Esquirol and an American writer, Dr Isaac Ray, who had written one of the most important books on medical jurisprudence of the time, published in 1838.[8] It was Ray's belief that the legal tests for criminal responsibility were too narrow. In particular, they did not take account of the new thinking about the role played by impulse in the criminal acts of the mentally ill:

We have an immense mass of cases related by men of unques-
tionable competence and veracity, where people are irresist-
ibly impelled to the commission of criminal acts while fully
conscious of their nature and consequences ... They are not
fictions invented by medical men for the purpose of puzzling
juries and defeating the ends of justice, but plain, unvarnished
facts.[9]

The moral insanity defence was successful in the case of
McNaughtan, and this was because irresistible impulse was
accepted as a factor. Doctors who had interviewed him said
he was 'deprived of self control' and had 'no restraint over his
actions'. But for the majority of judges, and certainly most politicians, irresistible impulse, or, as one lawyer critical of the notion
called it, 'unresisted impulse', was an outrageous proposition.[10]
The public outcry that followed the jury's decision to acquit in
this case led immediately to the creation of a clear legal formula
for insanity cases.[11] Several senior law lords eventually confirmed
what judicial discretion had long acted upon – that to establish
such a defence:

It must be clearly proved that at the time of committing the
act the accused was labouring under such a defect of reason,
from disease of the mind, as not to know the nature and quality of the act he was doing; or if he did know it, that he did not
know he was doing what was wrong.[12]

The fact that a defendant could now be considered insane only
if he had lost some or all of his power of reasoning disappointed
the medical profession and placed it in continual tension with
its legal counterpart.[13] The existence of what became known as
the McNaughtan Rules did not end the insanity defence. The

intention behind their introduction was to prevent the new medical notions – impulsive insanity, instinctive insanity and the rest – from confusing jurors in the courtroom and letting the guilty go free. But the medical repertoire of mental illness was expanding at a rapid pace, new categories of disease were being created, and bright young lawyers were obliged to try out the medical testimony in cases where it seemed appropriate. Young William Allnutt's crime appeared to provide such an opportunity, especially given its seriousness and the unusual behaviour that had gone with it.

'Satan has got so much power over me'

The twelve-year-old was already on remand in Newgate when he was given the news that he would have to stand trial for murder. His initial crime had been theft; he had stolen his grandfather's gold watch and was also responsible for stealing ten gold sovereigns that had gone missing weeks earlier. If he had hoped for a charge of theft only, he would have been disappointed but not surprised; he knew what he had done. Samuel Nelme was not a favourite with his grandson, as the old man's truculence had resulted in a beating for the boy on more than one occasion. At 73, he was still strong, and it appears that he was an overbearing figure in the household.

William's beginnings in the Allnutt family had certainly not been ideal. His birth was difficult, and his mother's mind was 'considerably affected' for many months after his arrival. Puerperal mania, an illness that affected women after childbirth, had only become widely understood in the nineteenth century. The novelist Thackeray wrote of a serious episode that his wife suffered after the birth of their third child: 'At first she was violent, then she was indifferent, now she is melancholy and silent and we are glad of it.'[14] The extent to which William's mother was afflicted is not known, but he was the sixth child in what must have been an unhappy household, overshadowed as it was by the violent outbursts of an alcoholic father. Mr Allnutt was a farmer on land in the countryside east of what was then the leafy London suburb of Hackney. The atmosphere in the family cannot have been helped by his fits of epilepsy that appear to have worsened with his continued desire for drink. He died in his late thirties, leaving his wife with eight children. The five eldest were sent to boarding school, while the two youngest remained in the countryside with friends. William was the only child to accompany his mother back to their original home in Hackney, where they settled with the boy's grandfather and his new wife. In the two years they were there, William's behaviour began to go awry and got steadily worse. His mother chastised him for a number of 'misdemeanours', but as she would later tell the court, 'he did not feel he was doing wrong'. She described her son as 'sharp and clever, but sometimes very sullen in his manner'. There was also evidence that his mind was troubled; he had begun sleepwalking at night, and on other occasions he would wake screaming from unsettling dreams.

He began stealing – in once instance several guineas went missing from the house, but suspicion initially fell on the maid, who resigned protesting her innocence. Days later William admitted the theft, but his confession must have appeared shallow, coming as it did in the wake of further, more serious behaviour. His mother and grandparents received a visit from the boy's schoolmaster, who told them that he had been found in possession of a gun. The police were called and William was questioned, but he insisted that he no longer had the weapon and was let go with a warning.

Then one afternoon, while William was walking in the garden with his elderly grandfather, the old man was jolted by the deafening crack of a gunshot close by. William shouted that he'd seen a man firing, but said that the stranger had quickly disappeared out of sight over the wall. As deputy chairman of Hackney's Board of Guardians, Samuel Nelme may well have made a few enemies, but it was doubtful whether any of them would have taken a shot at him. The mysterious event remained unsolved, and only became meaningful in the light of what was to happen later. Meanwhile, life resumed its customary rhythms at the house in Grove Place; a new maidservant was taken on, the family were seen going to church, and Mr Nelme continued to attend his meetings of the Board, dispensing poor relief to many of Hackney's rising population. William, however, had already fixed upon the plan for which he would eventually stand trial.

One late autumn evening after supper the old man began to feel ill, and went to bed with what his wife believed was a seasonal chill. The following day he was low in spirits, but physically he appeared much improved. His daughter made sure he continued to rest and eat well over the next couple of days, and as a treat one evening, she sweetened their gruel supper with a generous helping of sugar. Her father had always been fond of breaking pieces off from the large conical sugar loaf that was popular among families who could afford it. Usually, the domineering Mr Nelme only allowed himself the treat, denying it to other family members, but because his daughter shared the meal that night she too became violently ill. They had intense burning pains in the stomach and could not stop vomiting 'thick turbid matter streaked with blood'. These agonising symptoms went on through the night, with the grandfather suffering the worst. Mr Nelme was 73 years old, but he was strong and had enjoyed good health. At first light, the family doctor was called. Dr Toumlin knew the respected

family well and called at the house often. He was shocked to find
the body of Samuel Nelme, once so commanding and robust,
now convulsed in agony, and he immediately suspected cholera.
The daughter was not so severely affected, but was still very ill
and would remain so for several weeks. Her father, on the other
hand, succumbed later the same afternoon, suffering a horrifying
death.

In the days immediately afterwards, a coroner's inquest was
convened and then adjourned to await the surgeon's report on
the cause of the old man's death. It must have been an acutely
anxious time for those remaining in the house. Mrs Nelme had
lost her husband, her stepdaughter was not yet out of danger, and
the staff would have been concerned that the doctor's diagnosis
of cholera meant that they too were at risk. Distracted by these
concerns, their attention became focused on William only when a
gun was accidentally found in the garden, wrapped in a handkerchief that had belonged to his sister. When it was also discovered
that his grandfather's gold watch and monocle had gone missing,
the police were called and the house was searched. Under questioning, the boy admitted to stealing and told the police where
the items could be found. Their search also uncovered two bul-
lets hidden away, but it was the discovery of a key concealed
behind a chair in the parlour that most alarmed them. The key
had belonged to his grandfather, and it unlocked the drawer of a
bureau in which the old man kept arsenic, which he used as rat
poison. William had apparently watched his mother mix it with
butter, spread it on pieces of stale bread and then leave it down
for the vermin. This gave him the idea for how he could conceal
the substance in his grandfather's treasured bowl of sugar.

William was taken to the police courts in central London
where he was questioned and charged, at this stage only with
theft. However, by now, of course, his name was on the lips of

everyone who knew anything about the events in the house at Grove Lane, and the suspicion that he was responsible for his grandfather's death was entertained by them all. The new maid would later say that William had twice asked her if she thought Mr Nelme would be dead quite soon, and she had wondered what had made him ask such a question, especially as the old man was so strong and healthy. He was kept in custody, ostensibly while the police searched for other missing items of jewellery, but almost certainly because the coroner's hearing was soon to reopen and more information on this troubling death was expected to come to light. When it was revealed that the stomach contents of the deceased showed lethal amounts of arsenic, the twelve-year-old was charged with the murder. News of the charge reached him in his cell off one of the more dismal passages of Newgate prison, to where he had been transferred. It is known from the testimony of one of the jailers that on 22 November, three weeks after the murder, the boy asked for pen, ink and paper in order to write an astonishing confession.

As his mother lay ailing from the partial effects of her son's poisoning, he addressed her directly: 'My dearest mother, as you cannot come to see me, I hope you will write to me and tell me what I ought to do to get forgiveness for what I have done, for I know I have sinned against God and deserve to be sent into Hell.' He had been greatly impressed by the sermon that he had heard the previous Sunday at the prison chapel and no wonder, as it was replete with fearful images of hell and damnation. The boy writes that after the service, the prison chaplain came to him in his cell and told him, in his words, 'if I don't confess what I have done, God would not forgive me, and everyone was sure I had done it, and he told me I had better confess it to you, and he told me what you have told me, that if God was to strike me dead, where would my soul go to? Therefore, dear mother, I have no one to blame but myself. If I had only attended to what you were teaching me, I should not have come to such a place, but Satan got so much power over me.'[15]

Without doubt, a great part of the confession has the mark of the chaplain himself, who almost certainly fed most of it to the boy word for word. William writes that he dreamt of the Resurrection:

I felt so happy whilst I was dreaming it. I dreamed there was a God seated on his throne, and Satan was on his left hand, and God called us all up and asked us a question. It was an English word to make French, and those that had confessed all their sins and left off all their wickedness, he said unto them, 'Come ye into my kingdom which I have prepared for you'. And he said unto those on his left hand, 'Go ye into the furnace of fire prepared for Satan and his angels'. I dreamed I was happy, and you and my brothers and sisters, but I hope all the disgrace will fall upon me and no one else.

Reverend John Davis, prison chaplain at Newgate between 1843 and 1865, had on more than one occasion been accused by lawyers and the government of putting confessions into the mouths of his prisoners before they had received their conviction.[16] William's confession did not go unchallenged but it was finally admitted by the court, and read out in full to the jury. Although clearly written under pressure from the priest, in some sections there appears to be evidence of the boy's authentic voice. He describes how he got hold of the poison while his grandfather's back was turned and how he mixed it into the sugar basin:

Why I did it was I had made grandfather very angry with something I had done, and he knocked me down in the passage, and my head went up against the table, which hurt it very much, and he said the next time I did it he would almost kill me … But if I am transported I know it will be the death of me. Therefore, I hope they will pardon me. What is the punishment of man to the punishment of God? It is an awful thing to fall into the hands of a living God. I dare say you will not believe the dreams but it is the truth. With kindest love to you and all at home, believe me ever your affectionate son.

William could not know that this confession, written by way of exculpation, would be used by one doctor who took part in the trial to confirm that he was mad.[17] Frederick Duesbury, a doctor of medicine in Clapton, east London, near to where the troubled family lived, saw the confession as not so much an expression of real regret and responsibility, but as a simple enactment of it. According to the doctor, the boy showed no genuine 'struggle of mind' over what he had done, no 'compassion or remorse', but most importantly, he had 'no apparent consciousness of having done wrong', something his mother also confirmed. Such judgements had no meaning for this child. The doctor would argue in court that the crime itself was a measure of the boy's moral indifference to others. He could not feel that his grandfather's killing was wrong even if another part of him knew it was, because such a response was beyond his emotional capacity; he was simply unable to share or recognise normal emotional responses. But in his summation, the judge countered that 'insensibility to shame, though utter and complete, does not of itself amount to insanity'. And this was the point upon which the trial turned. Doubtless some jury members thought that a boy of such a young age who had murdered his grandfather could not be anything but insane, but even they would recognise that this opinion must be borne out by fact, and that it was up to the defence to prove it.

Moral Insanity or Moral Depravity?

Insanity has always existed, but what was new about the plea in the nineteenth-century court was that it could now be backed up with science.[18] Doctors were bringing in novel ideas about human behaviour and casting a different light upon the psychology of motive, intention and the ability to tell right from wrong. The impaired, or limited, capacities that they were identifying in mentally disturbed adults were also being applied to children in cases of the most serious crimes such as murder – including Margaret Messenger and now William Allnutt. But how could a legal defence affecting responsibility, made with adults in mind, have any use in the case of a child on trial for a capital crime?

For over 600 years, the criminal liability of a child had supposedly been established in common law. Children below the age of fourteen were deemed to be not fully capable of criminal intent, and could not therefore be held fully responsible for a crime. Except, of course, they were. Being a child was only ever an excuse for crime if the perpetrator was very young indeed. Above the minimum age of criminal responsibility (seven years old, as it was in the nineteenth century), other factors had always come into play to test a child's culpability. In previous eras it was the capacity to distinguish good and evil that was pre-eminent, then later it became an ability to tell right from wrong. In this respect children were no different from adults as, in court, the same test applied to both – did the defendant know that what he or she was doing was wrong?

New scientific ideas, which threatened this legal test and undermined traditional rules defining insanity as a condition that affected cognition only, were important in an extraordinary case like William Allnutt's. This case was unique because, while it was not the first to attract legal controversy over a particular medical diagnosis, it was the first in which the defendant was so young. At twelve years old the boy already had partial protection from the law, so if he was to be found guilty of murder he would not face the same penalty as an adult – death at the gallows. Why then was an insanity defence entered when, as the prison doctor in the case would argue, the boy was perfectly sane, but because of his youth could not be judged to have the same reasoning ability as an adult? Would his age alone not have qualified the degree to which this boy was responsible for murder?

Forensic psychiatry was only just beginning in the mid-nineteenth century; it was a time in which the law relating to psychiatric excuse and mitigation was developing, but only with adult perpetrators in mind. Its use in this case therefore had no basis in any recognition of the special capacities, or indeed psychology, of childhood. Children were seen as underdeveloped adults rather than as individuals generating their own emotional lives and disturbances. Allnutt's trial would turn out to be one in which the age of the defendant was a less important issue than the wider one at stake – namely, the fundamental legal idea of a responsible self.

William was brought into the Old Bailey on 15 December 1847. The spectators in the gallery, who had paid to watch the unusual proceedings, looked towards the small boy as he sat with his head in his hands. 'Turn your eyes to the dock', wrote Dickens on a visit to the court some years earlier, 'watch the prisoner attentively for a few moments, and the fact is before you, in all its painful reality. Mark how restlessly he has been engaged for the last ten minutes … observe the ashy paleness of his face when a particular witness appears, and how he changes his position and wipes his clammy forehead, and feverish hands, when the case for the prosecution is closed, as if it were a relief to him to feel that the jury knew the worst.'[19]

William's mother, who had recovered enough to attend her son's trial, wept as she listened to his confession being read out. But despite her fragile state she took the stand and gave evidence for her child. Maria Louisa Allnutt spoke of how ill she had been after her son's birth and about what a difficult boy he was, always resisting her attempts to discipline him. She recalled a severe blow to the head he had received earlier in the year after falling on some ice, which she believed had permanently affected his health, giving him headaches and disturbed sleep. She said that when she admonished him over his conduct he would sometimes answer that a voice in his head said to him: 'Do it – do it – you will never be found out.'

The response of the six medical experts in the case was ambiguous, to say the least. Dr Henry Letheby was the first witness to be called by the prosecution. As a physician and lecturer in chemistry at the London hospital at Whitechapel, Letheby had been sent by the coroner's surgeon three jars containing the contents of the deceased's stomach, intestines and liver for examination. He gave a lengthy technical account of the procedures by which he had discovered the arsenic, and eventually stood down. The judge recalled him some time later, and this time the interrogation was about the prisoner rather than his victim. Baron Rolfe inquired whether the boy's reported episodes of sleepwalking could have consequences for his mental health. Asked, 'Are you able to say whether walking in the sleep is indicative of a disordered state of mind?', Letheby replied: 'Yes, it might be occasioned by some organic cause, or by some disordered state of the stomach, and the same observations would apply to talking in sleep.' Furthermore, Letheby said that a blow to the head could also cause 'mischief to the brain', possibly giving rise to an 'alteration in its formation'.

The judges' own lengthy summation, published in full after the trial, gives a clue to the rationale behind his questioning.

He was trying to establish whether or not the Allnutt child had a diseased mind and, if so, what were the corresponding bodily diseases or injuries that might have accounted for it:

Strict inquiry into the symptoms of bodily disease is the best guide to determine sanity of mind in a doubtful case ... there has been too much disposition [by our medical brethren] to envelope the subject of insanity in a murky atmosphere of its own – to assume that the mind, in its pure essence, is susceptible of disease which the body does not share, much less occasion.[20]

The line of bewigged barristers for the prosecution was, however, worried by the judge's interrogation. Letheby was after all their witness, speaking for the side that was hoping to disprove insanity and get a straightforward conviction of murder. When they called Gilbert McMurdo, Newgate's prison doctor, they were on safer and more reliable ground. McMurdo was retained by the corporation of London to keep a close eye on prisoners who were deemed likely to proffer an insanity plea. His task was to detect signs and consistency in a prisoner's behaviour that might convince him whether or not such a plea was genuine. He rarely concluded that it was, and this case was no exception.[21] The doctor told the court that he had seen and spoken to the prisoner a number of times and 'had not observed anything in his conduct to induce him to believe that he was not of sound mind or incapable of distinguishing between right and wrong'.

An attack of ringworm and scrofula that the boy had suffered when he was nine, and which Letheby and other doctors said could have affected his brain, was also dismissed as irrelevant by McMurdo: 'I have not seen any madness result from it ... it is not within my experience that scrofula driven inwardly is liable to produce a certain character of insanity.' Under close cross-examination by the defence, the prison surgeon alluded to the general controversy over the moral insanity diagnosis, and was clear, if polite, in his disparagement of it. He suggested that if the boy's reasoning ability was compromised it was not because of an insanity affecting his moral faculties, but rather caused by his youth: 'I should consider that in an infant the mind is rather a matter of feeling than of understanding – they understand from others that a thing is right or wrong and do not reason upon it.' However, as if to remind the jury that they were there to decide whether the defendant, young though he was, should be held accountable for his crime, the judge interrupted to ask McMurdo directly: 'Did the boy appear to you to be a person capable of distinguishing between right and wrong?', to which he gave an unequivocal 'Yes'.

William Allnutt's defence barrister, William Ballantine, was a lawyer of some standing and a regular presence at the Old Bailey. His book, *Some Experiences of a Barrister's Life*, ran into several editions and contained the haunting recollections of the tales of murder that had been told to him by his nurse and have been mentioned in chapter 2 of this book. It also contains an account of his first visit to the famous criminal court that he made with his lawyer father, an experience that gave him a taste for the profession in which he came to excel.

However, he was having some difficulty with this case. As well as the opinion of the prison surgeon, there was his client's confession. Though he attempted to discredit it, arguing that it had been made under pressure, the statement made it obvious to the jury that besides the fact that he had killed his grandfather, Allnutt had planned beforehand to do so and fully knew that it would result in his death. What the lawyer had to demonstrate was that although his client was undoubtedly the agent of the deed, he could not be held to account for it because he was not acting with the moral facility of a normal individual. He had to convince a jury that this was not a case where the criminal had retained his reasoning mind and simply set his heart on evil, but that, in fact, the boy had no capacity to feel such a thing in the first place. In 1847, well before psychology's litany of emotional disorders existed, such a defence would have dismayed a jury. In fact, this idea of emotional insanity went right to the heart of the law's conception of a legally responsible person who acts with reference to right and wrong. It represented an enormous challenge to legal tradition, so it was perhaps unsurprising that Ballantine, who was known for his formidable intellect, was confident he could rise to the occasion.

He called Frederick Duesbury, who had visited the home several times in the six months prior to the murder to treat the boy for scrofula a second time. At that time he had also been made aware of the boy's occasional sleepwalking, which alerted him to a disturbance in the youngster's mind, but not one whose cause he could specifically identify. By the time of the trial, however, the doctor was in no doubt about his diagnosis. He believed that the boy had been in the early stages of moral insanity, marked in particular by a murderous impulse. This was a pivotal point in the trial's proceedings. The judge was obviously willing to entertain a madness that had clear physical origins, but he saw the 'moral insanity' argument as pure philosophy with no factual signs from which a juror, or a judge for that matter, could deduce any mental disorder. The prosecution barrister interrogated Duesbury about the boy's state of mind, and the doctor replied:

> My opinion is that it is the early stage of insanity, implicating the moral sentiments … and not as yet having reached the

intellect in any marked degree, or interfering with his judgement of right and wrong.

Mr Ryland [prosecution]: What do you mean by a marked
degree? Has it gone to the length to injure the intellect, so as
not to know he was poisoning a person when he did it?

Dr Duesbury: He might know [right and wrong] as a
principle of hearsay, but not as a controlling principle of his
mind – I think he would understand that he was poisoning
his grandfather, if explained to him, but at the time the sense
of right and wrong was not acting with sufficient power to
control him. I mean a morbid state of the moral feeling, or the
sense of right and wrong – I think he knew what the act was
that he was doing but that he did not feel it as being wrong – I
am speaking of moral feeling.

Mr Ryland: Do you consider when he did this that he did
not know that poisoning his grandfather was a wrong act?

Dr Duesbury: I think he has not the moral sense of wrong
distinguished from right or right distinguished from wrong
to give him a moral sense of feeling: it was an irresistible
impulse on his part – I draw that conclusion from his having
perpetrated it without any hesitation, or struggle of mind, or
remorse or compunction and without any sensible object, and
also another circumstance which I heard [not specified], leads
me to believe his conscience is diseased, that he could not
feel it as an influential agent to distinguish between right and
wrong, although his intellect leads him to understand what
others tell him.[22]

The last expert witness to be called was the most influential in
the field of early-nineteenth-century psychiatry. John Conolly
had been superintendent of Hanwell public asylum in Middlesex,
and was still a visiting physician there at the time of William

Allnutt's trial. With 900 patients, Hanwell was one of the largest madhouses in the country, and Conolly had pioneered some techniques of moral management, such as banishing forcible restraint, that had been popular in mainland Europe but which were still unpopular in England. Conolly had given evidence at many insanity trials and was an adherent of the theories of Franz Joseph Gall, the Austrian phrenologist who believed that the brain was the organ of the mind, and that it housed all our psychological faculties including those of language, self-esteem and destructiveness. If any of these became damaged, this would result in extraordinary behaviour. Furthermore, because these faculties functioned separately, one of them could become impaired while the others remained safely intact. Hence, a person knowing but not feeling that their actions were wrong. Cognition functioned, but the register of moral feeling did not. It was this thinking that underpinned Conolly's view on insanity and led him to testify that this twelve-year-old boy was 'imperfectly organised and, taking the word "mind" in the sense in which it is used by all writers, I should say he is of unsound mind ... his brain is either diseased, or in that excitable state in which disease is most probable to ensue ... the future character of his insanity would be more the derangement of his conduct than in the confusion of his intellect'.[23]

The principles of phrenology appeared to offer a coherent hypothesis for the physical basis of insanity that might have satisfied the judge, but Conolly was given no time to elucidate, even at this special trial of one so young. Summing up, Baron Rolfe reminded the jury of the importance of this case, not only because it was a child committing murder, but because of the consequences it also had for the law. He conveyed his disapprobation of the defence's argument. Although he said he had no wish to disparage the evidence of scientific men, he proceeded to do so by telling the jury that, if they were to accept it, there might be 'disastrous results to society'.[24] Identifying the defence's claim of uncontrollable impulse, the judge instructed the jury to regard it with suspicion and not pay 'slavish obedience' to it:

[B]ecause it might tend to the perfect justification of every crime that was committed. What was the meaning of not being able to resist moral influence? Every crime was committed under an influence of such a description, and the object of the law was to compel persons to control their impulses.[25]

The jury acquiesced and returned a guilty verdict, though, as in so many of such cases, they recommended mercy on account of the defendant's tender age. Baron Rolfe declared himself 'extremely satisfied' with their good sense. They had accepted that the twelve-year-old boy had wilfully murdered his grandfather, and that he fully understood, and was responsible for, what he had done; he commended them for having 'thrown to the winds the idle sophistry' of the defence's plea of moral insanity.[26]

Beyond Good and Evil

Whether such a plea could ever have made a difference to the outcome of this case is doubtful. The defence lawyers themselves may have privately nurtured some doubt given that, at the start of the trial, they took the line that the boy was not mature enough to distinguish between right and wrong. Instead, they decided to focus on what the judge contemptuously referred to as 'the more captivating defence of insanity'. This approach backfired. From the judge's point of view, this was because the jury had treated the insanity defence as an attempt to 'trifle with their judgement

... they felt that [the boy] knew too well that the act he had committed would send his grandfather to the grave', and as a result, they had not 'hesitated to declare that he was guilty of the wilful crime of murder'.[27] In other words, in a clear assertion of judicial power, Mr Justice Rolfe argued that the law had its own rules and traditions that were not going to be compromised by what he perceived as vague grounds of excuse. Science may have its own insights, but in the courtroom the law must reign supreme.

Arguments over the medical jurisprudence of insanity continued well into the twentieth century, with various attempts being made to include the concept of irresistible impulse, among others, into the insanity defence.[28] It may have been the confusion caused by such discussion that led to subsequent trials of child murderers such as Margaret Messenger ignoring the issue of insanity altogether, despite clear evidence of mental disturbance. The time-honoured practice of adapting the full penalty of the law in cases of children over seven, as had occurred with previous cases throughout the centuries, prevailed.

In 1921, in a case that involved a dangerously psychopathic boy named Harold Jones, the judge said he was satisfied that no insanity was present because the boy had pleaded guilty to his crime, demonstrating (presumably) that he knew right from wrong and could thus be held responsible. The defence did not offer any expert opinion on the boy's mental state and the judge may have felt justified in his view that the boy was fully responsible, because of the efforts he made to try the boy before his sixteenth birthday, thereby saving him from the mandatory sentence for murder – the death penalty.[29] Strategies of this kind allowed the law to keep firm control over its own domain. They also had the advantage of reflecting an image of the law as flexible, and responsive to exceptional crimes. Judicial discretion had for centuries been an effective instrument in the administration of criminal law – it had a durable image as the best means of reconciling the claims of society on the one hand with the rights of the criminal on the other. Psychological incursions could be considered unhelpful to jurors, who were required to make judgements on matters of fact.[30] In the eyes of some lawyers, psychiatric evidence was based on opinion rather than fact, and was therefore viewed as at best a 'good servant' to the court, but certainly not its master.[31]

Medical opinion, however, when based upon clear evidence of physiological disease, did fare better in the courtroom. This much is made clear by the example of a case in 1945 where a fifteen-year-old boy, in a clear display of irresistible impulse, pushed his girlfriend over a cliff. The defence provided evidence that his behaviour had been affected by a bomb which had dropped near his home during the war. He had since been subject to nervous attacks and disruptive behaviour, and was receiving treatment at a London nerve hospital. The court also heard that his probation officer was trying to get him into a home for epileptics – at the time, epilepsy was thought to be an incurable mental illness.[32] Whether any of these diseases were really behind the boy's behaviour we will never know, but the judge, no doubt assured by the incontrovertibly physical nature of the boy's problem, told him: 'For some reason or other, you are not very well. You will be well looked after and given the chance to get out of this miserable illness that catches you now and again and be just as good a boy as before.'[33] It was recommended that he be detained for a year in an appropriate institution.

This was more than a century after the case of William Allnutt who was almost certainly sent to Parkhurst, the only children's prison in the country at the time. It is possible that he failed to escape the punishment he most dreaded and that he was among the last cohort of boys shipped to the convict outcrop of Point Puer before it was closed down in 1849. In the year after his trial, the *London Medical Gazette* carried an article on the controversial case and the medical testimony that had been offered in favour of his plea. Written by Dr Duesbury the main proponent of the concept of impulsive insanity, the editors were at pains to distance themselves from his contentious views, writing: 'We can find nothing in the report of the case to alter our opinion that the young criminal was properly convicted.'[34]

Judge Rolfe had also been 'joyous' that the jury had rejected this medical testimony and 'had not shrunk from the discharge of a duty which men of weaker minds might have recoiled from, and that they had not returned a verdict which they felt their conscience would not sanction'. Criminal responsibility had been established according to the law as it had existed for centuries, and penalties were adapted accordingly. If not openly hostile, judges were certainly suspicious of psychiatric grounds for excuse, and preferred to use narrower conceptions of liability that were assessed by the ancient principles of *mens rea* and *doli incapax*. The problem was that judicial scepticism over the new kinds of insanity defence meant that, by the beginning of the twentieth century, the law was lagging far behind the rapidly developing study of child mental health. By the 1900s, fresh scientific theories and findings about children's mental capacity were identifying psychological phenomena that had important relevance to the unusual cases of children who kill.

Chapter Eight

FAMILY CRIMES

The Light of Lights
Looks always on the motive, not the deed,
The Shadow of Shadows on the Deed alone.
W.B. YEATS, 1909

The haunting behaviour of William Newton Allnutt, and Margaret Messenger's inscrutable motive for murder, were each seen through a medical lens where their thought and conduct were identical to that of an adult of unsound mind. The abnormality perceived in these cases of children who had killed was of interest to doctors, but only insofar as it aided their understanding of mental disturbances in adults. The child's mind as an entity in its own right, inscribed by the psychic dramas of its own experiences of love and fear, only received attention from scientists with the arrival of Freud.

Many of Freud's ideas have been widely criticised by doctors, academics and some feminists. His theories are trivialised by today's pop psychology, but his descriptions of childhood as it is lived in families has had a lasting impact on our culture – bearing this in mind, it is worth taking a brief look at where it all began, if only because the influence of Freud is so marked in contemporary perceptions of children who kill. Freud's work established a paradigm for twentieth-century research on child psychology. Like other scientists before him he used observations of children mainly for his theories about adult selfhood, but he also introduced the first real child as a subject for psychoanalysis in the case history of Little Hans.[1]

The story of the troubled emotions of five-year-old Little Hans became an illustration of Freud's theory of the Oedipus complex and the later controversial idea of the death drive. Little Hans' fantasies of violence and killing were, according to the analyst's view, symbolically identified with the intense family dynamics of Oedipal rivalry, and the full range of chaotic and overwhelming emotions that arise from it.

In the theory of the Oedipus complex the male infant's first love is its mother; she is the source of all his nourishment and pleasure, and is associated with the feelings of fear and love, specifically the loss of love. The child's main rival for the mother is, of course, the father, with whom the child becomes psychically engaged through feelings of jealousy and competitiveness. As one Freudian psychiatrist summarised it: 'In the Oedipus stage the small boy wishes his father dead in order to occupy his place in the mother's bed.'[2] The power of the father is central to the Oedipal drama, not least because of its symbolic role in the history of human society.[3] Freud positioned the taboo on incest at the heart of the Oedipus complex. It was the first social sanction that would play its part in his view about how a moral sense develops in a child. The sexual desire for the mother, which Freud saw as common to all male infants in all societies, must be renounced, as the health of human civilisation and the authority of the father is paramount. In the child's mind, the once obliging father also becomes a punishing figure, and the feeling of threat associated with him in this phase of Oedipal rivalry is, according to the theory, represented by a fear of castration that the father will, in the child's fantasy, undertake in revenge for the child's forbidden desire for his mother.[4]

The case of Little Hans provided evidence for Freud of the 'castration complex'. The boy was fearful of his father, and his anxiety was represented symbolically through a dream of a large and threatening horse, a beast whose sexual organ had been revealed to Hans, and whose death he had witnessed in real life. In Freud's interpretation of the dream, the child's wish for the death of his paternal rival, represented by the powerful figure of the horse, was entangled with the fear that his father might vent his disapproval through the punishment of castration, the boy's sexual organ being the means of his desired transgression.

This conflict was central to the story of Little Hans, but there was also a further plot in the family drama. The envious and competitive feelings the boy had in relation to his father, the most feared rival, were also induced by the birth of a sibling (though the similar feelings aroused by the sibling had a different meaning in Freud's system). The threat felt by the child at the arrival of a baby in the family was chiefly one of annihilation, the fear that the demands and needs of the newborn will absorb all the attention and love of the mother.[5] It was unsurprising, then, that this dynamic should provoke violent emotions:

When other children appear on the scene the Oedipus Complex is enlarged into a family complex. This, with fresh support from the egoistic sense of injury, gives grounds for receiving the new brothers or sisters with repugnance and for unhesitatingly getting rid of them by a wish [6]

Little Hans screamed that he did not want his baby sister and, more than a year after she was born, urged his mother to drop the child into the bath so that she might die. In the 1920s, Melanie

Klein's extensive observations of children also identified the death wish in the very young. She believed that their sources of anxiety were the fear of deprivation and the sense that the mother will thwart the infant's desire for nourishment. Klein believed that this arouses ambivalent feelings of love and hate within the child, as the mother has the power both to provide and to with-hold satisfaction and pleasure.[7]

The exposition of these theories is, of course, highly detailed and involved. But, uniquely, Freud attributes to the child an entangled mental complexity of drives and emotions all operat-ing within the maelstrom of family psychodynamics. The child, for the first time in science, becomes an agent in these processes and carries their meaning and development well into adult life. Oedipal rivalry and fantasies of death were, for Freud, a normal part of a child's development:

Children are completely egoistic; they feel their needs intensely and strive ruthlessly to satisfy them – especially as against their rivals, other children, and first and foremost as against their brothers and sisters ... And it is right that this should be so; for we may expect that, before the end of the period which we count as childhood, altruistic impulses and morality will awaken in the little egoist and a secondary ego will overlay and inhibit the primary one ... If this morality fails to develop we talk of 'degeneracy', though what in fact faces us is an inhibi-tion in development.[8]

In Freud's view, a child's moral sense, which at the bare mini-mum was taken to mean his knowledge of social mores and prohibitions, could not be taught by simple education, though this could be attempted; rather, in order to have any lasting hold over us, such matters needed to register at a level deeper than mere behavioural function. Other mid-nineteenth-century psychiatrists had focused on 'disorders of the will' as the cause of immorality, the 'will' being identified as a biological entity that can go wrong through poor heredity.[9] For Freud, however, bad behaviour was an indication of the discrepancy between an ideal, or standard, of how we should behave and the unconscious processes that often undermine our ability to keep faith with this ideal. In the psychological system that he outlined, the agency or structure that the influence of parents, and later teachers, acted upon was the superego, or conscience. He believed that it was only through the workings of the superego that man could achieve control over his destructive impulses. Parental authority was significant for Freud's concept of the superego, not just because of its obvious role in enforcing moral behaviour, but because of the identification we make with our parents during childhood. Through a childish idolatry of our mother and father we become ourselves partly in their image, even in our reactions against them, and our values are moulded, in part at least, according to their contours.

This moral development can go horribly wrong, of course, especially in families where children feel a constant atmosphere of danger. One psychoanalytically-trained reformer of 'wayward' children, August Aichorn, believed that the aggression expressed by many of those in his care was a reaction to the aggression that they had seen in their parents:

> The family constellation was never perfect in these cases. The parents lived in an atmosphere of hatred and discord; insults and fighting were part of their daily life; either that or their parents were divorced, re-married, with the children raised by a step-parent, or else the parents were dead and the children wandered about in unfamiliar places.[10]

Aichorn was director of two reformatories for difficult children in his home city of Vienna in the years after the First World War. He was urged by Anna Freud, Sigmund's daughter, to undertake psychoanalytic training, and soon became a pioneer of its methods and insights in his attempts to re-educate 'delinquents'. He set up a child guidance service for the Vienna Psychoanalytical Society, but his real influence was on the children in his charge. According to him, the violent youngsters needed to model a different ego ideal from that of their threatening authority figures. Believing that discipline and punishment held no fear for these difficult children he gave them respect, warmth and gentle discipline, and had some success with these methods.

Unconscious Wishes

Freud's account of Little Hans' murderous aggression was, of course, far removed from the reality of these children's lives. The boy's neurosis was eventually contained by love and dialogue with his father through Freud's assistance. Hans was not a child whose circumstances were such that his death wish found concrete expression. But for psychologists confronted with such cases, psychoanalytic terms and ideas were important even if the elaborate theories behind them were never fully endorsed. The educational psychologist Cyril Burt, for example, was not a Freudian by inclination, but he was sufficiently persuaded by arguments about the defence mechanism of repression in children, and its connection to the unconscious, to make use of such ideas in his psychological study of a seven-year-old boy who had killed a child.[11]

Burt was the first educational psychologist to be appointed by London County Council (LCC) in 1913. Early on in the post, which was only a temporary move from academia, he was called upon to make an assessment of a young killer he named as Jeremiah Jones; 'When I first saw him, he was just seven and a half years old, a scared and tattered bundle of grubbiness and grief, with his name still on the roll of a school for infants. Yet, at this tender age besides a long list of lesser faults, he had already taken a young boy's life.' The case formed the basis of Burt's seminal study of young criminals, *The Young Delinquent*.[12]

Burt realised that the story of this young killer was in many respects 'typical' of those of the other delinquents he studied. He came from a poor home, and although he had a devoted grandmother she was elderly and worked at cleaning jobs all day in local hotels. His mother was also a chambermaid, and had become pregnant with Jeremiah after a brief encounter with a well-to-do London visitor. The boy grew up to be, as might have been said then, 'a bit of a tearaway'. When he was six, he had a serious accident when he tried to jump onto a moving lorry. He was hospitalised for over ten weeks, and when he returned to the basement tenement that was home, near London's Kings Cross station, he drifted. Avoiding school, he ate from food crates on the station platform and sometimes took pennies from his grandmother's purse. His mother was cautioned about her son's truancy and eventually fined when it continued. It was only when she paid a neighbour to look after him during the day that his wandering appeared to stop.

Then, one summer's morning, Jeremiah and two friends went fishing along the Regent's Canal. At that time, it was still a busy transport route to and from the Thames. One of the boys was carrying a toy aeroplane and began flying it near the bank side. It had a propeller made of bent tin and a coil of wire; with just a flick of the propeller, it flew and returned like a boomerang to its owner. Jeremiah was excited by the toy and wanted it; he asked his friend to hand it over. When the boy refused Jeremiah threatened him, and when he scoffed Jeremiah lunged at him, pushing his playmate into the canal. He watched, 'with jibes and taunts', as the little boy struggled for his life.[13]

At the inquest, the death was declared accidental. Jeremiah had lied to the coroner's jury, telling them that the boy had fallen backwards into the canal while trying to throw a heavy stone. But as the weeks passed after the inquest, Jeremiah's behaviour became erratic and disturbed; 'there were wild outbursts of inexplicable passion, half terror and half temper, such as, in an adult, would have been called hysteria or mild mania'. It was at this point that Burt was called upon to make a psychological examination of the boy. After the first interview he obtained, 'without much difficulty', a confession. When word of Jeremiah's guilt reached the family of the dead boy, the father raged and vowed that he would have revenge. He attacked Jeremiah's mother, dragging her by the hair and throwing her down a flight of steps. In desperation, she later wrote to Burt asking him to put her son away: 'The people are tormenting myself and the child down here so much and give no peace.' He was eventually transferred to a remand home far from London and it is likely, given the cost of travelling, that he was never visited by a family member at any point during his detention.

It was significant that Burt made this case so central to his study of youth crime. Though exceptional in nature, it was also commonplace in circumstance; he wrote: 'A crime is not a detached or separable fact, self-contained and self-subsisting.' By this, he meant that a crime like Jeremiah's has causes that are deeply rooted, and that punishment should be secondary to finding out what these causes may be:

The handling of the juvenile offender is, or should be, a practical application of known psychological principles. To whip a boy, to fine him, to shut him up in a penal institution, because he has infringed the law, is like sending a patient, on the first appearance of a fever, out under the open sky to cool his skin and save others from infection.[14]

One of the governing principles of the Freudian school was that through knowledge of the unconscious, unacknowledged or repressed emotions will surface in analysis and thus lessen the likelihood of such feelings being acted upon to the detriment of oneself and others. Burt took a very different approach, and used a more intuitive idea of the unconscious, in his work with Jeremiah. He also made a more general use of the mechanisms of fantasy and repression.

First, he observed that Jeremiah had indeed intended to kill the younger child, 'and knew that his act would do what he intended'.[15] Moreover, the boy demonstrated a 'state of intelligence relatively developed', suggesting that the psychological study of Jeremiah needed to go beyond any narrow legally-defined criteria about knowledge of right and wrong. Burt also cited Freud's comments on fantasies of murder in the young in order to argue that the subject of his own study could have no real conception of death or its meaning. Freud had stated:

A child's idea of being 'dead' has nothing much in common with ours apart from the word. Children can know nothing of the horrors of corruption, of freezing in the ice cold grave, of the terrors of eternal nothingness – ideas which grown-up people find so hard to tolerate ... to children ... being 'dead' means approximately the same as being 'gone'.[16]

Other influential child studies of the early twentieth century pointed to the fact of death as a finality beyond a child's
conception.[17] Indeed, this view was so widely accepted among
early child psychiatrists that it led one professional, who had an
expertise in cases of young children who had killed, to argue that
a death involving children so young could only ever be viewed
as accidental. An extraordinary claim, but in 1935 the American
psychiatrist Lauretta Bender, an expert on child suicides and violence, began a study of 33 homicidal children from as young as
five years old up to sixteen. After interviewing these children over
many years she concluded that they could not really comprehend
death, that they believe that it is reversible, and that, to them, it
represents some temporary form of deprivation: 'The hardest
task for the child is to believe in and accept the immutability of
the death of his victim.'[18]

Bender also pointed out that for a child who kills, the trauma
of this event works its way through the psyche. This was certainly
the case for Jeremiah Jones, the young murderer whom Burt
interviewed in depth and over many months. The death that this
little boy had caused, though not fully comprehended, had clearly
made an impact on his youthful unconscious. It was displayed
in the extreme symptoms exhibited in his behaviour for weeks
and months after the killing. Even though Burt reported that,
at his initial interview with the child, 'little or no reference had
been made to the original tragedy', he nonetheless saw that it was
'always near the surface of [the boy's] mind'.[19] Jeremiah showed
fears of drowning and suffered continuously from nightmares.
He was also 'susceptible to depression and grief'.[20] Lauretta
Bender also noticed this kind of reactive depression in her work
with murderous children and adolescents. One ten-year-old boy,
who had been involved in the drowning of another, developed
a phobia of water and experienced night terrors in which he,

or someone else, was drowned.[21] These anxieties may well have been associated with fears of punishment and feelings of guilt for something the child only subsequently saw as being his own fault. But the process of talking to sympathetic specialists trained to elicit the source of behavioural symptoms inevitably drew the child towards a more conscious awareness of his crime. The sorrow witnessed by these experts was indeed a sign of the children's guilt. In the case of Burt's young killer, he had for some time concealed the deliberate nature of his act, but it proved impossible for his mind to maintain such firm denial. The anxious dreamworld that the boy inhabited betrayed this; the closer these images came to his mind's surface, the more overwhelmed the child became. The corresponding despair he felt, and the diminution of his self-worth, almost drowned him in depression and grief.

In the cases of the children mentioned above, it was their unconscious minds that revealed the real meaning of the deaths that they had been involved in. But even in normal children a curiosity about death exists from quite an early age, otherwise there would be no satisfactory explanation for the delight that many small children show in the killing of insects or small animals. None of this is to suggest that a young child's sense of death is identical to that of an adult; after all, their sense of time and space is different. As Freud argued regarding children's inability to identify the relative differences between 'dead' and 'gone':

> A child makes no distinction as to how this absence is brought about: whether it is due to a journey, to a dismissal, to an estrangement, or to a death.[22]

A child's sense of death is not absolute because his or her ideas about life are not defined by the knowledge that it has a beginning, middle and an end – in other words, of the meaning of a lifespan. The seven-year-old in Burt's study had killed his playmate because he would not hand over his homemade aeroplane; a motive which on the face of it seems chilling, and destined for a headline in any newspaper. But we also learn that this victim had over many months taunted his killer with insults about his parents; Jeremiah was illegitimate and his mother was engaged in prostitution. According to Burt, it was this 'longstanding provocation, more than any passing whim for a twopenny toy', that was the real, but hidden, motive for the child's crime. He wanted to undo his connection to his tormentor by getting rid of him. He simply wanted him gone.[23] It was because Jeremiah was ignorant of the real consequences of his act that he could not be answerable for his terrible deed, and legally, aged only seven, he was of course protected from criminal prosecution.[24]

The Beginnings of Violence in Children

No matter how much Freud's theories were to be criticised throughout the century, he nonetheless gave meaning to things that science had never spoken of before: the unconscious, rivalrous emotions in families, death wishes, and death drives. Indeed, child psychology and child psychiatry might never have come into being were it not for his legacy. By the end of the Second World War, the concepts and ideas he introduced were being moved by later experts beyond issues of infantile sexuality and towards an emphasis on interpersonal relationships within the family and the importance of love in the bond between parent and child.[25] One group of psychiatrists, writing at this time on the subject of murderous aggression in children, argued then what today, because of Freud's influence, seems commonplace:

In response to firm, non-ambivalent parental example and direction, the growing child learns to control his impulses and to tolerate frustration. If the parental demand for compliance is supported by warm affection and is clearly delineated by adequate limit setting, the child develops a firm, well-founded conscience structure. Ethics that have no personification in a parental figure have no well-founded part in the life of the child.[26]

For Lauretta Bender, starting out as one of the first child psychiatrists in the United States, the conceptual tools provided by Freud's theories were invaluable to her work with emotionally disturbed children. She used Freudian ideas about drives and their explosive emotional energy to furnish her major study, *Aggression, Hostility and Anxiety in Children*, which was published in 1953.[27] Leo Kanner, one of the first academic child psychiatrists, was also enormously influenced by psychoanalytical ideas. His standard text, *Child Psychiatry* (first published in 1935), was used by professionals on both sides of the Atlantic, and showed the extent to which the projective techniques of psychodynamic models, such as play, creative activity, and the use of dolls and puppets, could play a central role in the assessment and treatment of child patients.[28] One of the issues which these techniques served to express was sibling rivalry, a problem to which Freud himself had only given brief attention in the case history of Little Hans and in *The Interpretation of Dreams*. Yet this was a problem that was routinely cropping up in child clinics.

Many of the studies that identified this dynamic through a child's play, or creative expression, involved children whose behavioural problems were disruptive, but not always malign. Their feelings of hostility towards siblings were fantasised and unconscious, and did not always result in acts of real violence.

But one study of 21 children admitted to a psychiatric unit because they were violent and dangerous showed that half of the children's violence was directed at siblings. All of them had been violent towards other children, and eight had made serious attempts to kill their mothers.[29]

In her work on homicidally aggressive children, Lauretta Bender deduced that sibling rivalry rarely resulted in real acts of destruction, unless it was aggravated by other external factors or circumstances. Then, she argued, the excitatory impulses aroused by the Oedipus situation, or sibling rivalry, increase to an unbearable extent. One of the precipitating factors she mentioned is a situation where normal feelings of jealousy and competitiveness are not dealt with lovingly and in an environment where the child feels safe. Without the positive emotion of love, or because this emotion is not strong enough, aggression can easily become overwhelming, leading to acts of destruction. Other factors she cites are those in which an inborn incapacity, such as so-called 'backwardness' or autism, can make a child feel inferior, and 'helpless and disorganised and in greater need of love of which he is deprived'.[30] An intelligent child who is having learning difficulties can also have problems controlling the rage and frustration he or she feels at an undeserved lack of status. These circumstances, together with a frightening pattern of violence within a family, could make a child feel murderous, even if this feeling is not acted upon.

Each of these studies was undertaken by research doctors who chose to work with disturbed and violent children, but what happened when a child killing occurred far beyond the sight of professionals who were especially attuned to such things? How might the child perpetrator be understood? Did any of this knowledge about children and death, murder and guilt, which had been developing over decades have any influence among doctors who encountered a crime of this kind by chance? What explanations would doctors reach for to account for such behaviour in a child, in an era that was post-Freud but pre-child psychiatry? And when it came to evidence before a jury in the trial of a child murderer, what role, if any, did psychological insights play in the outcome?

Psychiatric Knowledge and its Legal Limitations – The Case of Doreen Russell

Doreen Russell was fourteen when she strangled a neighbour's sixteen-month-old baby in a village just outside Rotherham.[31] On the surface, there were many straightforward elements to this case. A young child was put in charge of children, one of whom she could not control; the impulse to kill was thoughtless and sudden. After all, if this were to happen today, the parents themselves would stand trial – if a babysitter is under sixteen, the child's parents are still legally responsible for anything that happens while the child is in his or her care. Any spectator of this case would have good reason to recognise, if not sympathise with, the circumstances in which the infant June Smith died. A ten-week-old baby was also part of this large family of small children, all of whom were in the house under the sole care of this young girl. As the local medical practitioner observed at the time, 'assuming that children were crying at different times in different rooms, a girl of fourteen who had charge of them could become demented'.[32] As it was, there was nothing simple about this case. Further inquiry into the archive revealed that a great deal lay behind this tragic impulsive moment.

It was an October evening in 1958, and Doreen had gone to the small Victorian house to babysit the family's five children, all of whom were below the age of six. The father of the household was at the pub, and the mother had gone to a friend's house to watch their family's newly-acquired television. Brinton was a small village in a coal-mining area. It had row upon row of ter-raced houses, and was the kind of place where everyone knew everyone else. The family of the dead child, the Smiths, lived in Lyndhurst Avenue, only streets away from the young babysitter's home.

In many respects, the accused girl had tried to do a reasonable job of looking after her charges. On the night of the murder, the children had all been put to bed in different rooms around the house. One of the little boys woke up and wanted to come into the living room. Then the newborn awoke, and Doreen picked her up and placed her next to her little brother on the settee while she attended to the other crying child, June. Doreen failed to quieten her, and in her own statement to the police she describes what then took place:

> I was cross with first one and then the other crying, and I
> went into the living room where I got Mr Smith's scarf off the
> sideboard. I took the scarf into June – she was still crying and
> I wrapped the scarf round June's neck and tied it in a knot …
> then I pulled it tight.[33]

This was the first case of child murder in which photographic evidence appears in the official records. They provide sickening images of the infant shortly after her death. The grubby, unkempt bedroom in which she lies is stark and cold-looking. As a final thought in her statement, Doreen said she did not intend to kill June: 'I did not mean to harm her, I only did it to stop her cry-ing.' The pressures of taking care of these children were obvious enough. While today societal disapproval might focus on the parents for leaving such young children alone, in the working-class neighbourhoods of the 1950s it was commonplace and not considered wrong. Besides, the murdered child's mother had reason to feel confident that her children were in safe hands. Doreen had sat for them on at least three previous occasions. She had also come to the house several times to help out just after the baby was born. In her evidence Mrs Smith said defiantly:

> I would not allow anyone to baby sit with my children, unless I had complete confidence in that person. Doreen appeared to be a nice girl and very fond of children. I was satisfied that when I was out she was looking after them well.[34]

The reasons why Doreen Russell killed her infant charge were not addressed at her trial. The only issue on which the court had to be satisfied was whether the girl was responsible or not. Under the Homicide Act (passed the previous year), under which this case was heard, a reduced verdict of manslaughter could be given on the grounds of diminished responsibility. If a defendant was proven to be suffering from some mental abnormality, it could qualify his or her degree of responsibility.[35] To assist in this, the opinion of a psychiatrist was called upon in court.

Dr Cuthbert was the physician-in-charge at St Luke's Hospital in Middlesbrough. He also had an interest in psychological medicine, and was part of a joint hospital team doing work in this area. His expertise on children, however, had been only lately acquired through work at the Sunderland Child Guidance Clinic.[36] Nevertheless, his investigation into Doreen's background and personality was thorough.

In his written report for the Home Office, Dr Cuthbert dispensed with the old criteria concerning disease of the mind, defined by the McNaughtan Rules in terms of cognitive function only. He stated clearly in his conclusions:

I am of the opinion that Doreen Russell did not suffer from a defect of reason due to disease of her mind at the time of the crime and that she did know the nature of her act and that it was wrong. She has admitted that she acted as she did with the intent to stop the child crying and she has attempted to avoid responsibility for her actions since her part in the death was detected.

Addressing the new legal concept of diminished responsibility, however, the psychiatrist concluded that the girl was suffering from an abnormality of the mind which impaired her responsibility for the crime. In other words, like the generations of psychiatrists before him who had appeared in the cases of William Allnutt and Margaret Messenger, Dr Cuthbert was essentially arguing that the child's condition was not one of delusion and did not affect her ability to reason; she knew what she was doing and that it was wrong. The condition he believed she was suffering from was characterised by an impairment of normal emotions, rather than of cognitive function. This opinion was given in court, whereas the doctor's seven-page deposition took a more succinct form. According to *The Times'* report of the case, after he gave his assessment of responsibility, he spoke only of the girl's slightly below-average intelligence and commented that she was, emotionally, 'a very disturbed child'.[37] The statutory classification of 'psychopathic personality', required under the 1957 Homicide Act in order for the offence to be reduced to manslaughter, was given in the psychiatric report. As an expert medical witness, Dr Cuthbert was required to be as specific in his presentation of evidence as he could. Therefore a definition of terms was unavoidable even if, as a specialist, he might be frustrated by the way the legal process forced him to express what were, in their full form, complex findings.

In the Home Office document containing his assessment, he indicated that Doreen displayed all the characteristics of 'an adult psychopathic criminal, [who] after the commission of some bestial crime will frequently behave as though nothing abnormal had occurred and may, for instance, go to a theatre or visit friends who can detect no signs of abnormality, tension, shock, or difference from normality'.

In his capacity as medical witness at the trial, he was only asked to assess the legal concept of responsibility and provide a condition that accounted for its loss, but the result of this limited process was to give the impression of a murder entirely without motive. Yet it is known from the case of Cyril Burt's young killer that a crime that appears motiveless at the time, or callous or unfeeling, can disguise a range of disturbances that lie well beyond the child's own conscious awareness. The resulting picture of Doreen Russell's crime was that she committed it for no reason other than the fact that she was suffering from an abnormality of the mind that was later diagnosed as psychopathic. While this may have been sound as a defence, it provided nothing by way of an explanation for the motive behind her actions.

The Psychopathic Diagnosis and its Problems for Children

'Psychopath' was a controversial diagnosis even for adults.[38] It was a term used in its modern sense in the criminal courts only after the end of the Second World War.[39] It was supposed to have a generic meaning that encompassed a range of antisocial behaviours that ranged from disruptive to dangerous, but it acquired a more specific and fixed meaning in a legal context. One of the unintended consequences of this, for children, was that the diagnosis of a psychopathic personality created the impression that the child was set on a developmental continuum of aggressiveness that led inexorably towards the dangerous actions of a murderer. To the untrained eye of a juror, the diagnosis could easily be seen not so much as a condition, but an identity.

However, it is now known from subsequent medical research that children of Doreen's age, in the words of a recent report by medical experts, 'are subject to maturation and significant change'.[40] The opinion of these experts, which included the veteran UK child psychiatrist Michael Rutter, suggested a need to avoid any analogy with adult diagnosis.[41] This was not only because it is misleading, but also because it can set in train an assumption that the child, years later, will still fulfil the criteria for such a diagnosis as an adult. An example of the instability of this diagnosis for children was also shown by the case of the notorious child murderer Mary Bell. One psychiatrist, who had labelled her psychopathic at the time of her trial, effectively overturned his opinion three years later when he recommended her for early release.[42]

However, to understand the crime that Doreen Russell had committed, as well as the limitations of seeing it through the legal process, the description – 'psychopathic personality' – need not be dispensed with entirely. Just because the concept had run into some difficulties, this did not suggest that it was meaningless. One 1950s doctor posited the existence of four different groups of psychopathic behaviour, and he sketched out what he considered their respective causes to be. The first consisted of those whose environment has been wholly negative, and as a result a habit of antisocial behaviour had gone unchallenged. The second group comprised those whose violent actions in some way compensated for unacknowledged feelings of weakness or anxiety, or, in others, unconscious but prohibitive sexual drives. The third group included those for whom no management or containment of their early desires and frustrations had ever taken place. And finally, the fourth group covered those whose early life had been so singularly defeating and confusing that they lacked the ability to change their patterns of destructive response.[43]

When Dr Cuthbert reflected in his report on the motives underlying Doreen's crime, his observations conformed to many of the elements in the categories above. The child's father had been psychopathic, and her early life was described as 'unstable and insecure'. There was an added factor of 'maternal rejection acting very powerfully in the development of anti-social characteristics based on feelings of hatred and despair'.[44]

These observations also fitted a more Freudian description of a psychopathic character, in that such a person was defined as having an 'immature, relatively primitive and undifferentiated personality structure'. In Dr Cuthbert's more prosaic description, Doreen's emotional development was 'immature', and she was 'shallow in her capacity to react with normal depth of feeling'. According to one Freudian account, the psychopathic child has:

> Poor object relationships, a high degree of narcissism, pre-dominance of pleasure principle over reality principle, disturbance in the capacity to bind tension or tolerate anxiety, little sublimation of impulse, impaired superego formation with little capacity for feelings of shame and guilt, and a pregenital libido organisation.[45]

This latter phrase, 'pregenital libido organisation', refers to what psychoanalysts argue is the period before the basic organisation of the superego takes place and the ground plan of personality is established, usually around the age of five or six. Practising psychiatrists like Dr Cuthbert may not have directly deployed the psychoanalytic model, but even he could not escape its influence as he surveyed the young life of Doreen Russell. He speculated in his report that her strangulation of the baby 'represented, perhaps symbolically, some deep disturbance'. By 'symbolic' he was referring to Doreen's representation of her unconscious wish to kill one of her own siblings. The evidence for this in her background is indeed striking.

Doreen had a brother who was two years older than herself, and there were signs that he had been violent towards her and she towards him. When she was six her sister Beryl was born, and according to Cuthbert it was at this time that 'serious evidence of emotional disturbance had begun to make its appearance'. A year later her violent and criminal father was killed in an accident, and her mother, an 'unemotional' woman, married again twelve months later. Immediately, she became pregnant, and when this baby was two years old, twins were born. Finally, in September 1958, a month before Doreen killed the child she was caring for, another baby was born to the Russell family. All of these intrusions proved devastating to a girl whose early life appeared to be one full of confusion and danger and where there was little love.

It was understood from the work of Freud, Klein and others that the violent emotions arising from sibling rivalry do not often result in death. But the few psychiatric specialists who worked in the field of violent children found that in severe family situations it could, and did, result in murder. By the end of the twentieth century, it was possible to make a common-sense observation about sibling rivalry in the context of child murder and for it to seem unsurprising, perhaps even banal. The author Blake Morrison, attending the trials of Robert Thompson and Jon Venables, who were accused of murdering young James Bulger in 1993, noted the difficult family circumstances of these killers and speculated that among the reasons they might have had for killing James was that he stood in as a 'surrogate for their loathing of their siblings'.[46]

When it came to Doreen's trial, Dr Cuthbert's brief reflection on the psychological motives for the murder may as well not have been made. They played no part in the legal role assigned to him; establishing motive was not his purpose, whereas verifying the presence of mental disease was. It was only this that had any bearing upon the child's responsibility for what she had done. Lawyers were satisfied that the fourteen-year-old was suffering from a mental abnormality, and the disorder that described this defect was a psychopathic one. But the circularity of this legal reasoning meant that any lay observer of the case simply saw a girl who had committed murder because she was psychopathic and therefore given to impulsive acts. Her condition was the explanation for the crime, because aggressive acts were a symptom of her abnormality. The legal process squeezed out psychological insights on a more involved level, and the categorical description of her as a psychopath marked its limits. Although society sought to hold this child responsible for murder, an act in itself an indication of serious disturbance, no knowledge of its complex causes was ever considered necessary.

Medical Evidence and the Outcome of Child Murder Cases

The court accepted Doreen Russell's plea of diminished responsibility. Given the pattern of verdicts for most of the cases considered in this book, her mental condition could just as easily have been irrelevant to her manslaughter conviction. Similarly, her sentence – she was sent to an approved school for an unspecified period – was entirely dependent upon the discretion and sympathy of the judge.[47] In the case of the eleven-year-old child murderer Mary Bell (the subject of the next chapter), the same verdict, given following the same diagnosis of psychopathic personality, resulted in a sentence of lifetime detention.[48] In the trial of the James Bulger killers, the two children responsible were found guilty of murder, and the judge proposed a minimum sentence of eight years 'for retribution and deterrence'. In an interview after this case was over, a juror commented that the legal process had been designed for adults on trial for murder, and that, as a result, it was far too restrictive to be able to deal properly with children: 'We should have gone back into court, and we should have said, "Yes, we do have a verdict: these boys are in urgent need of social and psychiatric help".'[49]

When the distinguished seventeenth-century jurist Sir Edward Coke made his comparison between the reasoning ability of a madman and that of a child over seven, its purpose was to qualify the legal responsibility of the former. In the nineteenth century, when scientific theories of madness began to have a more significant role in the legal system, the behaviour of children was used to describe the origins of mental incapacity in adults. Their diseased minds had led to attributes that were identifiable in children such as impulsivity, lack of willpower and poor self-control. The science at this time went further than simple analogy. Faulty heredity was the suspected cause and children, together with 'savages', were at the bottom of the evolutionary scale. Any failure in the mental processes of an adult was therefore attributed to a failure in the development of the species. In this history, children were not separate from adults with shattering disturbances of their own; they were simply the raw material for theories of adult mental illness.

While the findings of the mental sciences, such as they were, slowly began to be used for adults facing trial in the criminal courts, psychological evidence was almost meaningless for children on trial for murder.[50] As is evident from the cases explored above, and those in previous chapters, the manslaughter verdict was by far the most commonly used. The law of diminished responsibility, developed with adults and their mental problems in mind, did nothing to change a child's liability for murder. As for sentencing, Doreen Russell's commitment to an approved school indicates that the criminal law could be seen to adapt and be child-sensitive. Mr Justice Hinchcliffe told the jury: 'You can take it the girl will be well looked after.'[51] The moral sensibilities of the post-war world were attuned, even in a legal context, to the deprivations of some childhoods and to the value and welfare of these children.[52] But the legal process was still too blunt an instrument for dealing with children who had murdered. Such children had, by their extreme acts, demonstrated heightened vulnerability; they were not so much suffering from an illness as having experienced trauma. It was inappropriate that they should stand trial like adults and be assessed by the same criteria as mentally ill adults. The most up-to-date psychological insights into children's mental and moral capacities, together with the one truly indispensable tool of psychological assessment – a child's life history – were far too complex for the constraints imposed on them by law.

Despite the fact that criminal law could be seen to have limitations, if not failings, when dealing with cases of children who had killed, it could hardly be made responsible for ignoring suffering of which it had no knowledge. In the first half of the twentieth century awareness of the needs of vulnerable children grew, but the hidden horror of abuse within a family was not yet something that society could contemplate. The case of Mary Bell shows how events within the life of a violent youngster can only really be fully understood once history has provided the concepts through which to interpret them.

Chapter Nine

A SPECTRE OF EVIL –
THE ENDURING IMAGE OF
A CHILD WHO KILLS

*I felt as though the age of innocence had been lost forever. My emotions
were of horror but also of pity for her. I didn't feel the hatred her name
has since come to inspire.*[1]

Laurie Taylor

Mary Bell has an unenviable place in the British imagination. In
one twentieth-century chronicle, she is so notorious that she has
her own entry as the eleven-year-old girl sentenced to lifetime
detention for killing two little boys.[2] She had been an unremark-
able child – bright, pretty and playful – but she came to be known
as a beast among innocents. In the minds of many commentators, child murder began with Mary Bell. In subsequent reports
of child killing, she is mentioned as if the seed of such dangerous
behaviour was sown back then in the 1960s.[3]

   The events that led to these killings took place in a land-
scape that has since disappeared. In 1968, Scotswood to the
west of Newcastle was a network of streets ribboned by gloomy,
nineteenth-century terraced houses. The twin factories of Vickers
and Armstrong dominated the area overlooking the Tyne, and at
the foot of the valley slope ran the city's east-west railway line

where the children of the area often played. It was here, below the railway bridge on a scrub of waste ground, that the body of three-year-old Brian Howe was found that spring.

The rail line has since closed and the factories it once served, which in their heyday gave work to thousands, have shrunk, and are now just a tiny fraction of what they once were. The old houses came down in the 1970s in the final wave of post-war slum clearance. Yet it seems that the area never quite shook off its blighted image. By the 1990s many of the houses that had been built, some of them less than twenty years old, were also taken down because of the problems of crime and drug abuse. Scotswood, like other areas of the industrial north-east, became a neighbourhood untouched by prosperity, and it is only in recent years that the hopes of the community have been restored by the prospect of regeneration.

In May 1968, Scotswood's slum areas were still in evidence, and it was in one of these condemned houses that three young boys, who had been on the lookout for old timber to use for a pigeon pen they were building, found the body of a small boy lying on his back in front of a shattered window. It was four-year-old Martin Brown. There were no signs of violence on his body, and no indication that he had struggled with anyone. The coroner's investigation into his death concluded that he had died accidentally. Two months later, another dead child was found, this time on waste ground in the same area. There were scratch marks on three-year-old Brian Howe's neck, nose and scrotum. This time the pathologist concluded that the boy had died from strangulation, but not at the hands of an adult, as the pressure marks were too light. He also believed that the nature of the sharp marks on the body were indicative more of curiosity than of sadism as they were shallow, leading him to suggest that a child or children, rather than an adult, had been involved in the death.

A widespread investigation was launched, the largest of its kind, in which 1,200 local children between the ages of three and fifteen were questioned.

Recalling the atmosphere much later, Martin Brown's mother, June, described the neighbourhood as 'swarming with police … people were worried – really worried, specially everybody who had small children. We kept looking out for them, calling after them.' As the police narrowed the circle of interviewees, detectives called at the homes of Mary Bell and her thirteen-year-old friend and neighbour, Norma. Detective Constable Kerr described the older girl as 'peculiar'. He said: 'She was continually smiling as if it was a huge joke. Her mother kept saying, "didn't you hear what he asked? Answer the question."' He remarked that although the house was overcrowded, and this was not unusual, the impression he came away with was of a 'close and happy family'. He encountered very different circumstances when he called next door.

At 70 Whitehouse Road, Kerr said the atmosphere was cold, 'no feeling of a home, just a shell'. He remembered the barking of a big Alsatian dog, known in the area for its ferocity, but to its eleven-year-old owner, he was her beloved friend. The detective described Mary Bell as 'the most evasive child I'd ever come across. And her father was very odd. I asked him, "You be her father?" and he said, "No, I'm her uncle." "Where are her parents?" I asked, and he answered, "She's only got a mother and she's away on business." All the questions I asked her she was continually looking at him for guidance.' When he went back to the house four days later to check some irregularities in Mary's statement, she answered the door but wouldn't let him in; 'Me uncle's not in', she told him, and when he asked where he was, she said he was in the pub. He told her to go and fetch him. According to Kerr, when they returned, 'Billy Bell was very hostile … and Mary was continually looking at him. Of course, I believed he was her uncle

– I had no reason not to. And I had the feeling that this uncle was only passing through – you know, not living there. I got no further information from them that evening.'

Mary's friend Norma had grown anxious since her initial interview with the police. She wanted to tell the police everything she knew. The man in charge of the investigation, Chief Inspector Dobson, went to see her. He said: 'She was pale and nervous, her eyes darted from one of us to the other and there was this nervous smile that turned to tears at the drop of a hat.' With her father by her side, she told Inspector Dobson that Mary had taken her to the waste ground on the day the boy had gone missing. They were playing around and suddenly, 'I tripped over something. I looked down and saw it was Brian's head. He was covered with grass but I could see all his face. He was dead.' She said that Mary told her how he had got there: 'I squeezed his neck and pushed up his lungs, that's how you kill them. Keep your nose dry and don't tell anybody.' After the interview, Norma took her father and the inspector to the spot where she had seen the dead boy, and showed them where they could find a razor blade that she said Mary had used to mark his body: 'She showed me a razor and said she had cut his belly. She pulled his jersey up and showed me the tiny cut on his belly. She hid the razor under a block and told me not to tell my dad or she would get into trouble.'

Norma was taken to the remand wing of a council's children's home in Newcastle. Police called to Mary Bell's house later that same night. She was woken just after midnight and taken away for questioning, but after three hours of interrogation she was allowed to return home. The two girls continually contradicted each other's evidence, each trying to blame the other, and the police had difficulty untangling what had really happened. Further statements were taken from Norma, but it was not until the day of Brian Howe's funeral, 7 August, that Inspector Dobson decided to call Mary into the station once more. He had watched her on that hot summer's day as the cortege of over 200 people followed the little boy's coffin through the streets. He claimed that she stood there, 'laughing and rubbing her hands'.

In custody, without either her mother or father as neither could be found, Mary, accompanied by her aunt, eventually gave a lengthy statement in which she implicated Norma as the sole person responsible. They were both formally arrested, and Norma joined her friend at the main police station in the West End of Newcastle. They spent the night before their initial court hearing in two small rooms at the end of a tiny corridor. Two policewomen tried to settle the girls separately, but neither child could sleep. The constable in charge of Mary recalled her shouting angrily about her mother. 'She was wearing torn old shoes and kept on saying, "I told mom I needed new shoes ... I sent her a message. I just hope she'll get new ones to me. What will people think if they see me like this?"' When the constable tried to get her to go to sleep, she said she was frightened of wetting the bed, something she said she often did: 'I told her not to worry about it but she did – she kept going to the bathroom.'

Mary's mother, Betty, had never been like other mothers in the neighbourhood of Scotswood. She was often away from her home for months at a time. Both Mary and her brother were often put in the care of relatives – sometimes their aunt, sometimes their grandmother – but they were always taken back again by their mother. She could be emotional in one breath but violent and hostile in another. She managed to attend every day of her daughter's two-week trial, but her behaviour there was erratic; crying on occasion and then shouting at what was said about her child. While Norma's parents were a comforting presence behind their daughter, Mary kept herself distant from her mother, whose heavy makeup and dishevelled blonde wig seemed to belie a desire for the court's attention.

A 'Macabre and Grotesque' Trial

The Newcastle local paper described the trial that took place at the assizes on 5 December as 'one of the most remarkable murder cases ever to come before a British Court'. But the coverage had few of the hallmarks of subsequent cases like the one that followed the murder of James Bulger in 1993. Then, the lurid headlines were everywhere, though in part this was due to competitive pressures that had arrived in the wake of a communications revolution. The numbers of media outlets were burgeoning in the 1990s: satellite, cable and the advent of breakfast television all added to the intensity of that story's coverage. None the less, in a show of restraint that would be inconceivable today, the broadsheet newspapers of 1968 confined their coverage of the Bell trial to the first and last day of the proceedings, the Sunday tabloids gave it no attention at all, and the *Sun*, which had emerged in 1965 from the left-leaning *Daily Herald*, even refused an offer from Mary Bell's parents to sell the story of her life; its correspondent declared himself 'sickened' by their approach. BBC television also excluded the story from the main six o'clock bulletin out of paternalistic concern, reinforced by sensibilities of taste and decency, that innocent children enjoying healthy childhoods might be disturbed by the details of the story.

Yet, in spite of all this restraint, there were few in the UK and even beyond who had not heard about the two girls standing trial for murder and who, by the end at least, had not formed the unshakeable view that one of them in particular was a monster rather than a child. At the trial's outset, the tactic of the prosecution was to present Mary as the key player in each of the murders. Mr Rudolph Lyons QC did not go as far as to suggest that Norma was innocent (this would have been legally inappropriate), but he gave a clear indication to the court that she played only a minor role as an accessory. Although over two years older than her co-conspirator, Norma was medically classed as 'backward', and was deemed to be a girl with 'subnormal' intelligence. By contrast, Mary was not only clever beyond her years, but according to the Crown's counsel, she possessed supernatural cunning. Lyons told the court: 'In Mary you have a most abnormal child, aggressive, vicious, cruel, incapable of remorse, a girl moreover possessed of a dominating personality, with a somewhat unusual intelligence and a degree of cunning that is almost terrifying.'4

Norma Bell's defence counsel, Roderick Smith, also sought to separate the two children in the minds of the jury. Regarding Mary, he told the court: 'This little girl who may have struck you, when the trial began, as a singularly innocent fresh faced child … was the cleverer and more dominant personality.'5 The ensuing days brought an ever-deepening strain to the faces of both girls, but they showed their anxiety very differently. While Norma was in tears for most of her cross-examination, Mary went through her interrogation with focused concentration, but at night she needed to be watched over constantly as she rarely slept. Of the two girls who had once been joined in friendship, it was Mary who seemed most alone. Norma sought the reassurance of her mother and father but Mary, though also in need, received little compassion from the court and none at all from her mother

At the close of the nine-day trial, Mr Smith again drew a clear distinction between his client and that of Mary, 'whom one was tempted to describe as evil'. He began by saying that it was not his duty to 'blacken' Mary's character:

Although this is a ghastly case and although some of the evidence may have made you ill, it is possible to feel sorry for Mary. She had a bad start in life ... Her illness – psychopathic personality – is said to be the result of genetic and environmental factors. It's not her fault she grew up in this way; it's not her fault she was born ...[6]

The facts alone in this case were sufficiently disturbing, but the Crown's barrister, Mr Lyons, made his concluding argument for Mary's guilt in terms that went above and beyond the facts. He took the opportunity to summarise Mary's character as unremittingly cruel and terrifying. He said that she had 'wielded over Norma an evil and compelling influence reminiscent of a fictional Svengali'.[7] He could not have overlooked the fact that this would have an excitable effect on the imaginations of those gathered in the press gallery. After all, this had been more than an ordinary trial, it was a public spectacle – a chance for a young, intelligent lawyer to display rhetorical brilliance tempered by an appropriate solemnity. Addressing the court, he said: 'It has been a tortuous tunnel, has it not, that has led us through the grimmest and almost unfathomable recesses of juvenile thought, in which we have plumbed unprecedented depths of juvenile wickedness.'[8] He spoke of the network of lies that Mary had spun. The impression given was that her lies were of a uniquely different order to those of Norma, who had simply tried to get herself out of trouble. Mary, on the other hand, constructed elaborate stories and followed them consistently. He dwelt at some length on what he saw as the worst lie of all, the one he described as 'fiendishly cunning', in which she tried to blame Brian Howe's murder on the little lad's playmate: 'One shudders to think of what might have happened to that eight-year-old boy if he had been in the area that afternoon instead of being, by happy chance, with other people six miles away at Newcastle Airport.'

The trial concluded on the ninth day – a bitterly cold December morning. The judge, Sir Ralph Cusack, took four hours to make his summary and the jury took a further three to reach their verdicts. When they returned to court, the press and public galleries were full to capacity. Norma and Mary were allowed to remain seated and told to listen quietly. The assize clerk waited for silence before asking the foreman if they were agreed on their verdicts, to which the reply was yes. He then asked:

'On the first count of murder do you find Norma Bell guilty or not guilty of the murder of Martin Brown?'
'Not guilty.'
'Do you find her guilty or not guilty of manslaughter?'
'Not guilty.'

At this, Norma let out an excited cry and turned to her parents. Her father gently indicated for her to turn around and remain seated.

A guilty verdict on both counts was read for Mary, but for manslaughter rather than murder, on the grounds of diminished responsibility. Doctors at the trial had declared her a psychopath. The relief of Norma's parents was palpable, while Mary's mother, Betty, appeared too immersed in her own tears to comfort her sobbing child.

Throughout the trial, the prosecutor, though unnecessarily sensational in his choice of language, had nonetheless touched upon an aspect of Mary's behaviour that was puzzling, if not sinister. This was her extraordinary persistence in maintaining her innocence despite overwhelming evidence to the contrary. Mr Lyon's speech and the medical opinion that Mary was a

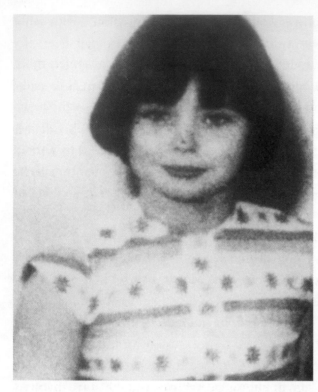

7. Mary Bell at the time of her trial, in 1968 © Hulton Archive/Getty Images.

psychopath did little to help anyone to understand why she did this. In fact, they only sought to portray her nature as inherently wicked. Yet Mary's deceit obviously had a purpose other than that of wanting to escape punishment. She knew that it was likely she would be found guilty of killing the boys, so what were her lies seeking to conceal?

Secrecy and Lies

Mary was an accomplished liar; that much became clear during the trial. It appears to have been something she had been habituated to throughout her life. More than likely, her noted cleverness had developed through this habit of dissimulation. From what has since been written about this case, we know that from the time she was a small child, Mary Bell had been taught to lie in accordance with her mother's wishes. She gained small gestures of approval for this, and for presenting an appearance to the world that concealed the true nature of her mother's behaviour towards her. In the inverted morality of their relationship, Mary's duty was to keep the secret about who and what her mother really was. It was a sad demonstration of faithfulness to her adored parent.

Guile was Mary's *modus operandi*; it was natural for her to protect herself, and more importantly her mother, through lies. Many years later, as an adult, Mary recalled that one of the things she remembered fearing most at the trial was that it would become known that her mother was a prostitute. 'That was the most frightening thing of all to me … that meant something to me, you see, everything else really didn't.'[9] In 1968 her lies were assumed to be a sign of her warped nature, and the more involved her lies were, the deeper her depravity was believed to be. Even the few psychiatrists who had an opportunity to interview Bell saw nothing by way of recognition of or feeling for what she had done.[10] In the words of one psychiatric witness at the trial, Mary was 'a manipulator … her social techniques take the form of automatic denial, bullying or violence'.[11]

Yet, according to the most thorough investigation of this case, carried out by the writer Gitta Sereny, most of what the well-intentioned medical profession said about Mary at the time was based mainly on their prior experience or intuition, because in doctors' interviews with her, they met a stubborn resistance to disclose anything.[12] They were not to know that Mary's mother had instilled a fear of psychiatrists in her child, that Betty Bell had sworn the whole family to secrecy, or that that any prying individual – be they psychiatrist, journalist or welfare officer – had to be treated with suspicion because they might unravel the lies that Mary's mother had involved her in.[13] Even when Sereny's *The Case of Mary Bell* was published, almost three years after the trial, it was impossible for anyone to know the extent of the experiences that Mary's lies concealed.

Sereny's was the most widespread and in-depth investigation of Mary's background that anyone had undertaken, but the facts that she uncovered were only the surface of what would later be disclosed as depths of terrifying depravity. No one in 1968 was equipped to detect the possible signs. As Sereny remarked some years later, 'troubled children were not yet in vogue'.[14] She was partly right, although in 1968 the Labour government did produce a number of discussion papers on the subject, one of which was entitled 'Children in Trouble'. It was supposed to address the problems of vulnerable children, but its emphasis was on how to protect society from children who were troublesome, rather than on the needs of those children who were in danger.[15] Psychologists of the 1960s were more aware of disturbances in children, but they regarded these 'troubled' souls as not unlike other children who encounter stresses in life, but are fortunate to have the right parents or resources to help them cope. In a comprehensive book on the subject of emotional disturbances in children published in 1969, cruelty towards, or sexual abuse of, children by family members received no attention.[16] The principle reason for this was that history had not yet revealed the widespread phenomenon of child sexual abuse.

Society's Late Discovery

It has been suggested that the phrase 'child abuse' was hardly in use before 1960, although sexual offences against children do have a much longer history than this implies.[17] A handful of such cases came before the Surrey assizes in the 1760s, for example, and they were successfully prosecuted, but many more allegations of this kind never came to trial because of the difficulties associated with a child's status as a witness, as mentioned in chapter 1.[18] It was only in the second half of the twentieth century that the term 'child abuse' began to encompass something more than a beating from a parent or stranger.[19] The most important historical influence that contributed to this change came from the women's movement.

The feminist movement of the 1970s and 1980s widened the understanding of child abuse.[20] Previously, the emphasis had been on the 'battered child', which American paediatricians had identified in their clinics in the 1940s. A disturbing number of small children, sometimes babies, were being brought in with scars from poorly healed fractures to their legs and arms. But it was not until 1955 that two doctors at Colorado University, Harry Kempe and his colleague Ray Helfer, dared to propose that this pattern of violence might be attributable to parental behaviour. Professional colleagues at the time urged caution because of the value judgements involved – it was, after all, difficult to prove – and the legal liabilities that might arise from too strong a suggestion that parents were indeed responsible for inflicting wounds on their own children. Eventually, however, awareness of what came to be called 'battered child syndrome' became more widespread, and grew across a range of sectors involved in the protection of children.

In Britain, campaigning work took off under the auspices of the National Society for the Prevention of Cruelty to Children. Their Battered Child Research Unit undertook groundbreaking work on child protection, as well as shaping the way in which the problem was perceived. The organisation interpreted signs of child abuse as a cry for help from a disturbed and dysfunctional family. The protection of the child was seen as paramount, and the view was taken that this was best achieved as part of a general plan of 'rehabilitation for the whole family'.[21]

The importance of the family and its favourable functioning was highlighted by the work of the post-war psychiatrist John Bowlby. His views on maternal deprivation and the value of securing close, nurturing bonds between mother and child for the latter's healthy development were enormously influential.[22] In 1951, his World Health Organisation report on children who had been left homeless after the war focused research and discussion on the role of maternal deprivation in producing psychiatric disturbances in children.[23] The study, developed and published as *Child Care and the Growth of Love*, proved significant, not least because it assisted the British government's agenda for the post-war reconstruction of the family.[24] Bowlby's work was also significant for the developing areas of social work and criminology. In 1961, a former chief of Scotland Yard cited the work of Dr Bowlby, and his theories of 'emotional development', to argue that good mothering or the absence thereof could be a deciding factor in causing crime.[25] However, the problems with the orthodoxy of the 'good' family approach, particularly for cases of sexual abuse, was that it focused policy on the family unit not, as one group of social workers put it, 'in order to expose problematic sexual behaviour, but in order to enshrine "normal" family relationships'.[26] The problem with Mary Bell's family, and as it turned out many others, was that although it may have appeared to the outside world as normal, it concealed unmentionable horrors and cruelty.

In the late 1970s, feminist commentators removed what they called a 'curtain of impunity' surrounding the sacred institution of the family to reveal the overwhelming evidence that child sexual abuse was more widespread than society had ever acknowledged, and that it was something that took place *within* the family.[27] Moreover, they demonstrated that it was a gendered practice, in that it was perpetrated mainly by fathers or other male relatives, and mainly upon girl children.[28]

The painful and terrifying events experienced by abused children could only be identified as 'child sex abuse' after the social and political 'consciousness-raising' produced by twentieth-century feminism.[29] The campaigns and insights of that movement created a sympathetic climate in which these stories could be heard, and the involvement of feminists in social services and parts of the criminal justice system changed the thinking about these crimes, so that abuse within the family, especially sexual abuse, became a legitimate focus of public outrage and condemnation.

As the feminist writer Beatrix Campbell has suggested, the detection of child sexual abuse was dependent upon a shared knowledge and understanding of what it is and why it is important:

If you don't believe it is possible for children to be sexually abused ... then you don't see the signs, even when they stare you in the face ... Detection is always contingent. It depends on co-operation and a consensus about what matters, what is wrong, what hurts, what is visible and what is knowable.[30]

There were signs that something was seriously wrong in Mary Bell's life, but without the knowledge to interpret these signals, they appeared meaningless and insignificant. Examples of Mary's extreme disturbance were not considered remarkable enough for comment. Even on the few occasions where her behaviour did draw the attention of those in charge of her, it never merited further official scrutiny.

First, there were the small signs of Mary's propensity to seek punishment.[31] According to Freud, certain criminals commit their crime out of a sense of pre-existing guilt. In a brief essay on the subject he observed that some patients engaged in criminal acts because it brought them mental relief, as the patient already suffered consciously or unconsciously from a heavy burden of guilt.[32] Taking this view, it is possible to see that although Mary lied about her crime, and determinedly claimed her innocence, this was not in itself an indication that she was incapable of guilt. The psychoanalyst Melanie Klein believed that the criminal child does not lack a conscience, 'but rather, has too cruel a conscience – an unmodified early superego which operates differently from normal children and drives him to crime by pressure of fear and guilt'.[33] When the matron at her remand home observed in Mary a desire to seek punishment, she was perhaps noticing the child's need to purge herself of some bad feelings, as if by inviting a beating she was seeking the punishment she felt she deserved. She was, after all, indifferent to her own penalty for the crimes she had committed, she didn't care, and she knew that she would be found guilty. By committing the worst crime imaginable, and bringing the worst punishment upon herself, she was, as Freud might have put it, 'setting [her] sense of guilt to rest'.[34] The day before the jury was to return their verdict, she asked the police-woman watching over her, 'What would be the worst thing that could happen to me? Will they hang me?' Then, over twenty years later, from her recollections of that time, she said:

In court, while they were talking and talking, I remember
thinking of what I would say when it was my turn. I'd tell them
I wanted my dog. I wanted him with me when they sent me
to be hanged. That's what I thought would happen: I'd be sent
away to the gallows and they might just as well have said that
right away because it was just as meaningless as life imprisonment or ... well ... death. None of it meant a damned thing,
not a thing ...[35]

There were other signs of the eleven-year-old's perturbed mind
that were noticed but not acted upon. Fourteen policewomen
were responsible for Mary while she was on remand; they
guarded her round the clock in eight-hour shifts. Each of these
women observed behaviour in her that was so unusual that they
submitted formal reports to their superiors. But, one of them
said later, 'it was just as if nobody wanted to know'. Another said:
'Nobody ever asked us questions about her, nothing about what
she said or what we thought or noticed.'[36] They remarked on
Mary's compulsion for personal cleanliness – she wanted baths
at all hours of the day and night, and she would ask for them
in a sudden, agitated manner. More than half a century earlier,
Freud had attributed the symptoms of obsessional neurosis such
as this to the displacement of the partially forgotten trauma of
'seduction'.[37] No connections of this kind were made at any time,
either before or after Mary's trial.

Similarly, Mary's precocious sexuality would almost certainly
be seen today as a warning sign of possible sexual abuse. Most
specialists now recognise that the abuse of a small child with no
fully formed boundaries of his or her own induces identification
with the behaviour of the abuser. From this perspective it is possible to see that Mary did not just want to protect her mother,
but that she *was* her mother, and as such she wanted to inflict

the same punishments on others who were even more defence-less than she.[38] The continuing murderous rage that was identi-fied before and after the killings was, curiously, never perceived as evidence of her profound and persisting disturbance.[39] Her attempt to strangle a cat, along with comments such as 'I'd like to be a nurse … because then I can stick needles into people. I like hurting people', were mostly seen as proof of her monstrous nature, rather than an indication of the heinous experiences that she had endured. As Sereny pointed out, if only the things that had been observed about Mary's behaviour had been 'accorded the importance they deserved', they might have played a part in 'helping the people who later had to decide her fate'.[40] However, this kind of acknowledgement and awareness was not simply absent by accident (as Sereny implies), but it was almost impos-sible without shared public knowledge of the existence of child sexual abuse.

While this recognition had come by the 1980s and played its part in Mary's understanding of her own experience – she read books on the subject while she was in Styal prison – her disclosures were all the more difficult to admit because of the intimate role that her mother had played in her damaged child-hood. The women's movement focused attention on the fact that men perpetrated most sexual abuse, and indeed they had in Mary Bell's case, but with the devastating complicity of her mother.[41]

The Ultimate Taboo

In *Criminal Tendencies in Normal Children*, Melanie Klein argued: 'It is evident that the deepest repressions are those which are directed against the most unsocial tendencies.'[42] The fact that a child could repress an experience of severe abuse, and that it could emerge as a memory many years later, became one of the most controversial theories of twentieth-century psychology. Mary Bell's revelations about her own childhood came amid the maelstrom of conflicting opinion about so-called recovered memory, and the effects of this are considered later on in this chapter. However, Freudian theory, for all its shortcomings, did provide a framework by which one might understand just how a child's mind would seek to defend itself not only from physical and emotional threats, but also from an overwhelming sense of personal shame.

Mary Bell's humiliations began the day she was born. 'Take her away from me', Betty Bell screamed when she was handed her newborn infant, and while the pathological feelings continued, evinced by threats on Mary's life, a much more painful set of experiences were still in store. From the time when Mary was four years old, Betty, an alcoholic prostitute, subjected her child to sexual abuse by her clients in which she also played her part. Mary related these experiences, 30 years later, to her biographer, Gitta Sereny. Coming very late in the course of their three-year interviews, they were told by Mary in a 'monotonous voice but more often in deep distress, her face growing paler and paler, breaking into a sweat, and finally, she would speak through desperate sobs, reverting at times, as she had done before under extreme emotional pressure, to the present tense'.[43]

The power that Mary Bell's mother had over her daughter was, in one sense, protected by the idealisation that society confers upon motherhood; it was inconceivable that a mother could be capable of inflicting such physical and psychological wounds upon her own child. In 1968, when it was more culturally acceptable, mothers smacked their children fairly routinely – they may even have resented their children's existence at times, fairly understandably, but Betty Bell's behaviour went beyond such careless misuse of motherly power. Unlike other mothers, she never redeemed herself by giving love and protection to her child. She was never capable, having had her own share of emotional disturbances that no one ever got to the bottom of. Whatever her story, as an adult she managed to get her daughter to keep the secrets of their life together, and it was a process that involved primitive defences on Mary's part as well as extensive and persisting denial.

There is no standard of causation to prove incontrovertibly that Betty Bell's abuse of her child was the direct cause of Mary's killing of the two little boys in that summer of 1968, but it does seem sensible to look in that direction. A change in Mary began when she told her mother that she no longer wanted to do the things that were being asked of her. She was about seven years old, and it was when she began to take refuge in the friendship of an adult outside the family that she appeared to gain some confidence, enough to challenge her mother.

Harry Bury was a rag-and-bone man who lived above the Bells. He was appalled when he woke one morning and found Mary unzipping his trousers, trying to get his penis out. He shouted, 'What the hell are you doing?' but then, seeing her startled, he reassured her and awkwardly changed the subject, saying, 'Let's go and have a cup of tea and feed the cat.' From this point on, it appears that young Mary adopted the gentle figure of Harry Bury as her new protector, and she followed him around everywhere helping him with his collections in the district. It was also around this time that an intense hatred began to take hold of Mary, a monstrous anger that developed and which she became desperate to discharge. She began to show signs of extreme violence and cruelty towards other children.[44] On these occasions the violence did not prove fatal, but the last such incident took place shortly before the first murder.

As an adult, Mary was asked if her rage towards her mother was in her mind at the time of the murders. In other words, had she killed because of the things done to her? She answered with an emphatic 'no'. Yet, as a child, there was a clear sign that she had believed that her guilt rightfully belonged with her mother. In an extract from a poem written for her mother, published in the *Sun* newspaper in 1972, Mary writes:

> ... I know you think I'm Bad so Bad.
> Please mom put my tiny Mind at ease,
> Tell judge and jury on your
> Knees,
> They will listen to your cry,
> of pleas.
> The guilty one is you not
> Me.[45]

The shocking details of what Mary Bell's mother made her do as a small child came to light two-and-a-half decades after this poem was published. Public acknowledgement that this kind of thing happened in some families had been slow to arrive, but it did eventually take form. Its shattering effects, however, were easily construed as inconsequential when confronted by a murdering child.

Forever Evil – Public Responses to Mary Bell's Disclosures of Sexual Abuse

In 1996, when so much more was known about children at risk, Mary Bell, aged 39, began a collaboration with Gitta Sereny on a book about her life which was published as *Cries Unheard: The*

Story of Mary Bell.[46] But if Mary thought the time was right for people to receive her story sympathetically, she could not have been more mistaken. The book sold over a million copies and was immediately mired in controversy. It contained her account of the sexual abuse that had remained absent from the records of her crime for nearly 30 years. However, the reception given to the book's revelations was overwhelmingly unsympathetic.[47] The evidence that such abuse had been present in Mary Bell's young life was treated with widespread doubt and suspicion. Her sympathetic biographer Sereny was cast as the fool, duped by the adult manifestation of a manipulative child.[48] Critics believed that Bell had made up her claims of sexual abuse, suggesting that she did this in order to receive an empathetic account of herself 'as a victim turned killer by abuse she suffered at home'.[49] Where commentators did grudgingly concede that abuse may have occurred, its meaning, remarkably, was detached from the crimes she had committed as if it was an event unconnected to the intimate tragedy of her life. Why did her disclosures invite so much hostility and disbelief?

The suspicion about her revelations of sexual abuse in particular was articulated on a range of grounds, but at each turn in every public argument there was condemnation. There was an eccentric view, put forward by a 'leading criminologist', that had Mary not been a 'naturally dominant' child who was always clamouring for attention, she might have responded to her home life by being ordinarily 'miserable and neurotic'.[50] The fact that Mary had not, in this sense, become a victim of her own experiences was sufficient reason to mark her out as 'evil'. The conclusion given by this 'expert' was that, if Mary Bell's parents had 'tanned her backside', the murders 'would never have happened'.[51] The peculiarity of such reasoning is easy to dismiss, but to do so overlooks the influential role it had on public opinion. One respondent to the article agreed that lax discipline was the main element at fault in Mary Bell's life:

> We are told by experts not to smack our children, to reason with them and to explain why what they're doing is naughty and unacceptable ... This form of punishment worked in the Sixties when I was at school ... I say bring back the cane, and most of the problems we have today would disappear.[52]

A different kind of incredulity about Mary Bell's early life was expressed by a group of men and women who gathered for a television debate on the publication of *Cries Unheard*. The programme was *Kilroy*, a triumph of populist current affairs television that assembled experts and members of the public in a studio for a gladiatorial debate. Among the participants was Paul Cavadino, at that time chair of the Penal Affairs Consortium, and clerk to the Parliamentary Cross-Party Penal Affairs Group. He made a valiant attempt to argue that most children involved in murder 'do, typically, have a history of abuse, emotional neglect or trauma in their own childhood'. But two women who said that they had been abused as children, but had not killed anyone, cut him down, insisting that their abuse had not affected their ability as children to distinguish between right and wrong.[53]

There are myriad reasons why the experience of these women might have been so, but one reason is surely to do with the historical change in the attitudes towards and treatment of abused children. One of the women making the challenge did say that after she disclosed her abuse, she received 'excellent counselling which was a big part of why I turned out the way I did'.[54] Mary Bell, on the other hand, had no psychiatric treatment or counselling. After the trial verdict, the judge and medical professionals had wanted to send her to a hospital for treatment, but there were none set up to accommodate such a young child. So, she spent the first six years of her sentence in a special unit of an approved school for boys. Twenty years after the Bell murders, a twelve-year-old boy who had suffocated a two-year-old girl was sent to a specialised youth treatment centre on the edge of London, where he underwent an intensive programme of psychotherapy.[55] One psychiatrist at the time said: 'My guess is that this child does not suffer from a psychiatric disorder. His behaviour is probably related to his upbringing and I would guess that his childhood was a lot worse than we have heard.'[56]

The editorial aim of this particular *Kilroy* broadcast appeared to be to reverse the balance of sympathy that might accrue to the Bell revelations. It was apparent from the chosen audience that they believed 'society' was giving too much attention to the plight of criminals, and not enough to the suffering of the victims. Victims and ex-criminals were gathered, ostensibly to confront each other over the issue of whether offenders should profit from their crimes. (Much of the controversy over the Sereny book was that she had paid Mary Bell for her participation.) Instead, all that was really on show were the open emotions of those whose worlds had been overturned by violent crime. Not all were victims in the commonly understood sense; for example, some had sons who were serving time for murder, but even they, together with the ex-criminals, courted the role of victim. Yet part of their contempt for Mary Bell was based upon the view that she was trying to masquerade as the injured party in the story of her life.[57]

Political Populism and the Judgement of
a Government in Waiting

In the late 1990s, the victim of crime received a centre-stage role in politics. After eighteen years of opposition, New Labour used crime as an issue from which to claim ground from the Tories.[58] Prime Minister John Major had already used the killing of two-year-old James Bulger by two young boys to make a speech in 1993 in which he said: 'Society needs to condemn a little more and understand a little less.'[59] As shadow home secretary, Tony Blair also responded to the disturbing events of the Bulger killing. In a widely-reported speech, Blair said: 'The news bulletins of the last week have been like hammer blows struck against the sleeping conscience of the country ...'[60]

He spoke to the sense of alarm that this child killing had generated, and he wove his rhetoric around wider anxieties about family values and moral crisis: 'If we do not learn and then teach the value of what is right and what is wrong, then the result is simply moral chaos which engulfs us all.'[61] In 1998, a year after Blair's election as prime minister, he intervened in the Bell controversy over the publication of Gitta Sereny's book. He condemned Mary Bell for taking part and receiving money for the book about her life: 'I think it is wrong for anyone to make money out of the most heinous and horrible crimes.'[62] The fact that Bell only received a small fee, and certainly not the £50,000 figure circulated by the tabloids, was irrelevant to the purpose of Labour's political discourse on crime.[63] The home secretary, Jack Straw, joined the denunciation, and in a perfectly contrived populist gesture he wrote to the mother of one of Bell's victims and published the letter in the *Sun*. In this public act of identification ('the Prime Minister and I understand and share the anger and frustration which you feel'),[64] Mary Bell received the full weight of government indignation. It was as if she had not paid the price for her crimes, had not served her time, and not been successfully rehabilitated.

The political instincts of New Labour were well placed; they received praise from the conservative *Daily Mail* who declared that the prime minister 'spoke for the whole nation'.[65] What a contrast this was to political opinion on Mary Bell in 1969. Then, the Labour home secretary Jim Callaghan was asked in the House of Commons if measures could be taken to prevent publicising Mary Bell's place of detention, to which he replied, 'I have much sympathy with this proposal', and expressed confidence that the media could be relied upon to show restraint.[66] Similarly, in 1972, when the BBC made incorrect allegations that Mary Bell was being allowed to take 'improper photographs' at the approved school where she was detained, the Conservative home secretary Sir Keith Joseph, who was not known for liberalism, condemned the coverage as untrue and argued that 'continuing comment and publicity about this girl is damaging to her'.[67]

Cries Unheard was published in a political climate that was marked by New Labour's desire for renewal. The leadership wanted to see the party break away from its collectivist traditions and focus instead on the importance of the individual. This involved bringing a specifically moral dimension to politics, with an emphasis on the ethics of personal responsibility.[68] New Labour wanted to be tough on criminals, and sympathetic towards their victims. A Manichean language, in which human beings were either 'good or bad', enhanced the status of the victim by placing him or her on the correct side of the moral boundary between right and wrong.[69] In the Bell controversy, the government had similarly left the public in no doubt about which side it was on. Both government and public sympathy was conditional, and it depended upon a clear identity of honest vulnerability;

however, Mary Bell's story was a lot murkier than this, and she eschewed any claim to victimhood. After all, the moral elevation upon which this identity was based would have been indelicate, if not preposterous, in this context. The real purpose of Mary Bell's story was not to convince a doubting public that she was a human being whose personality had been traumatised by a sadistic mother. Neither was it to do with money.[70] It was to answer her own poignant question: 'How did I become such a child?'[71] For many of Mary Bell's detractors, it was the very public means by which she chose to answer this question that became the focus of their rejection.

Popular Misconceptions and 'Informed' Opinion

Cries Unheard is not only a personal story, but also a process of historical interpretation. In it, Bell searches her past to try to make sense of the childhood she experienced. Unlike the modern therapeutic encounter, her conversations with Sereny were not those of an adult seeking to find the source of her grown-up troubles in her childhood; their purpose was to answer Bell's question to herself about how she became a child who had killed two little boys. Yet it was precisely this process of self-interrogation that formed the basis of further public dismissal of her story. Opinion-formers of a liberal persuasion took the unusual step of going further in their condemnation of her than the populist voices from which they were generally keen to distance themselves.[72] A major area of cultural controversy at this time revolved around the politics of memory as it related to the growing number of disclosures of child abuse. These influential commentators could not help but interpret the contents of Mary Bell's history in the light of this debate about memory.[73]

Important questions were raised about the validity of child sexual abuse claims in the 1990s. This issue had been partially stirred by the Cleveland scandal in 1987, in which 165 children had been taken from their homes because of suspected sexual abuse. The heart of this controversy was the medical diagnosis of doctors, which was later challenged by a coalition of parents and politicians.[74] These confusing events were the subject of an official inquiry.[75] Its conclusions focused only on the operation of statutory authorities, and are therefore not pertinent to the discussion here. But the scandal confronted Britain with a crisis; how was it possible to verify an allegation of child abuse? The Cleveland inquiry had brought the diagnostic techniques of doctors under scrutiny, but the controversy had wider reverberations for adults who had spoken out about their own recollections of abuse. Initially, popular commentators and some therapists assumed that revelations of childhood trauma were straightforwardly recalled by memory, as if the events of the past stood in a direct relationship to the mind's ability to recall it.[76] However, the evasions of memory were, as scientists demonstrated, more complex and persistent than that.[77]

Throughout *Cries Unheard*, Mary Bell viewed the events of 1968 through the prism of her older self. In the final part of the book, the non-violent adult revealed an understanding of her past through the experiences of having been an abused child, and, in so doing, strayed unwittingly into the controversial area of 'recovered memory'. The idea that an adult could repress memories of a childhood trauma and then recall it much later through memory and/or therapeutic intervention was beginning to be challenged by a number of scientists in the 1990s. The renowned cognitive psychologist Stuart Sutherland argued that the whole idea of 'repressed' or 'recovered' memory 'defies everything that is known about memory and trauma'.[78] The British Psychological Society took the opposite view and, in a special report on the issue, confirmed their belief in the 'accuracy of recovered memory of child sexual abuse'.[79]

This was fiercely contested ground, in which one side of the argument was used by conservative opinion to argue that politically motivated feminists and misguided therapists were exaggerating the extent of child sexual abuse.[80] There was also a suspicion that clients of medical specialists could manipulate doctors and counsellors with invented stories about their childhood. The media psychiatrist Dr Raj Persaud believed that Mary Bell was doing precisely this; that she was creating a history of abuse as a tactic to gain the sympathy of her confidante, Gitta Sereny. In an article entitled 'The Manipulator', Persaud writes:

> Mary Bell's outpourings appear to be a common rationalisation that disturbed criminals make to justify their actions. Although they claim to reveal all, they are a classic way of failing to take responsibility. And for someone as manipulative as Bell her choice of medium – journalist Gitta Sereny – is a perfect means of getting her own way.[81]

Dr Persaud had overlooked the fact that Bell had taken full responsibility for her crime, and paid for it through her punishment. Neither could he have read the full details of Mary Bell's experiences, as the book was not published until a month after his article appeared (although extracts had been serialised in *The Times*). He was not the only psychiatrist to issue condemnation before the book was published, but his opinion was by far the most influential.[82] As a consultant psychiatrist at the Maudsley, one of the UK's leading psychiatric hospitals, his position counted for something in the debate over Mary Bell's story. By lending his authority to the view that she was manipulating her biographer, he gave voice to the unformed suspicions of others. Yet his commentary betrays scant knowledge of the scientific discussion about the nature of memory. Those who question, though do not necessarily entirely disbelieve, 'recovered memory' tend to do so on the grounds that the nature of memory is uncertain and fragmentary. But it is precisely this uncertainty that Persaud picks up on in his attack on Mary Bell. He criticises her vagueness: 'She cannot even give a rough approximation of how often the abuse occurred ... she side-steps the question of exactly what form it took, and instead prefers to hint, allowing our imaginations to do the rest.'[83]

Whatever their position in the false memory debate, most scientists concur that memories do not simply reflect back external events unchanged. Yet in Dr Persaud's criticisms of Mary Bell's disclosures, the fact that they do not is grounds for his belief that she is telling lies. He concludes that only 'an experienced clinician' who could 'question her properly' could ascertain the 'real truth'. Persaud's model of memory was not one shared by most other contemporary scientists.[84] It was based on an outdated mechanistic idea that memory is like a storage system analogous to a computer or filing cabinet; it just has to be opened for the truth to be retrieved.[85] Cognitive psychology had moved beyond the more mechanical version of this model long before Dr Persaud took up his pen to attack Mary Bell. In the early 1990s psychologists, even those who still favoured the technical or 'computer' model of memory, recognised the incomplete nature of memory and the indeterminate process of recollection. The cognitive researcher Endel Tulving argued, in an interview in 1991, that it was not the storage model of memory that was the problem for his discipline, but establishing the processes of recall.[86] Some research suggested

that if certain experiences were not talked about they were more
likely to be forgotten,[87] while the experimental psychologist
Elizabeth Loftus argued that adults do not forget traumatic experiences such as child abuse, but they may have periods when they
do not recall them.[88] In a comprehensive overview of research
in this area published in 1997 by Martin Conway, professor of
Cognitive Psychology at Leeds University, the conclusion was:

> Some recovered memories may be essentially accurate, some
> may be largely inaccurate, but nonetheless partially based on
> experiences of the individuals other than actual abuse (for
> example, imagined abuse, or situations involving emotional
> abuse), and still others wholly inaccurate.[89]

For some commentators in the controversy over Mary Bell, it was
this uncertainty that appeared to drive them towards a choice
between the less complicated positions of 'truth' or 'invention'.
On a BBC radio programme, two female journalists criticised the
author Gitta Sereny for abandoning her 'disinterested' position as
a journalist, and suggested that she had become too fascinated by
Mary Bell and was therefore unable 'to know what the truth is'.
Having disagreed with their fellow participant (the writer Blake
Morrison, who argued that Sereny had 'gone as far as anyone can'
to get to what happened), one of the women remarked: 'Didn't
you find that it is rather neat that there was recovered memory
when that is so much the zeitgeist?' In quick assent, the other
woman pointed to the ubiquitous role that abuse could be put to
in the troubles of modern life: 'If I committed any kind of crime
– from joy-riding to killing someone – I'd say I'd been abused as
a child because now this is seen as the most mitigating.'[90]

Sereny had never claimed that her book had uncovered the
'truth' about Mary Bell: 'I'm not sure in this case that you can

know what the truth is.'[91] This did not make her any less rigorous in her search. This aside, however, and assuming that Bell was indeed weaving a web of deceit, her motivation would surely have had more significance than simply a desire to be part of the zeitgeist. Oddly, for all their truth-searching, these commentators make no reflection on Bell's possible reasons for inventing a sadistic mother. If they had, they would have found little reason. Clearly, Bell's revelations were not made to exonerate herself from the enormity of her crimes. She had served a twelve-year sentence, so the idea that she invented her abuse as a means to avoid judicial sanction could easily be set aside. Was she perhaps merely courting the good opinion of the public? Considerations about the public response to the book, though important, were not uppermost in her mind. Neither was money. She received only a small proportion of the advance given to Sereny for the book. On numerous previous occasions she had been offered six-figure sums for her story, and had turned each one of them down.[92] Of course, it is possible that her revelations could have been created as an explanation for her crimes, but what purpose would this have served if she really knew it to be untrue?

For all their appearance of reason, the opinions cited above rest on nothing more than a borrowed belief about Mary Bell that had haunted her for nearly 30 years. This belief was first inscribed on the popular consciousness at her trial in 1968, and it was that she was evil, dangerous and manipulative. There is nothing in *Cries Unheard* to suggest that Sereny took anything about her interviewee at face value. What she did was try to establish the meaning of those children's deaths and avoid drawing any absolute conclusions. Methodologically, the book is sound. Sereny meticulously scrutinised the available evidence, checking it against hospital records (where they exist), and cross-checking with remarks that had been made years previously to other authorities. Her research gives a definite enough picture of Mary Bell's past for it to be convincing. The early history of this child killer is of course indeterminate, because it has been recalled through the unreliable process of memory, but there are other sources of evidence.[93] However, commentators persisted in setting an impossible standard for Mary Bell, and not just out of their own fear of being duped. It was because they believed her to be, in essence, bad. Their suspicion was based upon the image that they had of her as a 'manipulative' child. Even as an adult, Mary Bell was spoken about as if she were still that evil child. This was not because the writers had forgotten that she committed her crimes as an eleven-year-old; on the contrary, it had everything to do with the fact that she had. As one commentator eloquently put it in an article on childhood:

> We think of young children as clear water, fresh and transparent. When a child doesn't fit this pure image as, most horribly, with James Bulger's young killers, then we comfort ourselves by demonising them – as if a foul pollution called evil had been dropped into their source and turned them into something that can no longer be called a child.[94]

It was difficult for the public to regard Mary Bell as a proper child; normal children did not commit murder and there appeared to be no adequate motive for her terrible actions. In the absence of any intelligible cause other than sickness or evil, the public, including those educated enough to know better, fell back on these explanations. At her trial, medical witnesses had declared her psychopathic. Thirty years later, on *Kilroy*, this had stayed in the public's imagination, one participant declaring: 'She's a very evil woman, she was diagnosed as a psychopath, well you can't lose that, that's with you for the rest of your life. You have no compassion when you are a psychopath.' No one could recognise the serious troubles that had afflicted this child, least of all Mary Bell herself.

When this 'child killer' sought to comprehend the events of her past, and to understand the young, shattered personality she had so successfully defended through her denials, she was judged as harshly as if she were on trial all over again. One clear basis of this condemnation was voiced by a Tory MP: 'She was described as manipulative and dangerous at her trial, let's not forget that. She is not, and never can be, properly rehabilitated.'[95] For people like this, Mary Bell was an icon of human depravity; she had been ineligible for childhood right from the moment of her birth. As a murderer, this child had failed to conform to an ideal of child-hood innocence, and had therefore forfeited her identity not only as a child, but also as a redeemed adult. This fall from grace was not a proposition that Gitta Sereny's moral outlook could ever entertain, much to the chagrin of her critics; and yet she shared their romantic idea about childhood innocence.[96] But while she kept faith with this idea, others were made disconsolate, perhaps seeing in Bell what the eighteenth-century writer Edmund Burke referred to as 'the defects of our weak and shivering nature'.[97]

Chapter Ten

MURDEROUS INNOCENTS

What was remarkable in the context of the 1993 incident was the
apparent dense public forgetfulness about earlier events.
CHRIS JENKS, 1996

Twenty-five years after the crimes of Mary Bell, the officer leading the investigation into another notorious child murder in 1993
believed the case to be unique. He told a journalist that the two
ten year-old boys who had killed James Bulger were the youngest ever to have been accused of murder. The crime they had
committed was, he said, unlike anything he'd ever encountered,
and he hoped he'd never see its kind again.[1] Yet there had been
other similar crimes in the intervening period. One occurred in
the same city, Liverpool, where an eleven-year-old boy drowned
a two-year-old in a pool of rainwater in 1973. And nearby, in the
district of Birkenhead in 1982, a nine-year-old stabbed and killed
a boy three years his senior. All in all, there were fourteen cases of
children murdering other children between 1968 and 1993, and
there may have been others that took place beneath the radar of
publicity.

Detective Alex Kirby's view that the Bulger killing was a one-
off, horrific but exceptional, shows how quickly we can be caught

up in the immediacy of a dramatic event. Yet so many features of this tragedy have their echo in crimes past.

The most salient comparison is the Stockport case in 1861 where the eight-year-olds, James Bradley and Peter Barratt, took the toddler George Burgess by the hand and led him to a scrap of waste ground on the edge of town. There, they stripped the two-year-old naked before beating him with a stick and drowning him in a shallow pool. 'Abduction' was the word used to describe how Robert Thompson and Jon Venables managed to get James Bulger to accompany them so far across a main road and towards a railway track. It is a modern word for a modern crime, conjuring the image of that which parents fear most – adult predators with adult horrors in mind. But in each of these cases the two small boys were more spirited away than snatched, which doesn't make their disappearance any less alarming, but does suggest something more ambiguous about the intentions of those who took them. In the nineteenth century this was something the judge, jury and public opinion appeared able to accept. It seems that they saw an ambiguity in what, in the context of an adult crime, might have been more sinister and deliberate. The boys' motives were not innocent – but neither were they, at the outset at least, murderous.

Thompson and Venables were troubled children, and of course troublesome ones too. After suffering the humiliating blow of being held back a year at their Church of England primary school, the two became allies. Naughty and disruptive in class, they had to be moved because of their effect on other children. They truanted regularly, hanging around the area of Walton Village or Bootle Strand – bored, mischievous, annoying – nicking this and that from the shops they idled in. The Stockport youngsters, whose crime bears such an uncanny resemblance to the one that the Liverpool boys went on to commit, had also given grief to their church school. In a century when it is often assumed that children were better behaved, Peter Barratt and James Bradley tore to pieces the brand new bibles that they had each been given, and ripped apart two boys' caps. Failing to appear appropriately contrite, they were expelled and told that they could not return until they were willing to cooperate with their teacher. Their parents' pledge to discipline them was never realised; within a week, the two eight-year-olds had been arrested for murder.

Each pair of boys found their little plaything quite by accident. One April afternoon in 1861, George Burgess was amusing himself outside, directly within the eyesight of his nurse. He was playing while she worked away at her chores, but when she next looked up he was gone. James Bulger had let go of his mother's hand several times on their shopping trip around Bootle Strand – he'd been playing up for most of their time there, kicking and pulling things about for fun. When they went into the butcher's shop, he was hanging around the entrance picking at the butt of a cigarette. His mother's attention was momentarily distracted, and in that instant, James was gone.

Little boys respond to the attention of older ones, and when Jon Venables took the younger boy's hand in his, there must have been a sense of awe and expectation – 'a little boy with blonde hair, skipping as he went along' was how one woman in the shopping centre saw it. But curiosity can sour when the interest of bigger boys turns to irritation or just plain boredom; it is then that torments can begin. Andrew O'Hagan describes such a moment in his book *The Missing*. It was the mid-1970s, a time of 'a new sort of independence' for this eight-year-old: 'In that year, I think we found out how bad we could be.' He and a group of three friends were playing in a field; with them was a toddler whom they'd often allowed to join the group. They came across a swamp and played at throwing stones, but they soon wearied of this game and turned their attentions to the little one:

> We got him to sit down in the marsh, and started trying to press him in deeper with poles. He was crying, and soaking, and we would cuddle him better then put him back in. We didn't know what we were doing, I think, but we knew that it was dangerous and it was giving a dangerous thrill.[2]

Maybe this type of encounter is necessary for some boys; a rite of passage, perhaps, towards a much-coveted identity. The dangerous pleasures of cruelty are, after all, the ultimate in power, a game in which masculinity, or one idea of it at least, can take shape. O'Hagan and his friends had an attachment to an ideal; they didn't come from Glasgow tenements themselves, but they knew that the boys who did were hard, and their machismo was magnetic. Toughness is the carapace that some boys need; it offers watertight protection against the darts of ridicule and disapproval that target young lives. Inflicting torment can bestow strength on a perpetrator; the suffering of another can lighten the burden of any secret humiliation hidden in the soul of a tormentor. Robert Thompson, cast as the bad boy to his friend Venables' weaker personality, had in fact been teased in the years before the crime for having the cherub-faced looks of a girl.[3] His fascination with troll dolls, too, did not go down well with his friend who snubbed it as 'girly'.[4] Was this 'fatal flaw in masculinity'[5] a source of some of Thompson's aggression?

When the American killer Gary Gilmore returned home from a stint at reform school, one of the many different institutions where he spent his teenage years before going on to kill two men years later, he described the 'merciless codes of his new life' to his younger brother. He told him about the 'soft boys' who did not have what it took to survive that life. He shared a room with one of them who would cry at night, 'wanting to disappear into nothing'. Then he gave his brother some advice: 'You have to learn to be hard. You have to learn to take things and feel nothing about them: no pain, no anger, nothing.'[6]

As working-class Liverpool lads, neither Thompson nor Venables was a stranger to violence. In Venables' case it was the ordinary bullying kind, mainly from kids on the estate and often about his older brother Mark, who had learning difficulties. It was the usual macho belligerence that is typical among young boys, but in a child whose emotions were already precarious because of difficulties at home it had an unsettling impact. He became abusive to his mother and unmanageable; his teacher at the junior school noticed his behaviour becoming increasingly odd. When he wasn't being disruptive and unpleasant, he would sometimes bang his head against the furniture, and rock backwards and forwards as if in some unseen turmoil. Then, one day, he took a wooden ruler and held it tightly against a classmate's throat. It took two teachers to force away his grip, and he never returned to that school again.

For the first five years of Robert Thompson's life, he witnessed brutality that was almost lethal. It was a family of seven sons, and at its centre was a powerful, wounding and loveless father who bullied his wife and children senselessly. Once, when Ann Thompson answered back to one of her husband's commands, he dragged her to the kitchen by her hair, filled the sink with water, pushed her head into it and held it down. On another occasion, when one of the boys was caught smoking, his father made him eat a packet of cigarettes – 'see the evil in my eyes, twat', was what he would say to frighten his children. One of Robert's siblings had been put on the child protection register following physical abuse when he was only four. Thompson senior abandoned them for another woman when Robert was five years old. He did not see his father again until his grandmother's funeral some years later. His mother, broken and unable to cope, also became violent, and the siblings tortured, battered and bruised each other in the poverty of their family life.[7]

When little James Bulger was carried some of the way out of the shopping centre by his new friends, to them he was a plaything, an object with which they could have some fun. They were seen several times on the journey, just as the Stockport boys had been seen with their foundling. Some onlookers thought they were brothers. In 1861, the sight of two young boys dragging a small, naked child towards a field was not quite odd enough to warrant intervention, though perhaps the eight-year-olds gave a plausible reason for this extraordinary scene. Thompson and Venables told one woman that they had found James lost and wandering and were taking him to the police station; they even stopped a lady for directions. Another passer-by who noticed James' distress felt uneasy and returned to check that he was all right, but by then they had gone. There were other tiny events that might, just might, have saved this little boy's life – a fire distracted them at one point, as did a weather loach fish that was said to jump out of its tank in stormy weather – any one of these might have turned things in a different direction and prevented a wicked prank from spiralling out of control. But it was too late; the boys knew that they were in trouble and maybe, like many of the children in this book, they wanted the crying to stop.

Death represents the greatest mystery to a child; such total finality is difficult to grasp. The experts back this up, saying that the children of their studies believed that those who die 'must be reborn again'.[8] Or, as was the case with the little child killer in Cyril Burt's study, he just wanted his persecutor out of the way. James Bulger was not the one inflicting torment in this uneasy threesome, but he received the blows because when the game was over and things got serious, he had become an unwanted presence. The cut to his head, his little frame spattered with paint, and the insistent cries for his mummy were proof enough of the magnitude of the crime that Thompson and Venables had already committed. Rather than return home and face the music, they beat their plaything with bricks and bars until it cried no more. They left the body on a railway track, perhaps in the vain hope that the power of a train's wheels would make it disappear forever.

The missing boy became a national story almost overnight, and as Robert and Jon rose from their beds, had breakfast and played separately in their neighbourhoods, their grainy CCTV images were being enhanced and broadcast to every living room in the country. If the two killers were trying to forget the horror of what they'd done, the picture of them outside Mothercare made it impossible. Their families, like all those in Liverpool and elsewhere, could think of little else, and they followed the news intensely: 'If I see them lads, I'd kick their heads in', Jon told his mum as they watched TV. A friend of Robert's mother thought that one of the boys looked like her son, and quietly took her suspicions to the police. Robert told his mates that he'd seen 'those boys' take the little one, and he took what his mother said was an unusual interest in the case, even adding his own floral tribute to the dead boy to the growing heap on the railway embankment.

Was the laying of the rose a mark of feeling or just a cunning alibi, one that might fend off mounting suspicion? Mary Bell had called to see Martin Brown four days after she had killed him; was this for the same reason, or because she didn't quite believe that he was dead? How unreal it all must have seemed in those few days after the crime, with the hope that it had never really happened and the terrible fear because it had. Therapists often use the metaphorical term 'splitting' to describe a coping process whereby a profoundly frightening experience may be obliterated from the mind. To the psychoanalyst Melanie Klein, it had a different meaning; splitting becomes a necessary partition that allows the mind to keep apart the good and bad aspects of the self. While Robert Thompson laid his rose, Jon, long after they had both been found out, hoped that James would revive, like the doll they had seen in the film *Child's Play 3* that is endlessly brought back to life.

They must both have entered the realm of fantasy, hoping and desiring that having removed their bawling nuisance, they could return home unblemished by his blood. But although James' death was absolute, they could never eliminate all traces of him as if he had never existed. He not only lived on in the painful memories of his parents, but he also haunted the boys and invaded their sleepless nights. Like the children of Lauretta Bender's studies, mentioned in chapter 8, the behaviour of these two deteriorated from the moment of their arrest. Jon suffered flashbacks, and told his mother of a recurring image of blood coming out of James' mouth. In another dream he performs an impossible trick – he rescues his victim and returns him to his mother. Robert, too, had dreams, in one of which he was killed by a car; he told the psychiatrist who interviewed him that when this happened, he tried not to go back to sleep in case the dream returned.[9] Both boys, in their own way, tried to avoid all conscious memory of the murder, and this required some effort. But it seeped through anyway in their agitations, tears, anger, and above all in their burgeoning obesity.

The level of psychological probing that these boys received was unprecedented in its refinement. As well as being asked about the crime itself, the children were asked about their families, how they felt about their parents, and their siblings. The psychologist who saw Jon Venables submitted him to a battery of tests: the Bene Anthony Family Relations Test, the Child's Depression Scale (revised), the Culture Free Self-Esteem Inventory and the Children's Manifest Anxiety Scale (also revised). The aim of all this scrutiny was to find out if they were suffering from an abnormality of the mind. Understandably, the 'nutter' label was not one the two mothers were keen to give to their sons. But the defence thought that a psychological assessment was necessary if they were going to try to get a conviction of manslaughter on the grounds of diminished responsibility. No wonder the children were not keen to talk – they didn't see themselves as mad, and no professional was going to make them say so. More than twenty years previously, the psychiatrist who interviewed Mary Bell had classed her as having a psychopathic personality disorder, which gave grounds for a lesser conviction; but trends change, even in matters of the mind, and professionals became unhappy with the label for children. They still are, and worry about the 'developmental appropriateness' of such a description and the 'potentially negative impact' of applying it to those who haven't yet reached maturity.[10] However, there is currently talk of reviving its use for the young, and so the debate continues.[11]

Remembrance of Trials Past

The trial went the way of others recounted in this history, the grooves of legal precedent having been driven very deep. Quite apart from the judge's wig and the crimson robe of centuries past, there was the necessary but sterile aim of proving that the defendants knew what they had done because they were able to tell the difference between right and wrong. These kids knew the difference, they'd gone to a church school, but what ten-year-old child learns these lessons according to strict rational principles? Rousseau believed that adults constantly attribute to children knowledge they do not really possess, but more significantly he said that feeling, especially in children, comes before judgement, and that 'the decrees of conscience are not judgements but feelings'.[12] Most people have probably nurtured murderous feelings at one time or another in their lives, for sleights and cruelties both big and small. But the act itself is so hedged with powerful prohibitions, internal and external, that we find the idea of carrying it out unthinkable. Thompson and Venables knew that what they were doing to James Bulger was wrong, but they did it anyway. They were propelled by vivid, destructive emotions so shameful that neither of them could admit what they'd done, and each blamed the other. Remorse was unforthcoming.

Yet the silence of the courtroom was cut through with their sobs – from twenty-four hours of taped interviews, played over a week. Not just tears, of course; there was larking about and cleverness too. Robert appeared especially adept at sticking to his story and, for his age, seemed to be good at anticipating what his interrogators might know and weighing up what he should tell them. But for one of those listening, the writer Blake Morrison, he sounded like a desperate little boy, 'slowly being caught up in the web of his own lies'. In his book on the case, Morrison said that Robert 'talks like a child – a child afraid of getting in trouble, more trouble than he's already in'.[13] Jon had a go at lying too, but he was tripped up after a couple of hours by the news that Robert had admitted they were both at Bootle Strand; he crumpled and cried like a baby. This was not the first time they had cried. During his interview with the psychiatrist Dr Vizard, Robert was asked to use the three dolls she had placed in front of him to help in giving an account of what had happened with James. He spoke of the 'baby', and when the doctor asked him about James, what he thought of him, Robert covered his eyes and began to cry. She told him it was understandable that he should cry, and that it might help him, but he was angry, and through his sobs he shouted: 'How does it help to make it all come back, I don't want to do it.'[14]

It seems difficult to imagine that the label 'evil' could be tagged on to these two, but the tabloids did so with repetitive ease, as if cruelty and violence did not belong to a realm that was human.[15] One or two people who were much closer to the case than the tabloid journalists actually believed that the boys were not human, but 'freaks who just found each other'. Phil Roberts, who conducted the police interview with Robert Thompson, told BBC's *Newsnight* that the boys were different from others he had known, that they could not be compared with ordinary badly behaved boys: 'They were evil. I think they would have killed again.'[16] The detective in charge of the investigation, Albert Kirby, said it was 'frightening to see two boys with such strong evil criminal intent'. He believed that they had every intention of abducting a little boy that day and causing him serious damage.[17] However another police officer, as if sensing a discrepancy between appearance and reality, drew an intuitive parallel with Mary Bell. For him, the respective behaviour of each boy resembled the contrasting aspects of hers. On the one hand, Robert Thompson reminded him of the girl's performance in court, guileful and intelligent. 'He winds you up, you don't feel any sympathy for him', he said, and 'whether it's right or not, the impression I got from the book I read was that Mary Bell transmitted that type of lack of sympathy, a hard-nosed, streetwise kind of kid.' But in Jon Venables he recognised a vulnerability that Mary Bell had also shown.[18]

He did not elaborate, but he was perhaps hinting intuitively that fear and confusion can be difficult to read. Even a child can mask emotional turbulence with an unfeeling demeanour. But the apparent lack of emotion can also be real, a signal that this person is capable of dissociating; not in the full-blown sense that gives rise to double consciousness or multiple personalities, but a defensive kind which allows the self to cope with the frightening, and sometimes traumatic, demands of the external world. Freud believed that this kind of dissociation requires significant mental focus that might make a person appear vacant or unintelligent, but could it also make him appear chillingly lacking in human feeling?[19]

Margaret Messenger, William Allnutt, Mary Bell – each appeared callous and unfeeling after committing their terrible crimes. The sight of the latter smiling as she joined the onlookers at her victim's funeral was enough to chill the heart of the detective who watched her. Psychiatrists believed that her icy character was a symptom, not of her catastrophic childhood, which they knew little about, but of her mind, as if this were an entity in the skull housed separately from the lived experience of its owner. In 1968 there was no agreed classification for psychiatric disorders in childhood, so experts in the Mary Bell case used the adult one. The *Diagnostic and Statistical Manual* (DSM) was sacrosanct in the psychiatric profession. First published in 1952, its diagnostic criteria and therapeutic protocols were of central importance in assigning the profession the status of a biomedical science.[20] In Bell's case, specialists used the second version of the DSM to give a medical name to what they saw. She ticked the box for displaying a lack of feeling, the murders also showed that she was vicious, and she lacked shame or remorse for what she had done. The 'negative features' of her illness, in other words the things she *didn't* have, were depression, schizophrenia or a criminal motivation. So she was, according to the manual, a psychopath.

If things had not moved on in the field of child psychiatry, Thompson and Venables might have acquired the same label. The cruelty of the murder that they perpetrated, their remorseless lies and their unrepentant denials all fitted the old psychiatric nomenclature. The scientific manual was supposed to be an objective system of classification, but at times it now appears uncomfortably close to the idiosyncrasies of subjective judgement. If any of us had seen the *Sun* for 7 October 1993, we'd have said that the picture of the boys sucking lollipops as they attended a court hearing was confirmation of what we already suspected that they were cruel and heartless in their disregard. The swaggering, shaven-headed coolness of Robert Thompson during the trial also presented a disturbing picture of a hard-bitten youth. And as if our own projections were not enough, there was the phenomenal worldwide media coverage, a lot of it devoted to portraying these killers as monsters without a conscience.[21]

When it came to the insights of psychology, however, these two boys were much better served than Mary Bell. It wasn't that her interviewing doctors were incompetent, far from it – merely that much more attention had been given to disturbances in children in those intervening years, and clinicians could not help but benefit from this work. Dr Eileen Vizard was a specialist consultant who worked with extremely violent children, and the doctor who reported on Jon Venables; Susan Bailey, also had a professional background in the mental health of violent young offenders. But, as with the 1950s doctor referred to in chapter 8 who interviewed the baby-killer Doreen Russell, the function of these professionals had not changed in the criminal justice system, and it had a limited legal aim – to declare whether the boys had the intellectual capacity to know right from wrong. This was, and in this type of case still is, psychiatry's forensic role; not to tell us what kind of children Thompson and Venables were, nor what kind of families they came from, but whether they understood that what they did was wrong. Eileen Vizard got less than five minutes in a trial that lasted over a month, and Susan Bailey got little more. It was the only time in which the mental health of the boys was ever mentioned in court.

There was, however, something distinctive about this trial compared to all the others in this history. The lawyers involved in the case felt some disquiet about the whole process: 'We were dealing with two children who were profoundly damaged, if by nothing else than their participation in the offence itself.' In an interview for the *Guardian* on the tenth anniversary of the case, Dominic Lloyd, the solicitor for Robert Thompson, said he believed it was unclear whether or not his client really understood what was going on throughout the trial proceedings: 'It was completely out of his range of experience. I just remember how people looked at him.' In the same article, the boy's barrister David Turner said:

I still believe that the English adversarial process was inappropriate for children of this age. In other countries, social and psychiatric experts would have become immediately involved, rather than lawyers. I have always felt that the misery for both accused children was that they were unable to tell anyone what had really happened – their mothers, their families, or their lawyers. It must have been a dreadful experience for each of these boys.[22]

Our adversarial system, in which lawyers are required to make cut-throat defences on behalf of their clients, was, in this case, like using a sledgehammer to crack a nut. It worked against the boys' disclosure of what had happened because it only ever held out the possibility of punishment and wounding betrayals; if you tell your parents you did it, they tell the police and you're done for. Outside of this system, Thompson and Venables might have confessed their crime more readily and felt more able to talk about it.

The Alternative?

The legal systems of other countries take a very different approach. In Italy, for example, where the minimum age of criminal responsibility is fourteen, no trial would have taken place. And even if the boys had faced criminal proceedings, they would not have appeared before a jury. They would have had a preliminary hearing in front of two judges who were schooled in 'psycho-pedagogical issues'. In other words, these judges would have an in-depth understanding of children and how they understand and make sense of things. Then, using information provided by social workers and child psychiatrists, they might decide to pardon or put on probation, though a murder case like this one would almost certainly have gone to a proper trial. This would consist of a tribunal of four judges with specific expertise in children and crime, but it would be a private hearing rather than one held in the full glare of the world's media. If sentenced, the youths would be sent to a secure accommodation unit exclusively for children, where they would serve only a third of the punishment period given to adults for the same offence. The entire aim of this process, and of the principles guiding it, is the psychological and social rehabilitation of the child.[23]

The Norwegian approach has evolved along even more radical lines. There are simply no criminal proceedings for children, whether they steal a packet of Smarties or kill another child. In 1994, a mother lost her five-year-old daughter when two young boys stripped her, brutally beat her unconscious with a heavy stone, and left her to die in the cold. It was an event no less shocking to the population of Trondheim than James Bulger's killing was to the people of Liverpool. One man who lived there at the time wrote: 'Its effect was entirely traumatic. People were stunned, there was disbelief, there was no understanding of how such a thing could happen.'[24] The police were involved from the beginning, not with the aim of gathering evidence for a prosecution, but to establish what had taken place. The boys knew exactly what they had done and described the details to the police. Incredibly, within weeks the two killers were allowed to return to their school and community, and there was no dissent at all. The authorities wanted to return the children to as normal a situation as was possible, accepting that they, too, had been involved in a traumatic event.

Each day a psychologist accompanied the boys on their journey into school. Trond Andreassen, who was in charge of the child protection team that dealt with them, recalls their shock at what they had done: 'They were very afraid and confused. What we wanted to do was give the boys the chance to talk about what happened, help them make sense of it.'[25] Andreassen believed that punishing them would have achieved nothing; their conscience would do that job. He said:

I don't think making them suffer is the way to make them realise what had happened. When you are continually punished for something you can't undo you have to do something to protect yourself so you begin to imagine it's not really you who did it. You develop a split personality.

The strategy adopted by the welfare services appears to have had some success. According to the last report in 2000, one of the boys was making good progress – he had adjusted quite well and was 'functioning normally'. For the other boy normal life was still a struggle, and his difficulties were continuing: 'We later found out that there were reasons for his problems, reasons that could explain what happened with Silje [the girl].' When Andreassen was asked if the boy had been abused, he would only reply, 'something like that'. Nonetheless, the fact that this child was still receiving help was confirmation of how the system worked not just for the boys and their families, and for the victim's family as well, but also for the city of Trondheim.

The dead child's mother, of course, had her heart broken and, as for Denise Bulger (now Fergus), it is a pain that 'never goes away'.[26] Their families never return to normal, because there is always an empty space at the centre. But Silje's mother has different feelings about the boys who killed her daughter. Unlike Denise Bulger she cannot bring herself to hate them, and she believes that they were 'punished enough by what they did. They have to live with that. I think everybody has got to be treated like a human being. The children had to be educated, had to learn how to treat other people so they could get back into society.' It is not easy for her, and she continues to suffer her grief, but her feelings towards these boys are shaped and supported by a culture very different from our own. James' mother aims her grief squarely at Thompson and Venables, and who can blame her when even the government of the day was urging us all, in the light of the crime, to 'condemn a little more, and understand a little less'.[27]

Would it Work Here?

It would be unthinkable for the government of Norway to inflame what was already a crisis with a comment like this. In their country, the humiliation of young criminals is not a condition for success when it comes to dealing with them. Governments everywhere have to take note of the 'climate of opinion', which was particularly vengeful in the British case, but it appears that the Conservative leadership of 1993 chose to listen in one direction only. In Norway, there was no mood of retribution; they seem to have cultivated a different habit of mind. In England, we are perhaps trapped by a more limited view of the world.

There was certainly something of a Hobbesian fear in the climate of the early 1990s, and the lead investigating officer on the James Bulger case felt it. He was deluged with letters giving views about the 'degraded state of society', and how people had become full of disregard for others and their property. Albert Kirby said: 'They wrote to me with very deep concern as to what is taking place in society generally, in the lowering of standards, and concern about the breakdown of the family unit.'[28] A headline in a Scottish newspaper shouted its opinion about this decline, 'Our Children's Minds Feast on Garbage', and the *Independent* had 'Daring to Agree About Our Moral Sickness'.[29] Among the scores of letters to newspapers, one read:

> I was not surprised by the murder. It seemed to me just the sort of thing that could happen in nineties Britain, just one symptom of the insidious brutalism that has permeated every aspect of life. Why should we expect children to have any sense of mutuality when they grow up in a society where human life is accorded no value.[30]

If anxiety was stirred by this crime, argued a columnist in the same paper, 'it was because children in a moral vacuum seem the most spectacular victims of a society in which people have ceased officially to count'.[31]

274

These concerned voices came from all ages; from the religious who believed that society was spawning 'little devils', to those who were not so committed, but who nonetheless believed that the Bulger killers must have 'a Satan bug inside'.[32] All manner of opinion was aired. The nation was in the grip of a moral panic, but it was not all falsely generated by a hungry media; there were real fears to play upon. Crime was high in 1993. If you take burglary, for example, the most common offence and one by which people are deeply affected, in that year it was more than double the figures in more recent years.[33] People worried about crime a great deal, and when the killing of James Bulger occurred there was something, at last, to which they could attach their anxiety.

People do not have such worries in Norway, where crime is low and violent crime even more so. Rich in minerals, oil and gas, it has a generous healthcare system, a well-funded education sector, and is ranked first-class in the provision of child welfare.[34] It was the first country in Europe to outlaw the corporal punishment of children, and it has a tough regulatory regime for advertising aimed at the young. Male teenagers do compulsory military service, and those who conscientiously object serve time in civilian work. The population of Trondheim is 10 per cent of Liverpool's, and it has only recently emerged from being dependent on fishing. It is socially cohesive because it is small, recently rural and has no history of immigration. More than three-quarters of the country's population are members of the Church of Norway, and although less than half of them attend church regularly, the celebration of religious rites such as confirmation is the foundation of a strong social as well as religious identity. When the solicitor for Jon Venables visited the country for the BBC, he said that he admired their system of rehabilitation and saw it as a place 'so civilised' that the boys who killed five-year-old Silje Raedergard 'can survive without fear of retribution'. But he was pessimistic about whether it would work in England, saying: 'Look at the numbers you have to rehabilitate.' He sees little that would inspire trust towards the young criminals he encounters every day in his work, and believes that to raise the age of criminal responsibility to fifteen would just be cynically exploited. 'Imagine if we said to these kids you can do anything you fancy 'til you're fifteen', he said, 'they'd have a field day. There'd be absolute mayhem.'[35] As much as he admired the Norwegian approach, it is impossible not to agree with him that transplanting it to the UK would not work; any system, after all, is inseparable from the cultural context from which it has evolved.

Yet the case in history that resonates most closely with the killing of James Bulger shows that there is nothing inevitable in how people respond to such events. Media discussion of the crime carried out in 1861 by Peter Barratt and James Bradley also extrapolated imaginatively on the subject of what their crime said about human nature. It used the example of the French revolutionary terror and the American Civil War to argue, in effect, that we constantly have to invoke our better natures, our moral resources, to keep us from 'the evil principle within'. But it was also said that the 'practices of cruelty and oppression ... permitted in our great educational establishments are scarcely less mischievous' than the crimes of Bradley and Barratt. These boys, it was suggested, 'are only in a wild degree what all our boys would be without religion or education'.[36] Their crime, diabolical though it was, took place in a period where children's lives were beginning to matter, and where even childhood's failures could be reclaimed as part of an ideal.

The Ruins of Childhood

Whereas in the nineteenth century society appeared to discover childhood, the murder of James Bulger seemed to signify its loss. 'In essence', wrote one sociologist, 'what the British public seemed to have come to terms with in 1993 was that childhood could no longer be envisioned as a once-upon-a-time story with a happy and predictable ending.'[37] Like the other case histories recounted in earlier chapters, James Bulger's death was not a fringe criminal event, but it is set apart by the fact that in the late twentieth century a global media turned this one tragedy into a worldwide cultural phenomenon. Other killings carried out by children in France and Japan were linked to it, while in Britain, the sheer volume of commentary was staggering.

This widespread adult unease found varied expression. Added to the lamentations for the collapse of family values, for instance, was criticism of the so-called moral relativism of a liberal education.[38] Even the Church became a target; it was criticised by the government, no less, for failing in its duty to 'battle for the soul of our young'.[39] There were compassionate voices, too, marked by a sense that society had failed the two young killers in some way, either by failing to identify the links between crime and truancy or by being insufficiently alert to the difficulties of their family lives.[40] The view that the brutality represented in this crime had been nurtured in the cradle of Thatcherism was also voiced, and it was not just left-leaning commentators who agreed.[41] News reports showed us feral gangs and children wreaking havoc in their neighbourhoods, and schools spoke of kids preying on those more vulnerable than them through viciousness and greed. Something significant was changing in children's lives, and with it the old ways of thinking about childhood were also coming to an end.

When Peter Barratt and James Bradley killed two-year-old George Burgess in 1861, it did not undermine the idea of childhood innocence. At that time, Victorians did fear that for some children, those of the poor in particular, their innocence was ripe for corruption, but the threat was identified with the actions of dangerous adults, older criminals who would enlist them to participate in their nefarious acts, or employers who would exploit them for profitable gain. In the 1990s it was children's autonomy from adults that was the problem. They lived alongside their parents, but adult authority did not so readily control them. It started with teenagers in the 1960s but, three decades on, younger children were beginning to enjoy the pleasures of agency. As consumers of technology, fashion, alcohol and, on occasion, sex and drugs, children had fallen prey to what one writer referred to as the 'ruthless demands for profit and publicity'.[42] Parents, teachers and social workers were worried about the effects of big-brand advertising, and felt that film and television violence were having a malign influence. It did not matter that researchers had found no proven link between screen violence and aggression – for many adults, the brutal crime of Venables and Thompson was seen as the inevitable outcome of a society where the child is not only exposed to images of violence (the judge in the trial made a point of blaming video violence), but chooses such images in preference to sentimental ones. Children had become too knowing, and James' killing was emblematic of this knowingness in that it appeared to show a youthful contempt for the adult romance of childhood innocence.[43]

To an extent, the idea of innocence had been an invention all along, undermined by the reality that dangers as well as pleasures have been a feature of childhood experience for some time. But as an idea, it was still one of the most cherished in Western culture. From Rousseau's *Emile* to the cherubic images of Thomas

Gainsborough and Joshua Reynolds, and the blackened faces of Blake's chimney sweeps, innocence has been an enduring ideal of childhood. For many, however, it was an ideal that became lost in the dog-eat-dog world of modern life. The CCTV images of three young boys walking past Mothercare – one a toddler, his hand held by the bigger boy – appeared a perfect picture of innocence but became instead an iconic image of malevolence. The troubling transition of childhood did not begin with this atrocity, but the crisis it represented has had ongoing reverberations.

In November 2002, when ten-year-old Damilola Taylor was left to bleed to death on a stairwell in south-east London, the fear that children's lives were in danger because of the threat posed by other children became widespread. A school inspector, who had visited the one attended by Damilola only weeks before his death, described it as being 'like something out of Dante's *Inferno*'.[44] The children were out of control and beyond the discipline of their teachers. A decade after James Bulger's death, it seemed as if violence and danger were enduring features of many inner-city estates in Britain. After two young teenage girls were gunned down in Birmingham in 2003, one academic wrote that murderous boys 'learned their selfishness from Mrs Thatcher, their ruthlessness on the games console, their studied ignorance from the media, and their love of the bling-bling life from the celebrity culture that has debased our civil society'.[45]

The worry about children and the childhood they are seen to be missing out on continues, finding expression in the excessive caution that is exercised in relation to them and in efforts to protect them from strangers, bullying and disappointment. Their distress and depression is increasingly medicalised, and in the case of middle-class children they are cocooned in counselling and therapy. They consume too much junk food, and are not permitted to travel to school by themselves or play in the park unsupervised; the cautionary tales are endless. In the face of all this worry, children just cannot wait to grow up and be free from the anxieties and control of adults. They want to move from innocence to experience, and it is here that public feelings about children are in painful contradiction. If the true faculty of knowing is bound up with experience, then a child must be permitted to experiment with life. But if childhood is increasingly impinged upon by the 'experience' of an adult world, the result can be a knowingness that disqualifies children from protection. This is certainly the case if they cross the line into criminality.

In law, the knowingness identified in the criminal actions of modern children set off one of the most important legal debates of the twentieth century. In 1994, the High Court considered at some length whether the ancient doctrine of *doli incapax* – the presumption that gave partial protection to children between the ages of ten and fourteen – should still be part of English law. In favour of its abolition, Justice Laws argued:

> Whatever may have been the position of an earlier age, when there was no system of universal compulsory education and when, perhaps, children did not grow up as quickly as they do nowadays, this presumption at the present time is a serious disservice to our law.[46]

His view was that today's education system has made children cannier, and equipped them with greater capacity for understanding their own wrongdoing, than children in the past. Three years later, Jack Straw as home secretary declared that *doli incapax* would be abolished. Nowadays, a child of ten is regarded as having the same reasoning capacity as an adult.

Robert Thompson and Jon Venables were just past their tenth birthdays when they killed James, only just criminally responsible.

Young though they were, their perceived knowingness put them beyond sympathy. Because they were seen as having acted with conscious intentions like any adult, it was acceptable to a large section of public opinion that they be treated with appropriate retribution. The original trial judge said that Thompson and Venables had committed an act of 'unparalleled evil and barbarity' that would be punished with their detention for many years. He settled on eight years, an unimaginable length of time for a ten-year-old. The lord chief justice then increased it by two years and six months. Later, the Conservative home secretary Michael Howard, in a spirit of righteous fervour, raised their sentence to fifteen years to 'maintain public confidence in the criminal justice system'.[47] He was responding to 'popular' pressure. A television phone-in programme had asked what their viewers thought about James' parents' petition to have them detained for life, and 80,000 people phoned in support of the idea. The *Sun* joined in, asking its readers to send a cut-out coupon to Mr Howard that read: 'I agree with Ralph and Denise Bulger that the boys who killed their son James should stay in jail for LIFE.'

When the boys' lawyers appealed against the home secretary's decision, it was on the grounds that not only had Michael Howard not read the social and psychiatric reports associated with the case, but he had also failed to take into account their clients' extreme youth. They added that the deterrent part of the sentence was out of place, in that killings of this kind were so rare that it was unclear who exactly it needed to deter. The appeal succeeded and Howard counter-appealed not once, but twice, and then a third time to the House of Lords where he lost by a majority of two to three. Howard's attempt to increase the tariff was criticised by the European Court. The parading of these two children in front of the world's media, and the unusual act of releasing their names, was also censured. The British government had violated the right of the two accused boys to a fair trial, because the degree of publicity was intimidating and prejudicial to the outcome.[48] Had it not been for this court's ruling, it is likely that the moderate adaptations made to the British court process, in order to make it less overwhelming for children in future cases of this kind, would never have been made.

Redemption's Song?

While some people undoubtedly moved between horror and compassion over this case, others remained in the grip of a desire for vengeance. The knowledge that the rejoicing cries in the courtroom at their conviction were being repeated outside and beyond confirmed to these boys that they were outcasts. Their crime had made them notorious, and they would never escape its memory.

The trial was the last time that the boys saw each other. Thompson went to a secure unit in the Midlands, while Venables went to one in the north of the country. When Robert arrived at his accommodation, he lined up several of the troll dolls he had collected on his bedside table. He shared the unit with a small group of boys between the ages of ten and seventeen, all of whom had been involved in violent crimes. He soon got into a routine of education, therapy and recreation. A similar regime operated at Jon's unit. There were no bars or cells, although they were locked in their bedrooms overnight. At times it seemed that the unit was not secure enough for Robert Thompson; he told his mother he was afraid that someone would be able to break in and get him. By the time he had reached the age of sixteen, the troll dolls were gone and according to one other inmate, Robert had on one occasion stepped in when an older boy was bullying a lad: 'I thought it was weird considering what he did to James, but he always looked out for the younger boys in there.'[49]

They received one of the most expensive and intensive reha-bilitation programmes available in the country. It provided an education that neither of them could ever have dreamed of back on the streets of Liverpool, and it appears to have been a success. Robert, who showed a talent for art and design, once carried out a project that required him to create 'an object of beauty'. He chose a wedding dress, doing all the cutting and sewing himself. Both of them achieved academic success at 'A' level, and Jon Venables was said to be interested in going to university. As they lost their liberty when they were ten years old, there was concern that they might have become institutionalised and, given their noto-riety, terrified of the outside world. Each set of parents had left Liverpool and changed their identities. Their brothers and sisters had the murderous notoriety of their siblings to contend with, and suffered threats because of it. For all of them, their lives had become too large to control. If the boys hoped for an early release they must also have feared it, not knowing who or what they were returning to and whether they could ever escape who they were.

In the summer of 2001, the parole board declared that they no longer posed a threat to public safety and on this basis, together with that of other reports on their progress, the lord chief jus-tice, Lord Woolf, ruled that they should be released before their nineteenth birthdays, when they would otherwise have to be transferred to what he called the 'corrosive atmosphere' of a young offenders' institute.[50] Unrepentant, Michael Howard said he 'regretted the decision'. The circumstances of their release remained secret – quite an achievement given the lawless terri-tory of the internet. Despite two High Court legal injunctions protecting their identities, there were fears that the boys would be hunted down. Labour's home secretary called for calm, and

James' mother Denise, who was 'devastated' by their release, nonetheless urged the public not to engage in any vigilante action to kill them.[51]

There seems little doubt that Robert Thompson and Jon Venables have been rehabilitated, and this is as much a good for society as it is for them personally. But has their time in detention restored their humanity? Have they felt, deep down, for the life they extinguished? No doubt Denise Fergus would say that if they really felt remorse they would not ask to be released – how could you reconcile the shame of what you had done and not accept punishment for it? But this is an older, theological way of looking at things. It may appear, as some journalists have rather glibly reported, that the boys have 'come to terms' with this awful crime, and are keen to 'put the past behind them', but their inner punishment must continue because the momentum of murder can never end. Remorse and pity, which characterise an adult consciousness of guilt, inevitably contain depression and grief. Ever since Freud we have known that childhood has no cut-off point, that its pleasures, fears and traumas become part of our adult personal history and identity. As one writer, Jacqueline Rose, put it, 'like the unconscious, it is not something that becomes "resolved" – there is no resolution'.

Epilogue

In the swell of media commentary that followed the conviction of James Bulger's killers, it must have been tempting to try to resist the tide and inject a sense of rational calm into the public conversation. The BBC's social affairs correspondent made an attempt at this by arguing that there was really nothing special about the case at all: 'Plenty of children grow up deprived. There may be no more moral or social lessons in this case than in any other bizarre murder.' The lawyer representing the Bulger family agreed that 'this was very much a one-off: it's dangerous to extrapolate lessons for society'.[1] In a sense, these commentators were right; the very particular set of circumstances that came together almost by chance in this tragedy was nothing short of exceptional. With hindsight, it is possible to see that there were moments in the journey of that triangle of boys when things could have turned out very differently, and the fateful meeting may not have happened at all. The drama to which the killing gave rise, and which was sensationally enacted through CCTV images broadcast all over the world, would never have taken place. The commentators were issuing a useful warning to us all: to think before ascribing a meaning to this case that it never quite deserved.

At the same time it is surely naïve to think that these events do not gain significance once aired to a wider public, if only because we, as viewers of the spectacle, actively take part in it through our opinions, our values and our projections. As creatures of meaning, we cannot help but find meaning in an occasion of such horror, and in this respect the killing of James Bulger is not unique.

When John Bell attacked Richard Taylor in 1831, *The Times*, in its reporting of the murder, focused on the boy's physical appearance to account for his terrible atrocity. He had, the newspaper indicated, the features of a particular class prone to this type of crime:

> The culprit was of fair complexion, with the light hair so common amongst the peasantry; his forehead and upper lip projecting, and his eyes were deeply sunk in his head, altogether not an inapt prototype of the 'Idle Apprentice' portrayed in Hogarth's inimitable work.[2]

Evidence, if any were needed, that in asking even the simplest of questions about these crimes, for example, 'Why?', we always reveal something of ourselves in the answers. *The Times*, two centuries ago, showed its class prejudices, but perhaps similar preconceptions operate in today's racialised coverage of gang violence.

As well as our need to ascribe meaning, we also convey it. In our responses to child murder it is difficult to avoid giving something away about ourselves, whether it be emotions of revenge or benevolence, of fear or curiosity. What is it, for example, about adulthood that makes us want to demonise a child? The writer Marina Warner believes it is because a child who kills betrays 'an abstract myth about children's proper childlikeness'.[3] Adults react punitively and callously because the murderous young person destroys the hopes of childhood and the moral future it represents.

Sometimes these crimes appear to say something about our identity as human beings. For the religiously inclined, the human propensity for sin explains it all, and religious concepts of good and evil are revived in a spirit of medievalism. The moral judgements that some people make about these children have their origins in fundamental moral ideas of the past. Even at a time when religious concepts had been loosened from their Christian moorings after Darwin, they acquired a different meaning in late-nineteenth-century medical opinions on health and disease: 'In consequence of evil ancestral influences', wrote Henry Maudsley in 1867, '[some] individuals are born with such a flaw or warp of nature that all the care in the world will not prevent them from being vicious or criminal or becoming insane.'[4] The moral vice of children who kill comes from an inclination in their nature, he believed, a disease 'which makes the evil good to them and the good evil'. Contemporary science eschews the language of morality, but is still drawn to nature as the repository of all that is most troubling about human behaviour.

In his book *The Blank Slate: The Modern Denial of Human Nature*, the evolutionary psychologist Steven Pinker declared: 'There can be little doubt that some individuals are constitutionally more prone to violence than others', if not genetically then instinctively.[5] Being rational enough not to rely on a gene for criminal violence, Pinker believes instead that violence is an inevitable behaviour trait of our species. He quotes a fellow scientist who poses the problem in terms not dissimilar to those used by Maudsley; children, it seems, 'do not kill each other, because we do not give them access to knives and guns. The question ... we've been trying to answer for the past 30 years is how do children learn to aggress. But that's the wrong question. The right question is how do they learn not to aggress.'[6] According to Maudsley, evil was the natural state, and for him the interesting scientific question was why and how man chooses good. It was this view which led him to write that 'to talk about the purity and innocence of a child's mind is a part of that poetical idealism and willing hypocrisy by which men ignore realities'.[7] Pinker echoes something of this contempt when he criticises those who hold to the doctrine of innocence, which is derived from Rousseau but circulates widely to this day in assumptions about childrearing, education and violent behaviour; where the child is seen as naturally good but spoiled or ruined by the things that happen to him in human society. According to Pinker, we have blinded ourselves with this fallacy and followed the same creed since the days of the Enlightenment. For example, the statement that 'violence is learned behaviour' is, he believes, a mantra repeated by well-meaning public servants and social scientists, but it has no basis in 'any sound research'.[8]

There are many who would take issue with this, but the purpose of mentioning it here is to illustrate how our understanding of children who kill is continually informed by wider cultural meanings and interpretations. Behind the moral confusion that society may feel about these crimes lie long-established traditions of thought and feeling, not only about childhood but also about humanity itself. In the nineteenth century, the 'rare and exceptional' murder of two-year-old George Burgess by two little boys led to similar extrapolations about human nature expressed in more common-sense terms. Human beings, it was generally concluded, are essentially imperfect creatures, a mixture of good and bad, and no romantic notion of innocence or striving for perfectibility would alter that: 'The eye glances down to these horrors, and we are duly shocked and scandalised', wrote *The Times* in 1861, 'but there mingles with the disturbance caused to our humane feelings a latent perception of this being the proper and expected place to find brutality; keeping to which precedent and order of things, it has not, of course, any defence or palliation, but some explanation and account of itself to the present.'[9] In other words, such events are to be expected because they belong to an overall picture of human fallibility.

So much is invested in particular conceptions of our moral condition and in their corresponding views about what it means to be human. People with high, sometimes Utopian, hopes for social change, for example, come up against those who believe that human capacities have their limits. These differing aspirations are played out in the conflict between those who seek understanding for the terrifying violence of some children and those who say we should 'understand a little less'. We saw this in the political reaction to the publication of Mary Bell's biography, coming as it did in the wake of the Bulger case. The characterisation of her, and of her sympathetic listener Gitta Sereny, came at a high point of widespread public pessimism about crime. Unusually, though, it encompassed liberals and conservatives alike. It was as if all the doubts about the intractability of young people's bad behaviour were represented in the callousness of the killings that she, Thompson and Venables had perpetrated.

So if some of these cases of murder carry an undue burden of representation, it is perhaps because they appear to symbolise a flawed aspect of our humanity. As one public commentator said of the James Bulger killing, 'it was a sadistic mutilation of a toddler, the sort of murder that makes us uncomfortable about who we are and what we are capable of'.[10] A further reason for the shock and disquiet that these killings evoke, and one which is manifested in earlier historical examples, is that such extreme action in a child goes to the heart of a greater dilemma about the extent to which they are morally and legally responsible. When someone is found to be completely responsible for committing murder, the crime carries devastating punishments, and from the earliest cases to the most recent it has proved challenging for the law to reconcile the conflict in holding a *child* responsible for society's most reprehensible offence. For the most part, an acknowledgement that children and adults are different has been reflected in a lesser penalty for their crime. But for this to happen, a profound shift needed to occur beyond the conservative world of the justice system. In 1831 the adult understanding of the conditions in which some children lived, as well as the pressures that they had to withstand, had not changed enough to make the execution of fourteen-year-old John Bell unacceptable. Many years later, however, children involved in murder were to benefit from the same reforming initiatives as other criminal children.

It is self-evident to say that the fate of all these youngsters depended a great deal upon the times in which they lived, as well as the prevailing perceptions of childhood with which their crimes inevitably became engaged. But the most enduring theme that links them all, and is related to the problem of moral responsibility, is the inscrutable question of motive. As readers and viewers of these extraordinary events, we are inescapably curious, if only because we were once children or have children of our own, about a child's capacity to commit this heinous crime. We want to understand the passions and moods, to know something about the parents, siblings and community of the child who has carried it out. The problem is that in general, as one legal academic has pointed out, 'motive is not relevant to the criminal law'.[11] Yet a child's experience, judgement and emotions have more than a little to do with what they do and why they do it.

Early psychology was interested in the 'passions', and the element of volition that shapes and controls them. By the late nineteenth century, the emphasis had become biological. Henry Maudsley, for example, espoused what might be called neural Darwinism. He saw the organisation of the nervous system, its neurological structure and function, as pre-determined through inheritance. Relying upon a concept developed by his predecessors – the idea of a moral sense – he saw it as a faculty, a physical entity, which could become diseased through poor ancestral influences. This had significant implications for the whole question of legal responsibility. How could someone be held accountable if they were not in possession of the sense that might have prevented them from committing a criminal action in the first place? Judges resisted the incursions of such new science, believing it to be insufficiently based on either hard physical or psychological fact.

Meanwhile, the child only really came nearer to the centre of psychology with Freud. He gave childhood an entirely new meaning. According to him, the problems of adulthood were to be found in the early years and were located in the deep recesses of the psyche. He explored dreams, motives and desires in the psychodynamic framework of a loving and desiring self, entangled with those with whom we share intimacy. Psychoanalysis then moved forward by integrating studies of family dynamics and the power of parental attachment. It was transformed in child guidance clinics and juvenile detention centres. Medical research on violent children relied upon these expanding frontiers and still does, though the mark of Freud has long gone. The disorders of childhood that are now known to be buried in the psyche can also be identified through symptoms and by the way in which a child interacts with his or her environment. In the last two decades, the whole field of child psychology and child psychotherapy has grown, as has the amount of research being carried out on the childhood origins of cruelty and sadism.

One area of current thinking attempts to join elements of attachment theory, which emphasised the importance of the child's relationship with the mother for healthy development, with contemporary neuroscience. It goes further than citing the maternal bond as vital, and suggests that a mother's psychological difficulties while pregnant can have chemical effects on the growing foetus; her anxiety, alcoholism or drug addiction opens up negative brain pathways which can be added to by a poor parental environment after birth. Unlike some neuroscientists who argue that murder, violence and other antisocial behaviour is the result of a small, inadequately active prefrontal cortex, an area of the brain that controls impulse, this new research sees the child as a systemic organism with a biology that acts upon, and is activated by, its environment. The vocabulary of regions in the cerebral cortex, stress hormones, the amygdala, the hypothalamus and the hippocampus is deployed in this fresh attempt to understand trauma and abuse:

> The combination of sophisticated brain scanning machines and hormone measurements has resulted in our beginning to understand better the chemistry of terror. Early research is demonstrating that the capacity to control behaviour and make pro-social choices is very much dependent on the efficient and balanced functioning of the brain. Minute damage or neurochemical depletion may play a significant role in violence.[12]

But what exactly is gained by this new role for brain functioning in creating cruelty in a child, particularly when the evidence is at best unclear? Why the need to shore up otherwise excellent and compassionate practical interventions on the ground with the scientific ballast of neurobiology? Does it provide something different to, say, ideas about 'instinctual energy', which in itself is not the cause of anti-social behaviour, but rather its fuel when it occurs?[13] Even Professor Eric Taylor, the head of the Child Psychiatric Unit at the Maudsley Hospital in London, whose research interests lie in neuropsychiatry, believes that the jury is still out on what exactly non-invasive brain scanning can show about the full range of conduct disorders diagnosed in children.

And the biologist Steven Rose says: 'No cerebroscope, however powerful, could translate the activity of all the nerve cells in the brain into a full description of a person's thoughts and feelings at any given moment.'[14] Yet the claims of the new thinking about violence in children are substantial. As one conference blurb on the subject put it:

> With recent advances in psychological research and brain science, we know so much more about how the sadistic personality can unfold. We can trace the seemingly incredulous path from the fresh faced baby who begins life with openness, innocence and programmed to love, to the young person or adult who in a calculated, cut-off way, enjoys the suffering he causes.[15]

Psychology's long-standing drive to emulate the natural sciences betrays a crisis of confidence about its evidential basis. But rather than borrowing scientific terms from medicine without sufficiently concrete evidence for how they work in the mind, practitioners with a more interpretive approach should keep faith with their work in dealing with the behavioural difficulties of childhood. This will not improve its status in the courtroom, however, where the field's relevance to the crucial issue of legal responsibility is negligible. No court in the land would admit abuse, trauma or any other psychological material as evidence of motive in a murder trial, and even if it did, it would certainly not count as mitigation. The psychology of an individual child, no matter how putatively scientific, counts for nothing when he or she enters a criminal court

Some therapists working in the area would prefer violent children never to appear in the courtroom in the first place. But are they simply avoiding the difficult question of public safety and, more importantly, justice for those whose lives have been devastated by the murders committed by the children in their care? Their aim is of course different; they want to encourage us to understand and empathise with these frightening figures:

> If you meet a teenage mugger on the street one night, the last thing that you will be thinking about is his infancy. But the fear and rage evoked in you are probably the same feelings that have been with him since babyhood, which have been instrumental in transforming this particular baby into an anti-social thug … as victims or potential victims, we retaliate, with thoughts of punishment and imprisonment … our attitude seems to be: he clearly doesn't care about other people – so why should we care about him? It is very hard to even bother to imagine that this menace was once a baby.[16]

Others – such as Camila Batmanghelidjh, who has done excellent and extraordinary work with Kids Company, a charity that supports violent, vulnerable children – make convincing pleas against society's wish to punish them:

> So many of our current interventions with vulnerable children come from the perspective of the well-adjusted adult, needing to preserve our own sense of safety. Onto these fragile and marginalised children and families, we project our hate, and we disguise our revenge as legitimate punishment.[17]

The gravity of murder places a difficult burden on criminal law when it is dealing with a child. For the most part, as the stories in this book have demonstrated, judges and juries have tried to mitigate the full effects of due punishment. But there is still a question over whether these children should ever stand trial in the first place. Doreen Russell, for example, probably had learning difficulties, which would be recognised today in a way that they were not when she committed her crime. Were she to be involved in a similar killing today, it might be decided that there was no public interest reason for prosecuting her. A number of researchers, most of whom have worked with violent children, believe that the existing partial defences for children who kill, such as diminished responsibility, are inappropriate:

> There is a move now to think about the developmental immaturity of children as an alternative concept within which we could understand children who have learning disabilities or just aren't grown up enough to understand the consequences of their actions and this leads to the issue of whether or not they are really fit to plead.[18]

The Law Commission has also recognised this, albeit in a more qualified way, by suggesting in a recent report that a plea of 'developmental immaturity' should be allowed to provide the basis for a finding of diminished responsibility.[19]

This would amount to a radical change in the criminal responsibility of such children. The body of knowledge that it is based upon, and by which their fitness to plead would be assessed, is developmental psychology. Those who support these changes argue that children who kill never really intend to do so, because their moral awareness is underdeveloped due to their having suffered abuse or other trauma. Essentially, what is being attempted by this innovative approach is to expand the range of defences for murder in those rare cases where children are involved, on the grounds that they are by definition damaged and disturbed. But while a convincing case could be made on such grounds for the young killers who appear throughout this book, would today's public, politicians and judiciary accept the same conditions for adolescents, possibly with equally damaging life histories, who spread fear to other children in their neighbourhoods by stabbing and shooting their peers?

The fact that children who kill are tried in an adult court is linked to the way in which recent society, in particular, has viewed them. While there are examples from the past of such children being treated sympathetically by jurors (perhaps because they came from the local parish or village, or because the simpler society from which they came meant that they were not the object of international media attention and revulsion), recent cases show a less favourable response. In the twentieth century, the evidence suggests that a child who has murdered another child is placed beyond the realm of childhood and is seen to have committed an adult crime with grown-up intention. It is this perception that allows us to treat these children with a strong element of retribution. Were another Mary Bell or Thompson and Venables to appear in criminal history, the law as it currently stands would, in most respects, operate in the same way as it did for them.

The Labour government commissioned a major review of the criminal courts when it came to power in 1997, but it chose to overlook this review's recommendations that related to the small number of youth cases committed to the Crown Court.[20] The most radical proposal was that children and young people under eighteen charged with serious crimes, should have their cases heard by a specialist youth court. The report pointed out that the British system was an anomaly, in that most other European and Commonwealth countries have separate adult and youth criminal justice systems.[21] In recognition of the fact that atypical cases merit more – not less – specialist treatment, Lord Justice Auld, the report's author, argued that the younger the age of the defendant, the stronger the argument in favour of special arrangements. A further recommendation suggested that the age of criminal responsibility be raised to put England and Wales on a similar footing to most of Europe.[22] None of these recommendations have been acted upon.

There would appear to be something of a paradox in the general response to these crimes. When they do occur, they generate widespread attention, vast amounts of media coverage and, recently, political comment. All kinds of meanings are attributed to them, sometimes including pessimistic messages about human nature.[23] Yet, once the event has passed, it is as if it never occurred in the first place. Perhaps Blake Morrison was right in thinking that the moral panic about child killing is over. Given the narratives recounted here, though, I doubt it. In spite of the cumulative expansions of possible meanings given to these episodes of violence, the older, darker ones still resonate.

Legally, we have not done any better in addressing the moral status of these children than our ancestors, though I suppose raising the minimum age of criminal responsibility by three digits in over 700 years is something. No other substantial changes have occurred in the way the law is applied in practice – such children continue to be liable for a public trial in adult criminal courts, and it is perhaps only the horror that they evoke that explains this.

There is one clear hope for this book: that when a child kills another child, igniting our outrage and our fears, this history will provide the important comparisons and perspectives from other cases, mostly long forgotten, that can help our understanding of, and responses to, the alienating, complex behaviour of children who kill.

NOTES

PROLOGUE

1 Hugh Cunningham, *Children and Childhood* (London: Longman, 1995), pp. 65–8.

2 Gillian Avery, *Nineteenth Century Children: Heroes and Heroines in English Children's Stories* (London: Hodder & Stoughton, 1965), pp. 48, 59. Kingsley quoted in Peter Coveney, *The Image of Childhood* (London: Peregrine Books, 1967), p. 103.

3 Colin Heywood, *A History of Childhood* (Cambridge: Polity, 2001), pp. 23–4. A. James, C. Jenks and A. Prout, *Theorising Childhood* (Cambridge: Polity, 1998), pp. 13–16.

4 From a letter to a correspondent quoted in the introduction to Jean-Jacques Rousseau, *Emile*, by P.D. Jimack (London: Everyman Edition, 1993), p. xxi. Rousseau thought that the state of nature was a happy one in which man, left to his own devices, would be a self-perfecting creature. He believed that this original state was ruined by the requirements of civilisation. It was this view of human nature that created the romantic ideal of the noble savage. For a discussion of the concept of the noble savage see Roy Porter, *Enlightenment* (London: Penguin, 2000), pp. 357–8.

5 John Locke (ed. J. and J. Yelton), *Some Thoughts Concerning Education* (Oxford: Clarendon Press, 1989), p. 265.

6 Coveney, op. cit., p. 40.

7 Rousseau, op. cit., pp. 84–5.

8 David James Smith called the British edition of his book *The Sleep of Reason*, and quoted Rousseau at some length; David J. Smith, *Beyond All Reason*, (New York: Donald I. Fine, 1995), p. ix. Blake Morrison also made use of Rousseau's thinking in his analysis of the trial of the Bulger killers; Blake Morrison, *As If* (London: Granta Books, 1998), pp. 99, 126. Gitta Sereny, author of the biography of the child murderer Mary Bell, premised her thinking on a belief in the innocence of children. For a discussion of her views see BBC Radio 4, *In the Psychiatrist's Chair*, interview with Gitta Sereny, 6 September 1998.

9 See the High Court debate on the issue as to whether the legal presumption of *doli incapax* for children between the ages of ten and fourteen should be abolished in *The Weekly Law Reports*, Queen's Bench Division, 30 September 1994, vol. 3, pp. 888–98, and *The Weekly Law Reports*, House of Lords, 31 March 1995, vol. 2, pp. 383–404. See also the House of

Commons Debate on the Crime and Disorder Bill, 8 April 1998; *Hansard*, vol. 377, column 373.

10   Heather Shore, *Artful Dodgers* (Woodbridge, Suffolk: The Boydell Press, 1999), p. 67.

CHAPTER ONE

1   On what follows see Naomi Hurnard, *King's Pardon for Homicide* (Oxford: Oxford University Press, 1969), pp. viii, 152–6.

2   Ibid., pp. 123, 214.

3   J.H. Baker, *An Introduction to English Legal History* (third edition, London: Butterworth, 1990).

4   Hurnard, op. cit., p. 153.

5   *Year Books of Edward II*, vol. 5, edited and translated by A.J. Horwood (London: Rolls Series, 1863), pp. 148–9. These translations of the Rolls are located at The Institute of Historical Research (IHR), London.

6   A.W.G. Kean, *The Law Quarterly Review*, vol. 53, 1937, pp. 364–70.

7   *Year Books of Edward II*, vol. 26 (London: Selden Society, 1909), held at IHR, London, p. 20.

8   For a full doctrinal history see Bernard M.G. Reardon, *Religious Thought in the Reformation* (second edition, London: Longman, 1995).

9   Quoted in Hugh Cunningham, *Children and Childhood in Western Society Since 1500* (London: Longman, 1995), p. 49.

10   S. Smith, 'Youth in Seventeenth-Century England', *History of Childhood Quarterly*, Spring 1975, vol. 2, no. 4, pp. 439–516.

11   1 Corinthians 11:27–32.

12   Reardon, op. cit., p.72.

13   S. Smith, 'Youth in Seventeenth-Century England', op. cit., p. 496. See also Cunningham, op. cit., pp. 49–51.

14   Rev T. Thirlwall (ed.), *The Works Moral and Religious of Sir Matthew Hale* (London: Thomas Thirlwall, 1805), vol. 1, p. 209.

15   This was the test of moral discretion which was used for at least three centuries after Hale, until increasing scientific knowledge about children meant that there was greater emphasis on their capacities of understanding and judgement. Sir Matthew Hale, *History of the Pleas of the Crown* (London: S. Emlyn, London, 1736), vol. 1, p. 26.

16   Quoted in Nigel Walker, *Crime and Insanity in England, Volume 1: The Historical Perspective* (Edinburgh: Edinburgh University Press, 1968), p. 39.

17   Hale, op. cit., vol. 1, p. 30.

18   Hale, op. cit., pp. 43–4.

19   Hale, op. cit., p. 25.

20   William Blackstone, *Commentaries on the Laws of England*, vol. 4, pp. 23, 349.

21 Ibid., p. 349.

22 A record of the trial appears in *British Trials Series: 1525/IV, 2052/1, 2320/x*, located at the Guildhall Library, London.

23 Justice Willes *Appeal Letter to the King*, 24 February 1749, State Papers Domestic (SP) 36/110, located at the National Archives, Kew, London.

24 The eighteenth-century judge of the Court of King's Bench, Sir Michael Foster, wrote at some length on this case in *A Report of some Proceedings on the Commission of Oyer and Terminer and Gaol Delivery for the Trial of Rebels in 1746 in the County of Surrey and of other Crown Cases. To which are added Discourses upon a few branches of the Crown Law* (Dublin: Sarah Cotter, 1763), pp. 70–73.

25 Camden Pelham (ed.), *The Newgate Calendar* (London: Reeves and Turner, 1886), vol. 1, p. 127. *The Newgate Calendar* is not a single publication but a number of different works. The various editions tend to feature the same cases but some are also updated with contemporary examples. The most complete collection was edited by J. Rayner and G.T. Crook, *The Complete Newgate Calendar* (London: Navarre Society, 1926).

26 Edward Foss, *The Judges of England With Sketches of their Lives* (London: 1848–64), vol. 8, pp. 398–9.

27 Foss, op. cit., p. 401.

28 Barbara Shapiro, *A Culture of Fact: England 1550–1720* (Ithaca and London: Cornell University Press, 2000), p. 24.

29 Shapiro, op. cit., p. 13.

30 Hale, op. cit., p. 235. Elsewhere in the same volume he recounts the story of a man accused of 'wizardry' by a thirteen-year-old girl, but the man is acquitted and the girl is assumed to have made the accusation out of malice. (Hale, op. cit., p. 148).

31 G. Geis and I. Bunn, *A Trial of Witches: A Seventeenth Century Witchcraft Prosecution* (London: Routledge, 1997).

32 Patrick Wilson, *Children Who Kill* (London: Michael Joseph, 1973), p. 183.

33 R. Seth, *Children Against Witches* (London: Robert Hale, 1969).

34 J.M. Beattie, *Crime and the Courts in England 1660–1800* (Oxford: Clarendon Press, 1986), pp. 128–9.

35 Beattie, op. cit., pp. 128-9, note 121.

36 William Blackstone (abridged and ed. Samuel Warren), *Commentaries on the Laws of England* (London: W. Maxwell, 1856), p. 352.

37 *The Book of Oaths* (London, 1649), pp. 205–7, cited in Shapiro, op. cit., p. 223, note 59.

38 Quoted in Beattie, op. cit., p. 342, note 65.

39 The reports of this case, and the judge himself, remarked on the poor instruction that the boy had received with reference to referring to the teaching of the Bible, but also on his general comprehension. *Appeal*

Letter to the King, State Papers Domestic (SP) 36/110 (National Archives), p. 65.

40 *Appeal Letter to the King*, SP 36/110 (National Archives), p. 67.

41 Sir Michael Foster, *Foster's Crown Law*, p. 73.

42 Barristers of superior standing attended Serjeants' Inn. See Sheila Bone (ed.), *Osborn's Concise Law Dictionary Ninth Edition* (London: Sweet and Maxwell, 2001), p. 348. The respiting, or reprieving, of an offender was likely, though not certain, to result in a pardon. After transportation was enshrined in statute in 1718, this became an alternative sanction to death. See Beattie, op. cit., pp. 431–9.

43 *Appeal Letter to the King*, SP 36/110, p. 67.

44 Roger North, *The Life of the Rt. Hon. Francis North, Baron of Guilford* (London: John Whiston, 1742), p. 129.

45 *Appeal Letter to the King*, SP 36/110, p. 59.

46 The pardon was granted on 18 February 1749 and signed by His Grace The Duke of Bedford. *Appeal Letter to the King*, SP 36/110, pp. 59, 85.

47 Roy Porter, *A Social History of Madness* (London: Phoenix, 1987), p. 19.

48 Quoted in Roy Porter, *Enlightenment* (London: Penguin, 2000), p. 219.

49 The influential psychiatrist Jean-Etienne Esquirol (1772–1840) used this definition to describe an insanity of the emotions. See chapter 6.

50 *Annual Register* 1763 (London: E. Burke, 1758–1800), p. 71.

51 *Annual Register* 1763, op. cit., p. 71.

52 Roy Porter, *The Athlone History of Witchcraft and Magic in Europe* (Ireland: Athlone Press, 1999), p. 229.

53 Porter, *The Athlone History of Witchcraft*, op. cit., p. 229.

54 The classification of mental illness in children did not really begin until the nineteenth century. See chapter 6.

55 A. Knapp and W. Baldwin (eds.), *The New Newgate Calendar 1809–19* (London: 1826), vol. 1, p. 463.

56 The appeals archive at the National Archives contains nothing on this case. However, since there are also other records missing from the archive, this could just mean that they are lost.

57 *Annual Register* 1778, p. 179.

58 Ibid., p. 179.

59 *Foster's Crown Law*, op. cit, pp. 72–3.

60 Clive Emsley, *Crime and Society in England 1750–1900* (London: Longman, 1996), chapter 2. See also V.A.C. Gatrell, *The Hanging Tree: Execution and the English People 1770–1868* (Oxford: Oxford University Press, 1994), p. 7.

61 *The Malefactor's Bloody Register* (London: Alexander Hogg, 1779), vol. 1, p. 149.

62   The exact age of John Mead is not given, but the other unnamed boy was 'scarce sixteen years of age'. From G. Thompson (ed.), *Newgate Calendar*, p. 350.

63   *The Daily Register*, 10 December 1786. This publication was a precursor of *The Times*.

64   See Trevor Dean, *Crime and Justice in Late Medieval Italy* (Cambridge: Cambridge University Press, 2007), pp. 27, 32, 45.

65   It is important to mention that the examples of young gallows victims given by some twentieth-century writers are exaggerated. It appears that these unproven and sometimes apocryphal instances have been repeatedly used to overstate the cruelty of the eighteenth-century criminal code. One reason may be timing; some such writings were published at the height of the 1960s campaign against capital punishment. The image of young children being hanged by the neck strengthened the emotional case against the death penalty. By citing the imagery of past cruelty, a whole way of life and of punishment was signalled, which was remote from the changed times of the 1960s. See John Laurence, *A History of Capital Punishment* (London: Sampson, Low and Masters, 1932), p. 18, and Ivy Pinchbeck and Margaret Hewitt, *Children in English Society* (London: Routledge & Kegan Paul, 1973), vol. 2, pp. 351–2. Other writers who have used these unproven examples are G. Gardiner, *Capital Punishment as a Deterrent: And the Alternative* (London: Gollancz, 1956); A. Koestler and C.H. Rolph, *Hanged by the Neck* (London: Penguin, 1961); A. Koestler, *Reflection on Hanging* (London: Gollancz, 1956); and C. Hibbert, *The Roots of Evil: A Social History of Crime and Punishment* (London: Penguin 1966). For a full and accurate record see B.E.F. Knell, 'Capital Punishment: its administration in relation to juvenile offenders in the nineteenth century and its possible administration in the eighteenth', *The British Journal of Criminology*, vol. 5 (1965), pp. 198–207.

CHAPTER TWO

1   Edward Gibbon Wakefield, *The Hangman and the Judge* (London, 1863), pp. 5–6.

2   *The Times*, 2 August 1831. The numbers mentioned in other accounts vary from 2,000 to 5,000.

3   H. Potter, *Hanging in Judgement: Religion and the Death Penalty in England* (London: SCM Press Ltd, 1993), pp. 64–79.

4   Unknown author, *Narrative of Facts Relative to the Murder of Richard Faulkner Taylor* (Rochester: S. Caddel, 1831), p. 35.

5   *The Rape of the Lock, Canto III*, in *Pope's Poetical Works* (London: Macmillan and Co., 1907), p. 78.

6   V.A.C. Gatrell, *The Hanging Tree: Execution and the English People 1770–1868* (Oxford: Oxford University Press, 1994), p. 499.

7   This case is cited in Gatrell, op. cit., p. 512.

8   Norbert Elias (trans. Edmund Jephcott), *The Civilizing Process*; vol. 1, *The History of Manners* (Oxford: Basil Blackwell, 1978, first published 1939).

9   Peter Spierenburg, 'The Body and the State: Early Modern Europe', in Morris Norval and David J. Rothman (eds.), *The Oxford History of The Prison: The Practice of Punishment in Western Society* (Oxford: Oxford University Press, 1985), pp. 44–70.

10   David Hume, *Treatise on Human Nature*, vol. 2, p. 317. Cited in Norman Kemp Smith, *The Philosophy of David Hume* (London: Macmillan, 1941) p. 172. For a discussion on eighteenth-century sensibilities and their role in the history of punishment, see Gatrell, op. cit., pp. 225–41. For the emphasis given to emotion in this period, see J. Mullan, *Sentiment and Sociability: The Language of Feeling in the Eighteenth Century* (Oxford: Oxford University Press, 1988), pp. 29–42.

11   Edward Foss, *The Judges of England With Sketches of their Lives* (London: 1848–64), vol. 8, pp. 398–9.

12   Samuel Warren (abridged and ed.), *Blackstone's Commentaries* (London: W. Maxwell, 1856), quoted on p. 1.

13   Gilbert Burnet, *Exposition of the XXXIX Articles*, 1699, p. 529. Cited in Potter, op. cit., p. 11.

14   Kent Summer Assizes Felony File, 1831 (National Archives), ASSI 94/2097.

15   Both boys were executed on 6 July 1791 for robbery. G. Thompson (ed.), *Newgate Calendar* (London: J.S. Pratt, 1845), p.102.

16   *The Times*, 20 May 1790, and E. Blunden (ed.), *Autobiography of Leigh Hunt* (Oxford: Clarendon Press, 1928), pp. 70–71, both cited in Gatrell, op. cit., p. 246. The execution in Horsham is cited in Potter, op. cit., p. 22.

17   Mrs Mary Sherwood (born Mary Martha Butt) was a novelist with strong Calvinist views. The first part of *The Fairchild Family* continued to be popular Sunday reading for the best part of a century. See Gillian Avery, *Nineteenth Century Children: Heroes and Heroines in English Children's Stories* (London: Hodder and Stoughton, 1965), pp. 83–4.

18   A copy of Henry Sharpe Horsley's luridly illustrated book is available at the British Library, London. See Gillian Avery, op. cit., p. 218.

19   S. Romilly, *Memoirs of the life of Sir Samuel Romilly written by Himself* (London: T. Cadell, 1840), vol. 1, pp. 11–12.

20   William Ballantine, *Some experiences of a barrister's life* (sixth edition, London: R. Bentley and Son, 1882), p. 3.

21   C. Knight, *Passages of a working life during half a century, with a prelude of early reminiscences* (London: 1864–5), vol. 1, pp. 40–41.

22   *Narrative of Facts Relative to the Murder of Richard Faulkner Taylor*, p. 35.

23   *Maidstone Journal and Kentish Advertiser*, 2 August 1931.

24 Rev G.A. Cuxson, chaplain of Aylesbury jail, giving evidence to the select committee of the House of Lords on 'The Present Mode of Carrying into Effect Capital Punishments, 1856': *Report and Evidence*, paragraph 85.

25 *Maidstone Journal and Kentish Advertiser*, 2 August 1931.

26 Gatrell, op. cit., p. 100.

27 Sir Samuel Romilly (1757–1818) was a Whig politician who wanted to reform the criminal law of England. He began by writing *Thoughts on Executive Justice*, which was published in 1786. This drew upon the works of Cesare Beccaria. Beccaria and the Enlightenment philosopher Jeremy Bentham fought their reform battle with arguments in favour of a more efficient system of punishment. They pointed to the inefficiency of the capital code, on the grounds that it had failed as an effective deterrent. These writers saw the criminal as a rational individual who commits crime in a deliberate utilitarian fashion. They believed that on the basis of how the criminal code operated in practice, the offender could calculate that his offence of, say, stealing, might result in a capital sentence, but would rarely end in execution and was therefore worth the risk. Nineteenth-century reformers were influenced by these ideas. The writers of the *Report of the Committee for Investigating the Causes of the Alarming Increase of Juvenile Delinquency in the Metropolis* also counted the severity of the criminal code as a chief cause of crime. The thinking was that because there were no graded penalties to fit the crime, acquittals were the only reasonable option in many cases, which meant that several crimes went unpunished. The report's authors argued that if it was made clear that certain penalties appropriate to the crime would definitely be carried out, then they were more likely to be effective as a deterrent. They suggested that the aim of punishment needed to have more explicit rational grounds; but although they sought to make punishment less arbitrary, they held on to the belief that capital punishment should remain in place for offences such as murder. See *Report of the Committee for Investigating the Causes of the Alarming Increase of Juvenile Delinquency in the Metropolis 1816*, p. 10; C. Beccaria, 'An Essay on Crimes and Punishment', appears in English in J. A. Farrer, *Of Crimes and Punishments* (London, 1880); J. Bentham (ed. W. Harrison), *A Fragment on Government and an introduction to the Principles of Morals and Legislation* (Oxford: Clarendon Press, 1948).

28 B.E.F. Knell, 'Capital Punishment: its administration in relation to juvenile offenders in the nineteenth century and its possible administration in the eighteenth', in *The British Journal of Criminology*, vol. 5 (1965), pp. 198–207.

29 J.L. Rayner and G.T. Crook (eds.), *The Complete Newgate Calendar* (London: Navarre Society, 1926), vol.5, pp. 252–5. See also British Trials Series 2325/LXIV. pp. 252–5.

30 *Copy of the Indictment of John Any Bird Bell*, Kent Summer Assizes Felony File 1831, ASSI 94/2097 (National Archives).

31 The following story is taken from *Narrative of Facts Relative to the Murder of Richard Faulkner Taylor*, 1831. Other accounts appear in the *Maidstone and Kentish Advertiser*, of 25 and 31 May 1831, and *The Times* of 30 July and 2 August 1831.

32 *Narrative of Facts Relative to the Murder of Richard Faulkner Taylor*, 1831, p. 41.

33 Heather Shore, *Artful Dodgers: Youth and Crime in Early 19th-Century London*, (Suffolk: Boydell Press, 1999); Margaret May, 'Innocence and experience: the evolution of the concept of juvenile delinquency in the mid-nineteenth century', *Victorian Studies*, xvii (1973), pp. 7–29.

34 J.L. and Barbara Hammond, *The Village Labourer* (London: Longmans, 1966), pp. 242–4.

35 Ibid., p. 244.

36 *Annual Register*, November 1830.

37 Shore, op. cit., pp. 71, 168.

38 Francois Bedarida, *A Social History of England* (London: Routledge, 1991), p. 13.

39 William Augustus Miles (ed. H. Brandon), *Poverty, mendacity, and crime* (London: 1839), p. 45. Cited in Shore, op. cit., p. 1.

40 J.L. Rayner and G.T. Crook (eds.), op. cit., vol. 5, pp. 252–5. Also British Trials Series 2325/LXIV, p. 252.

41 Shore, op. cit., pp. 17–34.

42 R. Porter, *Enlightenment* (London: Penguin, 2001), pp. 383–96. It is easy to exaggerate the process of secularisation at this time. Nevertheless, the rational imperatives of the Enlightenment and of science inaugurated a radical shift in religious conceptions, and for some, such as the German philosopher Hegel, it was felt that this shift would annihilate faith altogether. See D. Outram, *The Enlightenment* (Cambridge: Cambridge University Press, 1995), pp. 32–3.

43 Emsley, op. cit., p. 59.

44 Jose Harris points out that concerns about the depraved morals of the young are often only attributed to evangelical beliefs, but they were much more widespread than that and in fact 'were prevalent in many early Victorian households of every ideological shade – evangelical, High Church, utilitarian, positivist and secularist'. See J. Harris, *Private Lives, Public Spirit: Britain 1870–1914* (London: Penguin, 1993) p. 85.

45 M.G. Jones, *Hannah More* (Cambridge: Cambridge University Press, 1952), p. 117.

46 *Report of the Committee of the Society for Investigating the Causes of the Alarming Increase in Juvenile Delinquency in the Metropolis* (London, 1816), pp. 21–22.

47   *A Narrative of the Facts Relative to the Murder of Richard Faulkner Taylor,*
     p. 41.

48   Eighteenth-century writers like Defoe, and later Fielding, had criticised
     the greed, vanity and corruption of the governing class. See D. Defoe,
     The Complete English Tradesman (Rivington: 1738), vol. 1, p. 93. See
     also H. Fielding, *Enquiry into the Causes of the Late Increase of Robbers*
     (Millar: 1751), pp. xi, xv. Although the concerns of these authors focused
     on the habits of the 'vulgar', they believed that the elite had played their
     part in corrupting those they ruled. See I.A. Bell, *Literature and Crime in
     Augustan England* (London: Routledge, 1991), p. 196, which shows how
     contemporary journals carried equally critical articles.

49   *A Narrative of the Facts Relative to the Murder of Richard Faulkner Taylor,*
     p. 42.

50   *The Criminal Recorder* (London: 1809), vol. 4, pp. 462–3 and A. Knapp
     and B. Baldwin (eds.), *The New Newgate Calendar* (London: 1809–19),
     p. 463.

51   J.L. and Barbara Hammond, op. cit., p. 242. See also E.P. Thompson, *The
     Making of the English Working Class* (Harmondsworth: Penguin, 1963),
     pp. 233–58.

52   William Cobbett, *Rural Rides* (London: Penguin Classics, 2001).

53   Stone believed that the late sixteenth and early seventeenth century were,
     in England, the 'great flogging age: every town and every village had its
     whipping-post which was in constant use as a means of preserving social
     order'. See L. Stone, op. cit., p. 122.

54   E. Pleck, *Domestic Tyranny: The Making of Social Policy against Family
     Violence from Colonial Times to the Present* (Oxford: Oxford University
     Press, 1987), pp. 44–7.

55   Edmund Gosse, *Father and Son* (London: Penguin, 1989). See also
     N. Robertson, 'Home as Nest: Middle Class Childhood in Nineteenth-
     Century Europe', in L. deMause, *History of Childhood* (London: Souvenir
     Press, 1976), pp. 407–31.

56   Rev E. Neale, *Experiences of a Gaol Chaplain comprising recollections of
     ministerial intercourse with criminals of various classes, with their confes-
     sions* (London: Richard Bentley, 1847), vol. 2, chapter 15.

57   Gatrell, op. cit., p. 333.

58   Hugh Cunningham, *Children and Childhood in Western Society Since 1500*
     (London: Longman, 1995), p. 74.

CHAPTER THREE

1   *Derby Mercury*, 30 July 1835, and *The Times*, 1 August 1835.

2   A comment made by Samuel Taylor Coleridge, cited in H. Cunningham,
     *Children of the Poor: Representations of Childhood since the Seventeenth
     Century* (Oxford: Blackwell, 1991) p. 64–76.

3   *Report on Employment of Women and Children in Agriculture*, 1843, vol. xii, p. 109.

4   'A Day at a Derby Silk Mill', in Irina Stickland, *The Voices of Children 1700–1914* (Oxford: Basil Blackwell, 1973), p. 148.

5   *The Times*, 1 August 1835.

6   Michael Ignatieff, *A Just Measure of Pain: The Penitentiary in the Industrial Revolution, 1750–1850* (London: Macmillan, 1989).

7   Gatrell, op. cit.

8   Edward Gibbon Wakefield, *The Hangman and the Judge, or A letter from Jack Ketch to Mr Justice Alderson*, 1833, pp. 5–6. Wakefield (1796–1862) had spent a period in Newgate prison after an illegal marriage to the fifteen-year-old daughter of a wealthy family. On his release, he committed himself to the cause of prison reform.

9   Gatrell, op. cit., p. 544.

10 Ibid., p. 616.

11 From the Appeal Archive, State Papers, Home Office, HO/0120 (National Archives).

12 The *Euryalus* was a special hulk for young boys. Convict records show that Wild was imprisoned on the *Euryalus* prior to transportation: *2130 William Wild per Lord Lyndoch* (2), located at the Archive Office, Tasmania (AOT), Con 31/37. After the loss of the American colonies in 1783 when there was a crisis in the transportation system and convicts could no longer be shipped out there, prison hulks moored on the Thames and at other shipping docks around the country were used to house them. The prison reformer John Howard visited all of the hulks on behalf of the Charles Bunbury Committee. He described one, the *Lion* at Portsmouth: 'The ship was clean and the prisoners had a healthy and placid look; but they laid two on a bed, with one blanket. Here were several to be transported for life and some whose sentences were for short terms: among them were boys of only ten years of age.' In a footnote to one of his reports Howard says: 'The gaoler at Reading told me, 12 July 1788, that of the 11 convicts he carried on board the hulks, 1 April 1787, all were dead but three.' *Report of the Select Committee on Penitentiary Houses*, 1811. Cited in William B. Johnson, *The English Prison Hulks* (London: Christopher Johnson, 1957), p. 31. The magistrate Patrick Colquhoun also calculated that between 1776 and 1795 out of 5,792 convicts serving their sentence on board, 1,946 had died, roughly one in three. See P.A. Colquhoun, *Treatise on the police of the metropolis: explaining the various crimes and misdemeanours which at present are felt as a pressure upon the community: and suggesting remedies for their prevention* (London, 1796).

13 Cited in Heather Shore, op. cit., p. 130.

14   *Second Report from the Select Committee House of Lords on Gaols and Houses of Correction in England and Wales*, Parliamentary Papers (PP) 439, 1835, vol. 11, pp. 519–74, evidence of Thomas Dexter.

15   Ibid., pp. 519–74. It would be very unusual for a child so young to be transported; according to the rest of Dexter's evidence, it was because his mother did not want him returned home after his offence.

16   E.P. Brenton, *Observations on the Training and Education of the Children of Great Britain* (London: C. Rice, 1834), pp. vi, xx.

17   *Report of the Select Committee on Police of the Metropolis* (1828), vi, pp. 104.

18   *2130 William Wild per Lord Lyndoch* (2), Archives Office of Tasmania, con 31/37.

19   Shore, op. cit., pp. 111, 141.

20   Ibid., p. 134.

21   *Report of Prison Visitors* (1843), appendix 1, pp. 1–2. Cited in Jeannie Duckworth, *Fagin's Children: Criminal Children in Victorian England* (London: Hambledon Continuum, 2002), pp. 114–15.

22   Robert Hughes, *The Fatal Shore* (London: Vintage, 2003), p. 622, note 40. See also Duckworth, op. cit., p. 117.

23   Hughes, op. cit., p. 152.

24   *Report of the Select Committee on Transportation* (1837–8), xxii, pp. 5–16.

25   A meticulous physical description of convicts was made on their arrival. *2130 William Wild per Lord Lyndoch* (2), Archives Office of Tasmania, con 18/13.

26   Hughes, op. cit., p. 408.

27   Ibid., p. 399.

28   This is based on a letter from the commandant in charge of Port Arthur, when the juvenile camp was set up: *Captain Charles O'Hara Booth to the Colonial Secretary John Montague*, 24 July 1847. Cited in Duckworth, op. cit., pp. 126–9.

29   N. Hargraves and P. MacFie, 'The Empire's First Stolen Generation: The First Intake at Point Puer, 1834–39' in *Exiles of Empire, Tasmanian Historical Studies*, vol. 6 (2), 1999, pp. 129–54.

30   Shore, op. cit., p. 135.

31   William's conduct report is extensive. *2130 William Wild per Lord Lyndoch* (2), Archives Office of Tasmania, con. 31/37.

32   The reports on this case are taken from the *Bristol Gazette* of 27 December 1849 and 11 April 1850.

33   *2130 William Wild per Lord Lyndoch* (2), AOT, con 31/37.

34   *26766 Alfred Dancey per Equestrian* (3), AOT, con. 33/111.

35   N. Hargraves and P. MacFie, op. cit., pp. 129–54.

36   Walter Lowe Clay, *The Prison Chaplain: A Memoir of the Rev John Clay* (Cambridge, 1861), p. 407.

37   Michael Ignatieff, op. cit., p. i.

CHAPTER FOUR

1   Charles Dickens, *Sketches by Boz* (London: Penguin, 1995), pp. 240–1.
2   Mary Carpenter, *Reformatory Schools, for the Children of the Perishing and Dangerous Classes, and for Juvenile Offenders* (London: C. Gilpin, 1851), p. 69.
3   Shore, op. cit.
4   William Beck, *Peter Bedford, the Spitalfields Philanthropist* (London: Friends Tract Association, 1903), p. 53.
5   Gillian Avery, *Nineteenth Century Children: Heroes and Heroines in English Children's Stories 1780–1900* (London: Hodder and Stoughton, 1965), pp. 189–202, 199.
6   Margaret May, 'Innocence and Experience: The Evolution of the Concept of Juvenile Delinquency in the Mid-Nineteenth Century', *Victorian Studies*, (September 1973), pp. 18–19.
7   Matthew Davenport Hill, 'Practical Suggestions to the Founders of Reformatory Schools', in J. Symons, *On the Reformation of Young Offenders* (London: Routledge, 1855), p. 2.
8   Quoted in Avery, op. cit., p. 170.
9   John Glyde, *The Moral, Social and Religious Condition of Ipswich in the Middle of the Nineteenth Century* (Ipswich: 1850, reprinted 1971 by S.R. Publishers, Wakefield), p. 66.
10   Mary Carpenter, *Reformatory Schools, for the Children of the Perishing and Dangerous Classes, and for Juvenile Offender* (London: C. Gilpin, 1851).
11   Ibid., p. 73.
12   In Carpenter's evidence to a House of Commons inquiry she criticised the imprisonment of boys in Parkhurst prison, believing it to be incompatible with her favoured aim of reform. However, she did accept that very hardened criminals might benefit from going there. *Report from the Select Committee of the House of Commons on the Treatment of Criminal and Destitute Juveniles*, PP (515), 1852, vol. 7, p. 102.
13   J.E. Carpenter, *Life and Work of Mary Carpenter* (London, Macmillan, 1973). Also Herbert McLachlan, *The Unitarian Movement in the Religious Life of England: its contribution to thought and learning 1700–1900* (London: George, Allen and Unwin, 1934).
14   *Second Report from the Select Committee of the House of Lords inquiry into the execution of the Criminal Law, especially respecting Juvenile Offenders and Transportation*, PP (534), 1847, vol. 7, appendix: 'Answers of Certain of Judges to the Questions submitted to them by the Select Committee', pp. 569–70. Cited in Leon Radzinowicz and Roger Hood, *A History of English Criminal Law: Volume 5. The Emergence of Penal Policy* (London, Stevens and Sons, 1986), p. 174.

15   Accounts of this case appear in *The Daily Post* (Liverpool) of 23 August 1855, *The Liverpool Mercury* of 24 August and 31 August, and *The Liverpool Albion Weekly* of 27 August 1855.

16   Anthony Miller, *Poverty Deserved: Relieving the Poor in Victorian Liverpool* (Birkenhead: Liver Press, 1988), pp. 7–20.

17   Silas Hocking, *Her Benny: A Tale of Street Life (in Victorian Liverpool)* (London: F. Warne and Co., 1879), p. 100.

18   Miller, op. cit., pp. 30–48.

19   *Liverpool Mercury*, 24 August 1855.

20   *The Daily Post* (Liverpool), 23 August 1855.

21   A report on the jail appears in the *Liverpool Mercury*, 31 August 1855.

22   For a general picture of prison life see Jeannie Duckworth, op. cit., pp. 57–79. Also Shore, op. cit., pp. 101–10, and Sean McConville, *English Local Prisons 1860–1900: Next Only to Death* (London: Routledge, 1995), pp. 350–61.

23   Walter L. Clay, *The Prison Chaplain: A Memoir of the Rev. John Clay* (Cambridge, 1861), p. 386. By the mid-nineteenth century, the role of the prison chaplain involved a great deal more than religious instruction. The chaplain was an internal inspector of the prison with responsibility for monitoring the conduct and education of the inmates. He was also charged with post-release arrangements for prisoners, helping them to find a job and a place to live. Sean McConville, *A History of English Prison Administration, 1850–77* (London: Routledge, 1981), p. 447.

24   Mary Carpenter, op. cit., p. 100, cited in Duckworth, op. cit., p. 73.

25   The description that follows is based on what is known about the regime and structure of Parkhurst Prison, upon which other juvenile departments or special prisons were modelled. However, it is important to keep in mind that these details were not replicated exactly in other institutions. In Liverpool, for example, even though the prison was built along the lines of the separate system, the problem of overcrowding meant that, after a few years, inmates were sleeping three to a cell. Sean McConville, *A History of English Prison Administration 1850–77*, op. cit., p. 365. Also B. Manser, *Behind The Small Wooden Door: The Inside Story of Parkhurst Prison* (Isle of Wight: Coach House Publishers, 2000), pp. 1–15.

26   *Chaplain's Report*, Borough Gaol, Liverpool, 29 October 1869 (Liverpool Record Office), p. 16.

27   Mary Carpenter, op. cit., p. 298.

28   *Chaplain's Report*, Borough Gaol, Liverpool, 29 October 1869 (Liverpool Record Office), p. 16.

29   Cited in Sean McConville, *English Local Prisons 1860–1900*, op. cit., p. 358.

30   *The Report of the Reformatories and Industrial Schools Royal Commission*, PP, 1884 (C3876), vol. 45, Minutes of Evidence, q. 3986, p. 149.

31   Cited in Michael Ignatieff, op. cit., pp. 207–8.

32   *Daily Chronicle*, 28 May 1897, reprinted in Rupert Hart-Davis, *Selected Letters of Oscar Wilde* (Oxford: Clarendon Press, 1979), p. 270.

33   Quoted in Philip Priestly, *Victorian Prison Lives 1830–1914* (London: Methuen, 1985), pp. 55–8.

34   Margaret May, op. cit., pp. 7–29.

35   *Chaplain's Report*, Borough Gaol, Liverpool, 29 October 1869 (Liverpool Record Office), pp. 16–17.

36   Gatrell, op. cit., p. 397.

37   There were a series of attacks involving garrotting in 1862; one of them involved a member of Parliament. It led to the reintroduction of flogging, through the Garrotter's Act of 1863. The Act also led to harsher prison discipline and tougher sentences for repeat offenders. See Emsley, op. cit., pp. 276–7.

38   Thomas Carlyle, 'Model Prisons', in Elizur Wright (ed.), *Latter Day Pamphlets of Thomas Carlyle* (Boston, USA: Phillips, Sampson and Co., 1850), p. 70.

39   Mary Carpenter, op. cit, p. 292.

40   These views were exchanged at a meeting of the Royal Society of Arts in 1855 and are recorded in Symons, op. cit, pp. 82–118.

41   Symons, op. cit., pp. 82–118.

42   She insisted that imprisonment was a 'useless method'. Juvenile offenders 'are almost certain to go on undeterred, unreclaimed, from one degree of crime to another'. See Mary Carpenter, op. cit., pp. 274–5. See also Mary Carpenter, *Juvenile Delinquents – Their Conditions and Treatment* (London: W. and F.G. Cash, 1853).

43   *Report from the Select Committee on Criminal and Destitute Juveniles*, PP 1852 (515), vol. 7.1, q. 821, p. 97.

44   Cited in Pinchbeck and Hewitt, op. cit., vol. 2, p. 477.

45   Victoria 29 and 30., c. 117, statute 14.

46   *Juvenile Offenders Bill* (24 April 1850), vol. 110, column 771.

47   See letter to Sir George Grey cited by him in the debate on the *Juvenile Offenders Bill* (24 April 1850), vol. 110, column 778.

CHAPTER FIVE

1   G.M. Trevelyan, *English Social History* (Harmondsworth: Penguin, 1964), vol. 4, p. 158.

2   Gertrude Tuckwell, 'The State and its Children' (1894) in H. Gibbins, *Social Questions of Today* (London: 1891), p. 5.

3   *Stockport Advertiser*, 19 April 1861.

4   *The Times*, 17 April 1861.

5   *Stockport Advertiser*, 19 April 1861.

6   This archive material is available from The Stockport Heritage Library, Wellington Road, South Stockport SK1 3RS. Other material is available at Chester Archive, Chester County Council, Cheshire CH1 1SF.

7   *Chester Chronicle*, 10 August 1861.

8   Cited in Margaret May, op. cit., pp. 7–29.

9   *Stockport Advertiser*, 16 August 1861.

10   Ibid.

11   *The Times*, 17 August 1861.

12   Ibid.

13   Jean-Jacques Rousseau, *Emile* (London: Everyman, 1993), pp. 60–85, 84.

14   Ibid., p. 85.

15   Ibid., p. 39.

16   Major General Sir Edmund Frederick du Cane, 'The Decrease of Crime', in *The Nineteenth Century*, XXXIII, 193 (March 1893), p. 481. Cited in Sean McConville, *English Local Prisons 1860-1900*, op. cit., p. 172.

17   In challenging the Christian tradition Rousseau did say: 'There is no original sin in the human heart', but this was because he believed that the state of nature was not a moral condition at all; it was a state of innocence more animal than man, and therefore beyond religious good and evil. Rousseau, op. cit., p. 66.

18   *The Times*, 17 August 1861.

19   The use of the term 'conservative' here is used to denote the non-radical character of the newspaper rather than any party political allegiance. In the changing political climate of the time, newspapers tended to support causes rather than parties. *The Times*, though, being the newspaper of the Establishment, was conservatively inclined even when it favoured reform. In 1867 the paper sought a compromised measure on parliamentary reform, believing that Lord Russell's bill had gone a step too far in its extension of the franchise. See *History of the Times 1841–1884*, 'The Tradition Established', vol. 2 (written, printed and published at the office of *The* Times, London, 1939), pp. 400–03. However, *The Times*, together with the liberal *Stockport Advertiser*, backed the factory reform movement in the 1830s, whereas the *Manchester Guardian*, which was also liberal, but also the voice of the northern textile manufacturers, had opposed it. See H. Barker, *Newspapers, Politics and English Society 1695–1855* (London: Longman, 2000), p. 209.

20   Melville wrote this in a review of Nathaniel Hawthorne's *Mosses from Old Manse*, cited in H. Melville, *Moby Dick* (London: Dent and Sons, 1969), p. vi.

21   'Spencer saw the universe as an organism, one that became steadily more organised. The progress of society from savagery to barbarism to civilisation as political and economic structures became more elaborate was a corollary of this universal principle.' T. M. Porter, 'Natural

Science and Social Theory' in R.C. Olby et al. (eds.), *Companion to the History of Modern Science* (London: Routledge, 1990), p. 1036. See also Peter J. Bowler, *Evolution: The History of an Idea* (Berkeley: University of California Press, 1989), p. 221.

22   Spencer eschewed any state-sponsored reform to help progress along. Such action, he believed, would interfere with the natural laws of development governing social change. It is this belief that has linked Spencer with the extreme doctrines of *laissez-faire* liberalism, and in this sense he can be seen as a conservative thinker. See D. Wiltshire, *The Social and Political Thought of Herbert Spencer* (Oxford: Clarendon Press, 1978), and J.D.Y. Peel, *Herbert Spencer the Evolution of a Sociologist* (London: Heinemann, 1971).

23   *The Times*, 17 August 1861.

24   *Stockport Advertiser*, 16 August 1861.

25   *The Times*, 17 August 1861.

26   For example, this complaint by the borough reeve and constables of Manchester: 'The hardest Heart must melt at the melancholy Sight of such a Multitude of Children, both Male and Female, in this Town, who live in gross Ignorance, Infidelity, and habitual Profanation of the Lord's Day. What Crowds fill the Streets! Tempting each other to Idleness, Play, Lewdness, and every other Species of Wickedness.' *The Manchester Mercury*, 10 August 1784. Cited in Fisher, 'Birth of a Prison Retold', p. 1290.

27   For a thorough account of these changes see Dorothy Porter, *Health, Civilisation and the State: A history of public health from ancient to modern times* (London: Routledge, 1999), pp. 73–8.

28   For the political leanings of *The Times* see Raymond Williams, *The Long Revolution* (London: Pelican, 1961), p. 211. Pamela Horn cites crime reduction and the maintenance of order as 'one of the main aims of the voluntary societies in building schools'. P. Horn, *The Victorian Town Child* (Gloucestershire: Sutton, 1997), p. 81.

29   The words of Henry Moseley, one of the first of Her Majesty's Inspectors in 1845. Cited in Richard Johnson, 'Educational Policy and Social Control in Early Victorian England', in *Past and Present*, no. 49, November 1970, p. 96.

30   *Chester Chronicle*, 10 August 1861.

31   Chester County Record Office has an archive of records on Bradwall kept by Robert Bygott, a local solicitor, who was secretary to the managers over this period.

32   Mary Carpenter, *Juvenile Delinquents, their Condition and Treatment* (London: 1853), p. 301.

CHAPTER SIX

1 The story of this murder is taken from contemporary newspaper reports and witness depositions. They are cited in the notes below.

2 Charles Darwin, *The Expressions of the Emotions in Man and Animals* (London: HarperCollins, 1998, first published 1872), p. 137.

3 Henry Maudsley, *The Pathology of Mind* (London: Appleton and Co., 1899), pp. 279–280.

4 Michael Collie, *Henry Maudsley, Victorian Psychiatrist: A Bibliographical Study* (London: St Paul's Bibliographies, 1988). See also T. Turner, 'Henry Maudsley: Psychiatrist, Philosopher and Entrepreneur', *Journal of Psychological Medicine* (1988), vol. 18, pp. 551–74.

5 Maudsley was also influenced by the neurologist John Hughlings-Jackson, who used Darwin's evolutionary biology as a model for the organisation of the human nervous system. See Michael H. Stone, *Healing the Mind* (London: Pimlico, 1998), pp. 116–17.

6 Maudsley, *The Pathology of Mind*, op. cit., p. 282.

7 Ibid., p. 283.

8 HO 144/52/4. 1881, (National Archives).

9 *Carlisle Journal*, 4 November 1881.

10 Maudsley, *The Pathology of Mind*, p. 283.

11 The deposition of Mrs Pallister, Cumberland and Westmorland Assizes, ASSI 52/4, 1881. Assize Records (ASSI) are located at the National Archives (NA), Kew, London.

12 Henry Maudsley, *Body and Will* (London: Routledge, Kegan Paul, 1884), p. 246.

13 *The Standard*, 18 November 1881.

14 Jean-Etienne Esquirol (trans. E.K. Hunt), *Des Maladies Mentales*, (Philadelphia, 1845), vol.1, pp. 362–78. Located at the Institute of Psychiatry, London.

15 *The Standard*, appearing as a supplement to the *Carlisle Patriot*, 18 November 1881.

16 Esquirol, op. cit., pp. 371–2.

17 William Hale, *History of the Pleas of the Crown* (London: S. Emlyn, 1736), pp. 367–8.

18 H. Maudsley, 'Criminal Responsibility in Relation to Insanity', *Journal of Mental Science*, vol. 41, no. 175 (October 1895), pp. 657–65.

19 *The Standard*, 18 November 1881.

20 Report of Drs Orange and Macdonald, pp. 1–11., HO 144/528 (NA).

21 Maudsley, *The Pathology of Mind*, p. 290.

22 Cited in the *Carlisle Patriot*, 18 November 1881.

23 Henry Humble, 'Infanticide, its Cause and Cure', in *The Church and the World: Essays on Questions of the Day*, ed. Rev Orby Shipley (1866), pp. 51–69, 57. Cited in Josephine McDonagh, *Child Murder and British*

Culture 1720–1900 (Cambridge: Cambridge University Press, 2003), p. 123.

24 In 1938 the law on infanticide was changed – it became a separate category of crime rather than one of simply murder. There were a range of penalties, but most women found guilty of it were put on probation. See A. Buchanan, *Psychiatric Aspects of Justification, Excuse and Mitigation: The Jurisprudence of Mental Abnormality in Anglo-American Criminal Law* (London: Jessica Kingsley Publishers, 2000), p. 102.

25 H. Maudsley, *Responsibility in Mental Disease*, (London: Appleton and Co., fourth edition, 1872; first published 1867), p. 58.

26 H. Ellis, *The Criminal* (London: 1890), p. 4. Published in *The Contemporary Science Series* (London: W. Heinemann, 1951).

27 Ellis, op. cit., p. 9.

28 Ibid., p. 11.

29 Maudsley, *Responsibility in Mental Disease*, p. 26.

30 Maudsley, *The Pathology of Mind*, p. 295.

31 Cited in Edward Shorter, *A History of Psychiatry from the Era of the Asylum to the Age of Prozac* (New York: John Wiley and Sons, 1997), p. 94 ref. 82, p. 325.

32 Maudsley, *The Pathology of Mind*, p. 282.

33 A. Tredgold, *Mental Deficiency (Amentia)* (London: Balliere and Co., 1908), p. 320. In their later work, both writers gave an increasing emphasis to the role of will and the abnormality that might result in a sudden harmful impulse. For a discussion on this history, see M. Thompson, *The Problem of Mental Deficiency* (Oxford: Oxford University Press, 1998). Also, for a discussion on the contrasting approaches of government and welfare organisations to the problem of dangerous children and children in danger, see Pamela Dale, *The Mental Deficiency Acts 1913–1948: Medical care, control and eugenics* (unpublished PhD thesis, University of Exeter, 2002), chapter 5.

34 Reports of Drs Orange and Macdonald, pp. 1–11, HO 144/528 (NA).

35 J. Burnett (ed.), *Useful Toil: Autobiographies of Working People from the 1820s to the 1920s* (London: 1974), p. 138, cited in A. Davin, *Growing Up Poor: Home, School and Street in London, 1870–1914* (London: Rivers Oram Press, 1996), p. 158.

36 *The Standard*, appearing in a supplement to the *Carlisle Patriot*, 18 November 1881.

37 Davin, op. cit., pp. 157–73.

38 Ibid., p. 256, note 12.

39 *Carlisle Patriot*, 4 November 1881.

40 N. Walker, *Crime and Insanity in England* (Edinburgh: Edinburgh University Press, 1968), vol. 1, pp. 128, 129–31. There were several attempts to change the law so that a woman accused of killing her child

could be given the sentence of manslaughter rather than murder, but it was not until 1922 that the law was changed.

41 *Carlisle Patriot*, 4 November 1881.

42 Home Office papers (HO) 144/528 National Archives (NA).

43 *Petition letter from Woking prison in Surrey*, HO 144/528 (NA).

44 *Letter from Fred A. Gardiner, visiting director of Woking prison*, HO 144/528 (NA).

45 *Letter from John and Margaret Messenger (senior)*, HO 144/528 (NA).

46 *Letter from H.B. Collingwood*, HO 144/528 (NA). According to the 1901 census, Margaret Messenger was working as a dressmaker. Her parents had both died, and she was living at the home where she was born in the parish of Westward, just outside Carlisle, with her two younger brothers. The 1901 census can be found at www.1901censusonline.com

CHAPTER SEVEN

1 Nigel Walker, *Crime and Insanity in England: The Historical Perspective* (Edinburgh University Press, 1968), vol. 1, pp. 186–7.

2 There are accounts of this trial in *Old Bailey Session Papers*, 1847–1848, case 290, second session, pp. 280–94; *The Times*, 11 November and 26 November 1847, and 16 December 1847. Also Joel Peter Eigen, *Unconscious Crime: Mental Absence and Criminal Responsibility* (Baltimore: The Johns Hopkins University Press, 2003), pp. 105–126.

3 'Baron Rolfe's charge to the Jury, in the case of the Boy Allnutt, who was tried at the Central Criminal Court, for the Murder of his Grandfather, on 15th December, 1847', in *The Journal of Psychological Medicine and Mental Pathology*, 1 April 1848, p. 215.

4 There have been three Bedlams in London's history. The Bethlam Lunatic Asylum was built in the 1670s at Moorfields. From the fourteenth century, St Mary of Bethlehem (also known as Bethlem) had been a hospital for the insane housed at Bishopsgate in London. The final building known as Bedlam was built in the early nineteenth century in Southwark. Peter Ackroyd, *London, The Biography* (London: Chatto and Windus, 2000), pp. 618–23. Roy Porter, *London, A Social History* (London: Penguin, 1996), pp. 38, 96.

5 *The Times* lead article, 6 March 1843.

6 Joel Peter Eigen, 'Delusion in the courtroom: the role of partial insanity in early forensic testimony', in *Medical History*, vol. 35, no. 1, 1991, pp. 25–49.

7 Walker, op. cit., p. 94.

8 Ray was an American psychiatrist whose text was influential in the formation of the legal concept of 'irresistible impulse'. The concept was adopted by a number of states in America. Alec Buchanan, *Psychiatric Aspects of Justification, Excuse and Mitigation: The Jurisprudence of Mental*

Abnormality inn Anglo-American Criminal Law (London: Jessica Kingsley, 2000), pp. 91–3.

9   W. Overholser, 'Issac Ray', in Hermann Mannheim (ed.), *Pioneers in Criminology* (London: Stevens and Sons, 1960), p. 121.

10   Walker, op. cit., pp. 104–11.

11   One of the important aspects of the insanity defence from the time of Coke until 1843 was that no specific rule applied. In true common-law fashion, legal precedent was the judge's guide on such matters. For extensive discussion of this debate see Walker, op. cit., pp. 84–103, and F.A. Whitlock, *Criminal Responsibility and Mental Illness* (London: Butterworths, 1963), pp. 20–53.

12   *R. v McNaughten* (1843) 10 Cl. and Fin. 200.

13   Whitlock, op. cit., p. 3.

14   Gordon N. Ray (ed.), *The Letters and Private Papers of William Makepeace Thackeray*, (Oxford: Oxford University Press, 1945), vol. 1, 'From Mr Thackeray to Mrs Carmichael-Smythe, 4 August 1840', p. 462.

15   *The Times*, 16 December 1847.

16   Potter, op. cit., pp. 47–8.

17   'The Plea of Insanity – Case of the Boy Allnutt', *London Medical Gazette*, also known as *Journal of Practical Medicine*, vol. 6 (1848), pp. 475–7.

18   Joel Peter Eigen, 'Sense and Sensibility: fateful splitting in the Victorian insanity trial', in *Domestic and International Trials, 1700–2000* (Manchester: Manchester University Press, 2003), pp. 21–35.

19   Charles Dickens, *Sketches By Boz* (London: Penguin Classics, 1995), p. 232.

20   'Baron Rolfe's charge to the Jury', *The Journal of Psychological Medicine and Mental Pathology*, 1 April 1848, p. 215.

21   Eigen, op. cit., p. 26.

22   *Old Bailey Session Papers*, 1847–1848, case 290, second session, pp. 293.

23   Ibid., pp. 293–294.

24   *The Times*, 16 December 1847.

25   Ibid.

26   Ibid.

27   Ibid.

28   Lord Justice Atkin's Committee on Insanity and Crime was set up in 1922 to clarify the issue, and its decision to recommend a change to the law was rejected by law lords and politicians. The most thorough and precise study of the criminal responsibility question was undertaken by the post-Second World War Royal Commission on Capital Punishment. See the report of that title, 1949–53, Command Paper 8932, sometimes known as the Gowers Commission. For a discussion of this, see Walker, op. cit., vol 1, pp. 108–11. See also Whitlock, op. cit., pp. 35–53.

29 The trial of Harold Jones was an extraordinary case in which he stood trial for the murder of one little girl, and amid huge protests from the local population and with not enough evidence for a conviction, he was acquitted. But after another neighbour's child was found dead only months later, he eventually pleaded guilty to the first murder. For coverage of this case see *The Times*, 15, 21 and 22 July and 2 November 1921. Also *South Wales Gazette*, 4 November 1921.

30 This was the opinion of many lawyers, who were unsettled by the 'vagueness and fluidity of some psychiatric concepts'. See Whitlock, op. cit., pp. 4–5.

31 These were the views of one barrister, Sir Leo Page, in his book *The Young Lag* (London: Faber, 1950), p. 58. For a magistrate's sceptical opinion on the psychological evidence, see F.T. Giles, *Children and the Law* (London: Pelican, 1959).

32 The probation system was established by the Liberal government in 1907. Initially it was confined to first offenders, and because their use was optional it took time for orders to gain more widespread use. By 1913, probationary orders were most commonly used in the summary courts. They were not used in murder cases, so it would appear that this boy had committed previous non-serious offences that were seen as being the result of his brain damage. See Radzinowicz and Hood, op. cit., pp. 642–7.

33 *The Times*, 25 July 1945; *Rochester, Chatham and Gillingham Journal*, 18 June 1945.

34 'The Plea of Insanity – Case of the Boy Allnutt', *London Medical Gazette*, 1848, p. 475.

CHAPTER EIGHT

1 Sigmund Freud, 'Analysis of a Phobia in a Five-Year-Old Boy' in J. Strachey (ed.), *The Standard Edition of the Complete Psychological Works of Sigmund Freud* (London: Hogarth Press, 1953–74), vol. 10. This was not psychoanalysis in the conventional sense. Freud did see the boy on occasion, but he was analysed through the father who brought descriptions of Hans' behaviour, and his expressions in conversations and through drawings, to Freud, who then suggested how they might be interpreted. The first discussion of Oedipal desire appears in Freud, *The Interpretation of Dreams*, vol. 4 (London: Penguin Freud Library, 1991), p. 351. See also Freud's essay 'The Dissolution of the Oedipus Complex' (1924), in *On Sexuality* (London: The Penguin Freud Library, 1986), vol. 7.

2 L. Bender (ed.), *Aggression, Hostility, and Anxiety in Children* (Springfield: Charles Thomas, 1953), pp. 42–56.

3 Freud, 'Civilisation and its Discontents', in *Civilisation, Society and Religion* (London: Penguin Freud Library, 1991), vol. 12.

4   Stephen Frosh, *The Politics of Psychoanalysis: An Introduction to Freudian and Post-Freudian Theory* (London: Macmillan, 1987), pp. 47–51.

5   Freud, 'Analysis of a Phobia in a Five-Year-Old Boy', pp. 86–7.

6   Freud, 'Introductory Lectures on Psychoanalysis' in J. Strachey (ed.), op. cit., pp. 333–4.

7   Melanie Klein, *Love, Guilt and Reparation and Other Works 1921–1945* (London: Vintage, 1991).

8   Freud, *The Interpretation of Dreams*, p. 350.

9   G.F. Still, 'Some Abnormal Psychical Conditions in Children' in *The Lancet*, vol. 1, 1902, pp. 1008–12, 1077–82, 1163–8.

10   Quoted in M.H. Stone, op. cit., p. 156.

11   Sir Cyril Burt, *The Young Delinquent* (London: University of London Press Ltd, 1925), pp. 560–79.

12   *The Young Delinquent* set out a methodology for the psychological study of delinquency, and this case was one the author kept returning to.

13   Burt, op. cit., p. 3.

14   Ibid., p. 5.

15   Ibid., p. 441.

16   Freud, *The Interpretation of Dreams*, p. 354.

17   J. Piaget, *The Moral Judgement of the Child* (New York: Free Press, 1965). Also P. Schilder and D. Wechsler, 'Studies of Children's Attitudes Towards Death', in L. Bender (ed.), *Aggression, Hostility, and Anxiety in Children* (Springfield: Charles Thomas, 1953), pp. 42–56. Also S. Anthony, *The Child's Discovery of Death: a Study in Child Psychology* (London: Kegan and Paul, 1940). In this interesting study by Sylvia Anthony, children's attitudes towards death were examined at different ages. She believed that it is only around the age of nine that a child begins to understand death more realistically.

18   L. Bender, 'Children with Homicidal Aggression' in *Aggression, Hostility and Anxiety in Children*. Also L. Bender, 'Children and Adolescents Who Have Killed', in *The American Journal of Psychiatry*, vol. 116, 1959–60, pp. 510–13. Bender had been studying this group of children since 1935.

19   Burt, op. cit., pp. 509–11.

20   Ibid., p. 511.

21   L. Bender, 'Children with Homicidal Aggression', p. 511.

22   Freud, *The Interpretation of Dreams*, p. 355.

23   Burt, op. cit., p. 9.

24   The case never came to court because the coroner's inquest had returned a verdict of accidental death and the boy, aged seven, was not considered criminally responsible. It was only through the sessions that the child had with Cyril Burt that the deliberate nature of the crime emerged. See Burt, op. cit., p. 3.

25 The psychiatrist John Bowlby being among the most important. His series of books on attachment and loss replaced the instinct theories of early psychoanalysis, as they studied the ways in which problems in the mother-child relationship affect children's behaviour. See J. Bowlby, *Attachment* (London: Penguin, 1989), vol. 1 (3); J. Bowlby, *Separation* (London: Penguin, 1987), vol. 2 (5); J. Bowlby, *Loss* (London: Penguin, 1987), vol. 3 (3).

26 William M. Easson et al, 'Murderous Aggression by Children and Adolescents', in *Archives of General Psychiatry*, vol. 4, 1961, pp. 27–35.

27 L. Bender (ed.), *Aggression, Hostility and Anxiety in Children*.

28 Leo Kanner, *Child Psychiatry* (Springfield: Charles Thomas, 1935).

29 The oldest child in the sample was twelve and a half. See Lewis et al, 'Homicidally Aggressive Young Children: Neuropsychiatric and Experiential Correlates', in *The American Journal of Psychiatry*, vol. 140, February 1983, pp. 148–53.

30 Bender, 'Children with Homicidal Aggression', p. 95.

31 The names and places in this case have been changed.

32 Deposition of Dr Harry Walker, Assize Records (Sheffield), ASSI 45/335 (National Archives), located at Kew, London.

33 Statement of Doreen Russell, ASSI 45/335.

34 Statement of Anne Smith, ASSI 45/335.

35 5 and 6 Elizabeth II, c. 72 (Section Two) of the Homicide Act for England and Wales 1957: 'Where a person kills or is a party to the killing of another, he shall not be convicted of murder if he was suffering from such an abnormality of the mind (whether arising from a condition of arrested or retarded development of the mind or any inherent causes or induced by disease or injury) as substantially impaired his mental responsibility for his acts or omissions in doing or being party to the killing.'

36 Psychiatric report on Doreen Russell, ASSI 45/335, pp. 1–7.

37 *The Times*, 28 November 1958.

38 Walker, op. cit., vol. 2, pp. 245–53.

39 Christopher Wardle, 'Twentieth Century Influences on the Development in Britain of Services for Child and Adolescent Psychiatry', *British Journal of Psychiatry*, vol. 159, 1991, pp. 53–68. Also Lionel Hersov, 'Child Psychiatry in Britain – The Last 30 Years', *Journal of Child Psychology and Psychiatry*, vol. 27, 1996, no. 6, pp. 781–801.

40 *Children and Homicide*, a pamphlet published by the campaign organisation JUSTICE, London, 1996.

41 Michael Rutter began his career at the Maudsley Hospital in London in the 1960s. He was responsible for some of the most important research into disturbed children that took place during this period. This, along with his subsequent work with children, was pivotal in the development

of child psychiatry. See Wardle, 'Twentieth Century Influences on the Development in Britain of Services for Child and Adolescent Psychiatry'.

42 Gitta Sereny, *Cries Unheard: The Story of Mary Bell* (London: Papermac, second edition, 1999), p. 112.

43 P. Scott, 'Some Issues in The Classification of Psychopaths', *British Medical Journal*, vol. 1, 1960, p. 1642.

44 Psychiatric report on Doreen Russell.

45 Joseph Michaels, 'Enuresis in Murderous Aggressive Children and Adolescents', *Archives of General Psychiatry*, vol. 5, 1961, pp. 490–93.

46 Blake Morrison, *As If*, p. 217.

47 *The Times*, 29 November 1958.

48 However, it was also the case that the judge in this case showed a great deal of sympathy towards Mary Bell. His heartfelt wish to see her treated was not possible because no hospital could accommodate such a young girl. See G. Sereny, *The Case of Mary Bell* (London: Arrow, 1972), p. 208.

49 Sereny, *Cries Unheard*, p. 123.

50 For the beginnings of forensic psychiatry see Roy Porter, *The Greatest Benefit to Mankind: A Medical History of Humanity from Antiquity to the Present* (London: Fontana, 1999), p. 501.

51 *The Times*, 29 November 1958.

52 There had been three Children's Acts since the start of the century. The first, in 1908, introduced a separate legal system for juveniles. Some scholars have argued that the Act 'reflected a revolutionary change of attitude from the days when the young offender was regarded as a small adult, fully responsible for his crime'. See Pinchbeck and Hewitt, op. cit., vol. 2, 1983, pp. 492–4. A consolidating piece of legislation was the Children and Young Persons Act 1933, which brought the care of delinquent and neglected children closer together and involved local education authorities. It also replaced reformatories and industrial schools with approved schools. Local authority children's departments were established by the Children's Act of 1948.

CHAPTER NINE

1 Laurie Taylor was a retired journalist who covered Mary Bell's trial for the *Daily Mirror*. Quoted in the *Daily Mirror*, 28 April 1998.

2 *Chronicle of the Twentieth Century* (London: Dorling Kindersley, 1995), p. 991.

3 For example, a report in *The Times*, 28 October 1988, features a picture of Bell alongside another child who had murdered. The caption read: 'The disturbing faces of child murderers.'

4 G. Sereny, *The Case of Mary Bell* (Arrow: London, 1972), p. 194.

5 *Daily Mirror*, 14 December 1968.

6 Quoted in Sereny, *The Case of Mary Bell*, p. 200.

7   *Daily Mirror,* 14 December 1968.
8   Sereny, *The Case of Mary Bell,* p. 193.
9   Sereny, *Cries Unheard: The Story of Mary Bell* (London: Macmillan, 1998), p. 129.
10 G. Sereny, 'Regina v. Mary Bell', *Daily Telegraph,* 12 December 1969.
11 *The Daily Mirror,* 13 December 1968.
12 G. Sereny, 'Regina v. Mary Bell', *Daily Telegraph,* 12 December 1969.
13 Sereny, *Cries Unheard,* p. 111.
14 Ibid., p. 33.
15 'Children in Trouble' Command Paper 3601 (HMSO, 1968). Cited in Nigel Parton, *The Politics of Child Abuse* (London: Palgrave, 1985), p. 45.
16 Sula Wolff, *Children under Stress* (London: Pelican, 1969).
17 Ian Hacking, *Rewriting the Soul: Multiple Personality and the Sciences of Memory* (Princeton: Princeton University Press, 1995), chapter 4.
18 J.M. Beattie, *Crimes and the Courts in England 1660–1800* (Oxford: Clarendon Press, 1986), pp. 127–9.
19 Hacking, op. cit., p. 62.
20 Islington social services adopted a policy on child sexual abuse that was drawn up by a group of feminists working in the department. For a full outline of the policy and a brief discussion, see M. Boushel and S. Noakes, 'Developing a Policy on Child Sexual Abuse', *Feminist Review,* no. 28, spring 1988, pp. 150–7.
21 Parton, op. cit., p. 67.
22 Karl Figlio and Robert Young, 'An Interview with John Bowlby on the Origins and Reception of his Work', *Free Associations,* no. 6, pp. 36–54.
23 J. Bowlby, *Maternal Care and Mental Health,* World Health Organisation, Geneva (London. HMSO) – published in abridged version as *Child Care and the Growth of Love* (London: Penguin, 1964).
24 H. Hendrick, *Children, Childhood and English Society 1880–1990* (Cambridge: Cambridge University Press, 1997), p. 32.
25 Sir Harold Scott (ed.), *The Concise Encyclopaedia of Crime and Criminals* (London: Andre Deutsch, 1961), p. 57.
26 For a critical discussion of the family orthodoxy from a feminist perspective, see M. MacLeod and E. Saraga, 'Challenging the Orthodoxy', *Feminist Review,* no. 28, spring 1988, pp. 16–25. This quote appears on p. 31 of the same article.
27 'Incest: Child Abuse Begins at Home', *Ms Magazine* (USA), May 1977; Linda Gordon, *Heroes of Their Own Lives: The History and Politics of Family Violence* (London: Penguin, 1988); Judith Ennew, *The Sexual Exploitation of Children* (Cambridge: Polity Press, 1986); Elizabeth Ward, *Father-Daughter Rape* (London: The Women's Press, 1984).
28 L. Gordon and P. O'Keefe, 'Incest as a Form of Family Violence: Evidence from Historical Case Records', *Journal of Marriage and the Family,* vol. 46,

no. 1, 1984, pp. 253–67; J. Herman, *Father-Daughter Incest* (Harvard: University Press, 1981); Department of Health, *Child Protection: Message from Research* (London: HMSO, 1995), pp. 75–7.

29   Hacking, op. cit., p. 55.

30   Beatrix Campbell, *Unofficial Secrets: Child Sexual Abuse – The Cleveland Case* (London: Virago, 1988), p. 71.

31   Sereny, *The Case of Mary Bell*, p. 80.

32   Freud, 'Criminals from a Sense of Guilt', The Pelican Freud Library, vol. 14 (London: Pelican, 1985), pp. 317–19.

33   Melanie Klein, *Love, Guilt and Reparation and Other Works 1921–1945* (London: Vintage, 1998), p. 424.

34   Freud, 'Criminals from a Sense of Guilt', p. 318.

35   Sereny, *Cries Unheard*, p. 125.

36   Sereny, *The Case of Mary Bell*, p. 102.

37   Freud's seduction theory of neurosis came in for a great deal of criticism in the late twentieth century when Jeffrey Masson published *The Assault on Truth: Freud's Suppression of the Seduction Theory*. Masson argued that Freud abandoned his belief that patients had suffered actual sexual abuse, in favour of a view that they had fantasised it instead. Masson's work has been roundly criticised by a range of scholars. One of their main arguments is that Freud never downplayed the existence of a 'real event', but believed that fantasised seduction, though not the *same* as actual seduction, was nonetheless real. Either way, the relevance of his diagnosis of obsessional neurosis is still relevant here. J. Masson, *The Assault on Truth: Freud's Suppression of the Seduction Theory* (London: Penguin, 1985). For an excellent critique, see A. Scott, 'Feminism and the Seduction of the "Real Event"', *Feminist Review*, no. 28, spring 1988, pp. 88–102.

38   For a psychoanalytic discussion of mothers who abuse their children, see Estela Welldon, *Mother, Madonna, Whore: The Idealisation and Denigration of Motherhood* (London: Free Association, 1988). The details of the abuse suffered by Mary Bell are recalled in Sereny, *Cries Unheard*, pp. 329–54.

39   Sereny, *The Case of Mary Bell*, p. 103.

40   Ibid., p. 101.

41   Research indicates that cases of this kind are extremely rare. Feminists did acknowledge that women sometimes abuse their children, but their campaigning emphasis was on the much more widespread abuse by men. See: Mary McLeod and Esther Saraga, 'Towards a Feminist Theory and Practice', *Feminist Review*, no. 28, spring 1988, pp. 16–55.

42   Melanie Klein, op. cit., p. 170.

43   Sereny, *Cries Unheard*, p. 334.

44   *Sun*, 7 December 1968.

45   *Sun*, 22 September 1972.

46   Sereny, *Cries Unheard*.

47   There were exceptions. Carole Malone wrote a very robust defence of Bell in the *Sunday Mirror*. She had grown up in a council house only seven miles away from Mary Bell's home: 'But it might as well have been seven million. Where Mary got cruelty, I got love. Where I got education, she got dirty old men pawing her body, courtesy of her prostitute mother who charged her clients for the privilege of sampling her young flesh.' *Sunday Mirror*, 3 May 1998. The media commentator Roy Greenslade attacked the way in which Bell was 'demonised' by newspapers (*Guardian*, 30 April 1998), and Andrew Marr for the *Independent*, though more equivocal, nonetheless accused the Blair government of 'confirming the tabloid agenda rather than challenging it'. *Independent*, 1 May 1998.

48   David Sexton, *Evening Standard*, 5 May 1998.

49   Fiona Barton, *Mail on Sunday*, 3 May 1998.

50   Colin Wilson, in the *Daily Mail*, 28 April 1998.

51   Ibid.

52   P. Wassell (Letters), *Daily* Mail, 1 May 1998.

53   BBC 1, *Kilroy*, broadcast 6 May 1998.

54   Ibid.

55   Ann Kent, 'Growing up behind locked doors', *The Times*, 28 October 1988.

56   Terry Bruce, a consultant psychiatrist at Bart's Hospital, London; quoted in Ann Kent, 'Growing up behind locked doors', *The Times*, 28 October 1988.

57   One of the more poignant comments came from the mother of the murdered child, Martin Brown: 'No one will publish books on the victims, no one is interested … It's as if victims are not human beings.' BBC 1, *Kilroy*, broadcast 6 May 1998.

58   John Rentoul, *Tony Blair* (London: Warner Books, 1996), chapter 13.

59   Quoted in Gatrell, op. cit., p. 5.

60   Speech given in Wellingborough, 19 February 1993, cited in Rentoul, op. cit., p. 290.

61   Ibid., p. 290.

62   BBC 1, *Nine O'Clock News*, 29 April 1998.

63   Sereny, *Cries Unheard*, p. 13.

64   *The Sun*, 29 April 1998. Also quoted in *Scotland on Sunday*, 3 May 1998.

65   *Daily Mail* editorial, 30 April 1998.

66   Hansard 1968–69, vol. 778, 17 February 1969 (Questions), column 45.

67   Hansard 1971–72, vol. 843, 18 October 1972 (Questions), column 90. Also, for an account of this allegation, see Sereny, *Cries Unheard*, p. 185.

68   Rentoul, op. cit., *Tony Blair*, chapters 11 and 13. For a critique of this 'project', see S. Hall, 'Parties on the Verge of a Nervous Breakdown', *Soundings*, issue 1, autumn 1995, pp. 19–35.

69 See Blair's essay on Christian socialism quoted in Rentoul, op. cit., p. 294.

70 Sereny indicated that Bell had received a small fee, although she did not specify the exact amount, but on numerous previous occasions Bell had been offered six-figure sums for her story and had turned each one of them down. Sereny, *Cries Unheard*, p. 13.

71 Sereny, *Cries Unheard*, p. 16.

72 A *Guardian* editorial spoke of the 'specious moralising' of the tabloids, while arguing that because the Sereny book had provided 'therapeutic benefits' for Bell, she should not receive any monetary reward; *Guardian*, 30 April 1998. Other *Guardian* writers also criticised Bell on a similar basis; Decca Aitkenhead called Bell's payment 'morally grotesque'; *Guardian*, 30 April 1998. Luke Harding believed that the Sereny book showed that Bell had only 'qualified remorse for her crimes'; *Guardian*, 28 April 1998.

73 Controversy over memory and child abuse began in the United States, where stories of ritualised abuse were being added to the child abuse agenda. In early 1992, the False Memory Syndrome Foundation was established in order to bring to light cases where individuals believed that they were being wrongly accused of child abuse. The organisation uncovered stories that were seized upon by the US media. The False Memory Association in Britain was involved in similar work. In 1990 there were a number of reported cases of ritual abuse in Britain – this led to an exhaustive official investigation chaired by Jean La Fontaine whose report was published in 1998. J. La Fontaine, *Speak of the Devil: Allegations of Satanic Abuse in Britain* (Cambridge: Cambridge University Press, 1998).

74 Campbell, *Unofficial Secrets*, p. 24.

75 *The Inquiry into the Cleveland Abuse Scandal*, by Mrs Justice Elizabeth Butler-Sloss, was published on 6 July 1988.

76 An example of how some therapists worked with this model of memory is shown in D. Bryant, J. Kessler and L. Shirar, *The Family Inside: Working with the Multiple* (New York: Norton, 1992).

77 Martin Conway, *Recovered Memories and False Memories* (Oxford: Oxford University Press, 1997).

78 Stuart Sutherland, 'Welcome to the Doll's House', *Times Higher Education Supplement*, 16 May 1997, p. 29.

79 British Psychological Society, *Recovered Memories: The Report of the Working Party of the British Psychological Society* (Leicester: British Psychological Society, 1995), p. 29.

80 Lesley Garner, *Daily Telegraph*, 1 July 1987. In a piece entitled 'Overboard on Child Abuse', she suggested that 'we are encouraging, even inventing, a newly fashionable problem'. In an implicit attack on feminism, Garner writes that awareness of child sexual abuse is being too 'zealously encouraged'. She goes on: 'Few people know what forces are unleashed

once society begins to tamper with the mechanics of the family.' During the Cleveland abuse scandal, Labour MP Stuart Bell accused two of the women professionals involved in protective action of a 'conspiratorial attack on family life'; *Daily Mail*, 15 July 1987.

81   *Daily Mail*, 30 April 1998.

82   See article by Dr Prem Misra, *Daily Record*, 1 May 1998.

83   *Daily Mail*, 30 April 1998.

84   Steven Rose, *The Making of Memory: From Molecules to Mind* (London: Anchor Books, 1992). This draws together some of the key scientific work on memory.

85   For an excellent discussion on the debate about memory, see Lynne Segal, *Why Feminism?* (Cambridge: Polity Press, 1999), pp. 116–45.

86   'Interview with Endel Tulving', *Journal of Cognitive Neuroscience*, vol. 3, 1991, p. 89.

87   Martin Conway, 'Introduction: What Are Memories?', in M. Conway (ed.), *Recovered Memories and False Memories*, pp. 4–5.

88   E.F. Loftus et al., 'Forgetting Sexual Trauma: What Does it Mean When 38% Forget?', *Journal of Consulting and Clinical Psychology*, vol. 62, 1994, pp. 1177–81. Also E.F. Loftus, 'The Myth of Repressed Memory', in M. Conway (ed.), *Recovered Memories*.

89   Daniel Schacter et al, 'The Recovered Memories Debate: A Cognitive Neuroscience Perspective', in M. Conway (ed.), *Recovered Memories*, p. 89.

90   BBC Radio 4, *Front Row*, discussion between programme presenter Francine Stock, journalist Dea Birkett and author Blake Morrison, 5 May 1998.

91   Pre-recorded interview with Francine Stock, broadcast on BBC Radio 4, *Front Row* programme, 5 May 1998.

92   Sereny, *Cries Unheard*, p. 13.

93   For example, interviews and other documentation given to Sereny by psychiatrists, counsellors and Mary Bell's probation officer.

94   Nicci Gerrard, 'What's Worrying Our Kids?', *The Observer*, 14 February 1999.

95   Tim Lawton MP on BBC Radio 4, *The World at One*, 29 April 1998.

96   In one interview, she said: 'I've had a great deal to do with small children. I've worked with damaged, deprived children and I've never had the belief that they were bad.' BBC Radio 4, *In the Psychiatrist's Chair*, 6 September 1998.

97   Edmund Burke, *Reflections on the Revolution in France* (first published 1790), reprinted in a joint edition with Thomas Paine, *The Rights of Man* (London: Dolphin, 1961), p. 90.

CHAPTER TEN

1   David James Smith, *Beyond All Reason* (New York: Donald I. Fine, 1995).
2   Andrew O'Hagan, *The Missing* (London: Picador, 1995), p. 91.
3   Blake Morrison, *As If* (London: Granta Books, 1998), p. 30.
4   Smith, op. cit., p .93.
5   This quote from Quentin Crisp appears in Sylvia Levine and Joseph Koenig (eds.), *Why Men Rape* (London: Star, 1983), p. 3.
6   Mikal Gilmore, in 'The Family', *Granta* no. 37, autumn 1991 (Penguin: London, 1991), 'Family Album', p. 17.
7   See Morrison, op. cit., and Smith, op. cit.
8   For references, see chapter 8.
9   Smith, op. cit., pp. 169–90.
10   Mairead Dolan, 'Psychopathic Personality in Young People', *British Journal of Psychiatry*, no. 10, 2004, pp. 466–73.
11   P.J. Frick, 'Callous-unemotional traits and conduct problems: applying the two-factor model of psychopathy to children', pp. 161–89, cited in D. Cooke, A. Forth and R. Hare, *Psychopathy: Theory, Research and Implications for Society* (Holland: Kluwer, 1998).
12   Jean-Jacques Rousseau, *Emile*, p. 303.
13   Morrison, op. cit., pp. 128, 132.
14   Smith, op. cit., p. 185.
15   The title of a *Daily Mail* supplement on the killing gives a flavour of the coverage: 'The Innocent and the Evil', 25 November 1993.
16   BBC 1, *Newsnight*, 24 November 1993.
17   From the transcript of an unpublished interview, 1996.
18   Ibid.
19   Freud, 'On Psychoanalysis', in J. Strachey (ed.), *The Standard Edition of the Complete Works of Sigmund Freud* (London: Hogarth Press, 1895), vol. 12, p. 207.
20   Michael Rutter, 'Classification and Categorisation in Child Psychiatry', *Journal of Child Psychology and Psychiatry*, vol. 6, 1965, pp. 71–83.
21   B. Franklin and J. Petley, 'Killing the Age of Innocence: Newspaper Reporting of the death of James Bulger', pp. 136–48, in Pilcher and Wagg (eds.), *Thatcher's Children? Politics, Childhood and Society in the 1980s and 1990s* (London: Routledge, 1996).
22   *Guardian*, 6 February 2003.
23   Matilde Azzacconi, 'The Italian Juvenile Penal Process and Children who Kill', in Paul Cavadino (ed.), *Children who Kill* (Waterside Press: Winchester, 1996), pp. 115–25.
24   Dr Graham Clifford, 'Norway, A Resolutely Welfare-Oriented Approach', in Cavadino (ed.), op. cit., *Children who Kill*, p. 142.
25   *Guardian*, 30 October 2000.

26 This is a quote from Denise Fergus fifteen years after the murder in an interview with the *Observer*, 2 March 2008.

27 Quoted in many places, but see D. Haydon and P. Scraton, '"Condemn a Little More, Understand a Little Less": The Political Context and Rights Implications of the Domestic and European Rulings in the Venables-Thompson Case', *Journal of Law and Society*, vol. 27, no. 416, 2000, p. 433.

28 From the transcript of an unpublished interview, 1996.

29 *The Herald*, 30 November 1993; *Independent*, 19 February 1993.

30 Letters page of the *Guardian*, 27 November 1993.

31 Walter Schwartz, *Guardian*, 27 November 1993.

32 *Sunday Times*, 28 November 1993.

33 National crime statistics showed that 140,000 burglaries were reported in 1993; in 2006, the figure was 60,000. Crime statistics should never be taken at face value, but these figures do take into account various legislative changes as well as changed methods of recording crimes, and under these conditions, the room for variability in the figures is estimated at only 5 per cent – see www.crimestatistics.org.uk

34 *The Human Development Index 2007 Report*, http://hdr.undp.org

35 BBC News, *Correspondent*, 30 June 2000, www.bbc.co.uk

36 *Stockport Advertiser*, 16 April 1861.

37 C. Jenks, *Childhood* (London: Routledge, 1996), p. 118.

38 The first in *The Times*, 2 December 1993, and the second in *The Times Educational Supplement*, 3 December 1993.

39 *The Times*, 25 November 1993 and 27 November 1993.

40 *The Times Educational Supplement*, 10 December 1993.

41 Franklin and Petley, 'Killing the Age of Innocence' in Pilcher and Wagg (eds.), *Thatcher's Children?*, op. cit.

42 Anne Higonnet, *Pictures of Innocence* (London: Thames and Hudson, 1998), p. 12.

43 'The Innocent and the Evil' was the headline for a nine-page supplement produced after the trial in the *Daily Mail*, 25 November 1993. The juxtaposition was made between the victim and his killers, but the distinctions also generated wider meanings about adult views of children.

44 This quote appears in Mary Riddle, 'The Mystery of Childhood' in the *Observer*, 17 March 2002.

45 Paul Gilroy in the *Guardian*, 8 January 2003.

46 The education comparison is unfair, since it ignores the high levels of poor educational standards of many of the children involved in crime. *The Weekly Law Reports*, Queen's Bench Division, 30 September 1994, vol. 3, pp. 888–98 and *The Weekly Law Reports*, House of Lords, 31 March 1995, vol. 2, pp. 383–404. Also House of Commons Debate on the Crime and Disorder Bill, 8 April 1998, *Hansard*, vol. 377, column 373.

47   Quoted in Cavadino (ed.), op. cit., p. 15.

48   John Sprack, 'Publicity Surrounding the Trial', in Mike McConville and Geoffrey Wilson (eds.), *The Handbook of The Criminal Justice Process* (Oxford: Oxford University Press, 2002), pp. 230–31.

49   Interview with Leon McEwan, *Manchester Evening News*, 19 February 2001.

50   Quoted in the *Independent*, 22 August 2007.

51   For the full text of David Blunkett's House of Commons statement see the *Guardian*, 24 June 2001. Denise Bulger appeared on the *ITV Tonight* programme, 28 June 2001.

EPILOGUE

1   Polly Toynbee and Sean Sexton respectively on BBC 2, *Newsnight*, 24 November 1993.

2   *The Times*, 17 August 1861.

3   A point made at her Reith Lectures and quoted in the *Guardian*, 17 March 2002.

4   Maudsley, *Responsibility in Mental Disease*, p. 26.

5   Steven Pinker, *The Blank Slate: The Modern Denial of Human Nature* (London: Penguin, 2002), p. 315.

6   Ibid.

7   Maudsley, *The Pathology of Mind*, p. 281.

8   Pinker, op. cit., p. 281.

9   *The Times*, 17 August 1861.

10   Ros Coward, *Guardian*, 3 July 2001.

11   Claire McDiarmid, *Childhood and Crime* (Dundee: Dundee University Press, 2007), p. 76.

12   Camila Batmanghelidjh, *Shattered Lives* (London: Jessica Kingsley, 2006), p. 91.

13   Cyril Burt borrowed from Freud an energy theory of the psyche, but formulated it differently to talk about inborn levels of emotionality and temperament. See Burt, *The Young Delinquent*, pp. 399–400, 420–537.

14   *Guardian*, 17 February 2007.

15   Conference on Childhood Origins of Cruelty and Sadism, organised by The Child Centre for Mental Health, 2–18 Britannia Row, London N1 8PA, held 10 June 2006.

16   Sue Gerhardt, *Why Love Matters: how affection shapes a baby's brain* (London: Routledge, 2008, fifth edition), p. 167.

17   Batmanghelidjh, op. cit., p. 153.

18   Dr Eileen Vizard on BBC Radio 4, *All in the Mind*, 24 April 2007.

19   Law Commission, *Report on Murder, Manslaughter and Infanticide*, Law Commission no. 304, 2006, pp. 106–8 and 247–60. The government has since rejected this suggestion.

20 A summary of the report's recommendations on young defendants was circulated to the relevant organisations for consultation. Home Office Juvenile Offenders Unit, 'Auld Report: Young Defendants', 12 December 2001; Rt Hon Lord Justice Auld, *Review of the Criminal Courts of England and Wales*, October 2001. The report can be found at http//www.homeoffice.gov.uk

21 Rt Hon Lord Justice Auld, *Review of the Criminal Courts*, October 2001, chapter 5, paragraph 208.

22 Ibid., chapter 5.

23 For example, the comments of Stuart Kuttner, managing editor of the *News of the World*, on BBC Radio 4, *The Message*, 14 February 2003.

INDEX